P9-DGY-069

True North

Warren Bennis (signature)

A WARREN BENNIS BOOK

This collection of books is devoted exclusively to new and exemplary contributions to management thought and practice. The books in this series are addressed to thoughtful leaders, executives, and managers of all organizations who are struggling with and committed to responsible change. My hope and goal is to spark new intellectual capital by sharing ideas positioned at an angle to conventional thought—in short, to publish books that disturb the present in the service of a better future.

BOOKS IN THE WARREN BENNIS SIGNATURE SERIES

Branden	*Self-Esteem at Work*
Mitroff, Denton	*A Spiritual Audit of Corporate America*
Schein	*The Corporate Culture Survival Guide*
Sample	*The Contrarian's Guide to Leadership*
Lawrence, Nohria	*Driven*
Cloke, Goldsmith	*The End of Management and the Rise of Organizational Democracy*
Glen	*Leading Geeks*
Cloke, Goldsmith	*The Art of Waking People Up*
George	*Authentic Leadership*
Kohlrieser	*Hostage at the Table*
Rhode	*Moral Leadership*

JB JOSSEY-BASS

True North

Discover Your
Authentic Leadership

Bill George

With Peter Sims

Foreword by David Gergen

BICENTENNIAL
1807
WILEY
2007
BICENTENNIAL

John Wiley & Sons, Inc.

Library of Congress Cataloging-in-Publication Data

George, Bill (William W.)
    True North : discover your authentic leadership / Bill George with Peter Sims ; foreword by David Gergen. — 1st. ed.
        p. cm. — (Warren Bennis series)
    Includes bibliographical references.
    ISBN-13: 978-0-7879-8751-0 (cloth)
    1. Leadership. 2. Organizational effectiveness. I. Sims, Peter. II. Title.
    HD57.7.G4582 2007
    658.4'092—dc22
                                         2006100386

Printed in the United States of America
FIRST EDITION
HB Printing   10 9 8 7 6 5 4 3

Contents

Acknowledgments

True North is the result of collaboration with my coauthor, Peter Sims, and my colleagues at Harvard Business School, Diana Mayer and Andrew McLean. They have been tireless in their dedication to exploring with me how people develop as authentic leaders, to interviewing these leaders, and to assessing their inputs. Peter, in particular, has proven to be a true collaborator; he has provided exceptional understanding of the next generation of authentic leaders and of the meaning and impact of authentic leadership. Diana did a superb job in interviewing leaders across the United States and sharpening our thinking. Andrew led the research methodology, keeping our team on track with proper protocols and knowledge of other leadership research studies. We also received very valuable insights and guidance throughout the entire process from Warren Bennis, our executive editor, as well as from Susan Williams and Byron Schneider at Jossey-Bass.

We are especially grateful to the 125 leaders who offered their personal stories and their perspectives on leadership during the interviews, and their willingness to share with the current and future generations of authentic leaders and all those who want to understand leading from the leader's inside point of view. Without their openness, this book would never have been possible.

During the editing process, John S. Rosenberg, Jean Martin, Jeff George, Penny George, Grace Kahng, David Gergen, Carolina Helmick, Doug Baker, Chi Nguyen, and Matt Breitfelder were especially insightful in sharpening the text and the writing. Richard Sheppard did outstanding work on the graphic designs. We also appreciate the inputs of Bill Buzenberg, Charlie Dimmler, Paula Goldman, Daisy Wademan, Ryan Frederick, Ron Sonntag, Michal Petrzela, Matt Cain, Bryan Droznes, Kathleen Kelly, Jeannette Lager, Renée Will George, Jon George, Christopher Gergen, Daniel Salvadori, Julian Flannery, Scott Starr, Fawzi Jumean, Ori Brafman, and Gigi Sims. Special thanks go to Carol Mierau, my assistant at Medtronic, and Kathy Farren, my assistant at Harvard, for all their efforts on the book and research project. My colleagues at Harvard—Nitin Nohria, Jay Lorsch, David Gergen, Joe Badaracco, Lynn Paine, Srikant Datar, Ronnie Heifitz, Rosabeth Moss Kanter, Howard Stevenson, Joe Bower, Scott Snook, the members of the Leadership and Corporate Accountability teaching group—and my MBA students at Harvard have been especially helpful to me in my understanding of leadership and in support of my efforts, as have Peter's colleagues at Stanford, Charles O'Reilly, Joel Peterson, and Beth Benjamin.

None of this would have been possible without the unwavering support, encouragement, insights, and patience of my wife, Penny, from whom I have learned so much about people and leading them.

To all of you, Peter and I are deeply grateful.

The Authors

Bill George was chief executive of Medtronic, the world's leading medical technology company, from 1991 until 2001 and chairman of the board from 1996 to 2002. Under his leadership, Medtronic's market capitalization grew from $1.1 billion to $60 billion, averaging 35 percent a year. Currently, he is professor of management practice at Harvard Business School and serves on the board of directors of ExxonMobil, Goldman Sachs, and Novartis. He has also served on the board of Target Corporation.

He is the author of the best-selling book *Authentic Leadership: Rediscovering the Secrets of Creating Lasting Value* (Jossey-Bass, 2003). He has made frequent appearances on television and radio, including *The Today Show*, *The News Hour with Jim Lehrer*, CNBC, *Bloomberg News*, and public radio. His articles have appeared in *Fortune*, the *Wall Street Journal*, *Harvard Business Review*, and numerous other publications.

He has been named one of the "Top 25 Business Leaders of the Past 25 Years" by PBS, "Executive of the Year—2001" by the Academy of Management, and "Director of the Year—2001–02" by the National Association of Corporate Directors. He is currently a trustee of the Carnegie Endowment for International Peace and World Economic Forum USA and has been board chair of Allina Health System, Abbott-Northwestern Hospital, Greater Twin Cities United Way, and Advamed.

Earlier in his career, he was an executive with Honeywell and Litton Industries and served in the U.S. Department of Defense. He has been executive-in-residence at Yale School of Management.

He received his BS in industrial engineering from Georgia Tech and MBA from Harvard University, where he was a Baker Scholar, and an honorary doctorate from Bryant University.

Peter Sims helped found the London office of Summit Partners, a leading global investment firm, and established "Leadership Perspectives," a course at the Stanford Graduate School of Business while he was a student there. He also served previously as part of the Deloitte Touche Tomatsu Global Strategy Team.

Sims has served as a member of the President's Visiting Committee at Bowdoin College and on the board of directors of Summer Search. He received his MBA from Stanford and an AB, *magna cum laude*, from Bowdoin. He lives in San Francisco.

Editor's Note

As the world becomes ever more dangerous and our problems more complex and dire, we long for truly distinguished leaders, men and women who deserve our respect and loyalty. Instead, we have suffered far too much bad leadership in recent years. The business media have exposed one scandal after another—criminally greedy CEOs, boards that do little more than rubber-stamp executive whims, companies willing to trade customers' lives for profits, and corrupt and partisan political leaders. Too many of our so-called leaders have functioned best as subjects of the brand of satire perfected on television by Jon Stewart and Stephen Colbert.

But Bill George and Peter Sims's *True North* is about a very different kind of leader, the kind that we can be proud to follow. In this ambitious and important book, one of America's most respected corporate leaders and his talented younger collaborator show that ethically grounded leadership is not only possible, it is often the most effective leadership of all. It is an optimistic message that falls on grateful ears.

To write their guide to authentic leadership, George and Sims interviewed 125 leaders in many arenas. The authors chose men and women whose leadership appeared to be grounded in their character. The subjects range in age from twenty-three to ninety-three and have distinguished themselves in corporate life, as entrepreneurs, as social innovators, in political life, and in the study of leadership itself. Some, like statesman and former Bechtel head George Shultz, have contributed in many fields. Some, like Starbucks founder Howard Schultz and educator and frequent political commentator David Gergen, are household names. Others are less well known but have quietly made important contributions to our lives, including young Wendy Kopp, founder of Teach For America. Financial entrepreneur Charles Schwab, Avon CEO Andrea Jung, Amgen head Kevin Sharer, philosopher of design David Kelley, Judy Vredenburgh of Big Brothers, Big Sisters—all the leaders who appear in *True North* offer firsthand insights into the nature of authentic leadership and the way to develop it.

One of the revelations of *True North* is how critical these leaders' personal stories are in shaping their leadership. Time after time, those interviewed describe a turning point in their lives—a crucible, I call it—that transformed them into the leaders they are today. These tales of how they became the people they are reveal their most deeply held values, their most passionate beliefs. Howard Schultz recalls how, as a child of seven, he was forever changed by the news that his delivery-man father had slipped on a sheet of ice and broken his ankle. The accident lost Schultz's father his job and the family its health insurance and economic security. That experience led Schultz to create a global business, one built not on lattes and frappucinos but on the conviction that every worker deserves respect and health care.

"Those early memories are with me all the time," Schultz tells the authors. "I wanted to build the kind of company my father never had a chance to work for, where you would be valued and respected, no matter where you came from, the color of your skin, or your level of education. Memories of my father's lost health care led to Starbucks' becoming the first American company to provide health insurance for every employee, including part-time workers."

Such autobiographical stories continue to inspire the leaders who lived them, keeping their moral compasses pointed toward True North. The tales are inspiring for readers as well and marvelous to read. Novartis Chairman and CEO Daniel Vasella's story is a saga of Dickensian proportions. It begins with the Swiss-born Vasella's achingly lonely childhood, filled with physical pain and emotional loss. At the age of eight, he was struck with tuberculosis and meningitis. He was sent away to recuperate for a year—a year in which his parents never visited him. As a teenager, he joined a rowdy motorcycle gang that drank too much and fought too quickly. But Vasella and the other leaders of *True North* are not defeated by their struggles and setbacks. Instead, they learn from them and find their futures in them.

In his gang, Vasella recognized his own ambition and began to fashion a career in which he had more control. He went to medical school and later rose to the top of one of the world's leading health care companies. Today his leadership is grounded in his personal knowledge of poverty and ill health. "As CEO," Vasella told the authors, "I have the leverage to impact the lives of many more people. I can do what is right, based on my moral compass. At the end of the day, the only thing that matters is what we do for other people."

There are more than one hundred such stories in this fascinating, important book. Some are funny, some are cautionary, all are compelling. After a friend of mine read *True North* before publication, he noted how different it is from most business books. Instead of simply telling readers how to get ahead, *True North* offers a practical five-part program for developing their best selves and shows how authenticity and integrity shape great leadership. My friend wants to give the book to his children to read.

As CEO of medical-device giant Medtronic, Bill George was known as much for his integrity as for his business success. Now on the faculty of the Harvard Business School, he (with coauthor Peter Sims) has written a worthy successor to his best-selling *Authentic Leadership*. Building on that book's wisdom, *True North* goes even further, revealing just how powerful authentic leadership can be—and, best of all, how to achieve it.

Warren Bennis
Santa Monica, California
October 2006

This book is dedicated to my wife, Penny,
my faithful partner for the past thirty-seven years,
who has helped me stay on course to True North, and
to our sons, Jeff and Jon, and our daughters-in-law, Renée and Jeannette,
who represent the best of the new generation of authentic leaders.

Foreword

Growing up in the shadow of a great university, I always believed that the smartest person made the best leader. That was only natural in an academic family where my dad was a professor of mathematics and two of my older brothers became professors of medicine and psychology. Our family and friends placed great store in intellectual achievement, so I just assumed that smart people were the best at most things, including leadership. Boy, did I have some things to learn.

Moving to Washington in my late twenties, I began my education in the real world in earnest. Over a period of some three decades, I had the privilege of serving as an adviser to four presidents in the White House and working alongside leaders in government, the press, business, and other fields. Many of them were outstanding individuals, and I shall always cherish their friendships. They also taught me a lot about leadership. Yes, there is no substitute for ability: to lead others, you must know what you are doing, have deep curiosity, and develop keen judgment. Competence counts. But what ultimately distinguishes the great leaders from the mediocre are the personal, inner qualities—qualities that are hard to define but are essential for success, qualities that each of us must develop for ourselves, and qualities that are explored here in these pages with great clarity and insight by one of America's most authentic leaders, Bill George. This is a gem of a book that will guide you on your own journey.

To illustrate the importance of you embracing your own True North, let me tell you a bit more about what I discovered along the way. In the early 1970s, coming out of law school and then the navy, I went to work for Richard Nixon and stayed in his White House for three and a half years, ultimately running his speech-writing and research team. My mentor, Ray Price, helped me to understand that Nixon was one of the most complex men to reach the presidency. He had a bright, luminous side that to this day has me convinced he was one of the best strategists the country has ever elected. Nixon could figuratively go up on a mountaintop and see twenty or thirty years into the future and then decide how the forces of history should be nudged to favor America's national security. Thus his trip to China and a good many other initiatives. If that were all there was to Nixon, he would have become one of our better presidents.

Tragically, Nixon also had another side that was dark, bitter, and twisted. The longer one worked with him, the clearer it became that he had inner demons that he had never conquered and perhaps never understood. But the resentments and furies that poured forth caused no end of harm: he set up teams inside the White House to pursue his enemies in national security, real and perceived, and those teams eventually focused their efforts on electoral politics. The crimes that were committed in his name inevitably seeped into the public arena, and eventually the whole enterprise collapsed. He became the architect of his own demise— a prime example of a man who had all the makings for the presidency but failed because he never developed what it took inside himself.

In the years that followed, I worked for Jerry Ford and then Ronald Reagan in the White House. Neither had any pretenses of being as smart as Nixon, but each one turned out to be a better leader, especially Reagan. Ford knew exactly who he was, understood his weaknesses as well as his strengths, and—because he was so well anchored—was comfortable in appointing people he thought smarter than he was to the cabinet. Within the brief time of his presidency, he assembled one of the best cabinets in modern times. While he stumbled more than once, he looks better and better through the rearview mirror—a man of integrity who brought honor to the White House and healing to the country.

Reagan, like Ford, had figured out who he was and liked it. He didn't just feel comfortable in his own skin; he felt serene. Reagan not only had a compass for his life but a compass for his political beliefs, and he communicated both with a contagious optimism that stirred people across the land. Whether or not one agreed with his policies, it is pretty clear that he was the best leader in the White House since Franklin Roosevelt. Reagan didn't pretend to be the smartest man to serve, but he was smart enough. Ultimately, however, a key to his success was how closely he fit the description that Oliver Wendell Holmes Jr. once applied to FDR: "A second class mind but a first class temperament."

Dial forward for a moment to Bill Clinton, the fourth president I've been privileged to serve. Most Americans now recognize that Clinton is truly gifted: he has mental and verbal capacities that far exceed almost everyone else on the public stage today. More than once, I had the same experience with him in the Oval Office as others: during an engaged conversation with three or four people, he could simultaneously be talking back and forth while also quietly filling out a *New York Times* crossword puzzle. More impressive, he sought out information and perspectives across the spectrum—not just his partisans but many others, especially those who traditionally lack a seat at the tables of power such as blacks, Hispanics, and women. He had what I have called "360-degree leadership"—an increasingly important quality for every leader in today's complex world—and it enormously enhanced his judgment. In the end, he made some excellent policy choices.

Yet, as the country knows in excruciating detail, Clinton also had cracks in his character that came to haunt him. From what I saw he was working hard to repair those cracks and didn't quite make it; I always felt that if he had come to the presidency a few years later in life, he would have been a more integrated, whole person whose arc would have been higher. In *Eyewitness to Power*, a book I published in 2000 (and in terms that show how closely my own views of leadership are aligned with those of Bill George), I wrote sympathetically,

> *Instead of a struggle between light and dark [as with Nixon], my sense is that Clinton's central problem has been the lack of an inner compass. He has 360-degree vision but no true north. He isn't yet fully grounded within. . . . [He] isn't exactly sure who he is yet and tries to define himself by how well others like him. That leads him into all sorts of contradictions, and the view by others that he seems a constant mixture of strengths and weaknesses.*

His critics, of course, have much harsher assessments. This is not the place to settle those arguments. What is clear to everyone is that Clinton had so much promise and that, mostly because of those cracks, his presidency fell achingly short of what might have been. Even as it was, I continue to believe that he was a better president than his critics will ever concede. In the years since leaving the White House, let us note, he has also become more authentic in the sense that Bill George means here—and as a result, he is doing great good deeds for mankind.

What does all this add up to? Simply this: ability matters to a president, but inner qualities matter even more. As historian David McCullough wrote in assessing the leadership of Harry Truman: "Character is the single most important asset of a president." I would add this thought: that character without capacity usually means weakness in a leader, but capacity without character means danger.

Bill George and his talented younger collaborator in this book, Peter Sims, make a persuasive argument that the journey toward authentic leadership—that finding and pursuing your own True North—is the key to leadership in all fields, whether in business, government, or the nonprofit arena. I agree. Over the past decades, I have had the opportunity to observe and sometimes counsel leaders who have been in every walk of life, some young and some old, some women and some men. For all of them, the authenticity that Bill and Peter talk about here is essential to their success as leaders.

And certainly no one knows better than Bill, whose own life story is a model for others. He is now devoting much of his energy to teaching and helping rising young leaders, and I have watched with awe as he has talked to students at Harvard about authentic leadership and their eyes have lit up.

What he says here, drawn upon the life experiences of the 125 leaders he and Peter have interviewed, is just the sort of thoughtful, practical wisdom that every aspiring leader needs. They have written not only an important sequel to Bill's earlier, acclaimed book, *Authentic Leadership*; they have also written an invaluable guide to self-discovery that will serve generations to come. I wish you a good read—and a good journey.

David Gergen
Cambridge, Massachusetts
October 2006

Introduction

True North

What is *your* True North?

Do you know what your life and your leadership are all about, and when you are being true to yourself?

True North is the internal compass that guides you successfully through life. It represents who you are as a human being at your deepest level. It is your orienting point—your fixed point in a spinning world—that helps you stay on track as a leader. Your True North is based on what is most important to you, your most cherished values, your passions and motivations, the sources of satisfaction in your life.

Just as a compass points toward a magnetic pole, your True North pulls you toward the purpose of your leadership. When you follow your internal compass, your leadership will be authentic, and people will naturally want to associate with you. Although others may guide or influence you, your truth is derived from your life story, and only you can determine what it should be.

Discovering your True North takes a lifetime of commitment and learning. Each day, as you are tested in the world, you yearn to look at yourself in the mirror and respect the person you see and the life you have chosen to lead. Some days will be better than others, but as long as you are true to who you are, you can cope with the most difficult circumstances that life presents.

The world may have very different expectations for you and your leadership than you have for yourself. Regardless of whether you are leading a small team or are at the top of a powerful organization, you will be pressured by external forces to respond to their needs and seduced by rewards for fulfilling those needs. These pressures and seductions may cause you to detour from your True North. When you get too far off course, your internal compass tells you that something is wrong and you need to reorient yourself. It requires courage and resolve to resist the constant pressures and expectations confronting you and to take corrective action when necessary.

Sara Lee CEO Brenda Barnes says: "The most important thing about leadership is your character and the values that guide your life." She added,

> *If you are guided by an internal compass that represents your character and the values that guide your decisions, you're going to be fine. Let your values guide your actions and don't ever lose your internal compass, because everything isn't black or white. There are a lot of gray areas in business.*

When you are aligned with who you are, you find coherence between your life story and your leadership. As psychologist William James wrote a century ago, "I have often thought that the best way to define a man's character is to seek out the particular mental or moral attitude in which . . . he felt himself most deeply and intensively active and alive. At such moments, there is a voice inside which speaks and says, 'This is the real me.'"

Can you recall a time when you felt most intensely alive and could say with confidence, *"This is the real me"*? When you can, you are aligned with your True North and prepared to lead others authentically. Professionally, I had that feeling from the first time I walked into Medtronic in 1989 and joined a group of talented people dedicated to the mission to "alleviate pain, restore health, and extend life." I felt I could be myself and be appreciated for who I was and what I could contribute. I sensed immediately that the organization's values were aligned with my own.

The Leadership Crisis

An enormous vacuum in leadership exists today—in business, politics, government, education, religion, and nonprofit organizations. Yet there is no shortage of people with the capacity for leadership.

The problem is that we have a wrongheaded notion of what constitutes a leader, driven by an obsession with leaders at the top. That misguided standard often results in the wrong people attaining critical leadership roles.

There are leaders throughout organizations, just waiting for opportunities to lead. In too many organizations, however, people do not feel empowered to lead, nor are they rewarded for doing so. The purpose of *True North* is to enable you to discover your authentic leadership so that you can step up and lead while remaining true to who you are.

During my time as chairman and CEO of Medtronic in the 1990s, I witnessed firsthand many of the wrong people being chosen to run corporations. Under pressure from Wall Street to maximize short-term earnings, boards of directors frequently chose leaders for their charisma instead of their character, their style rather than their substance, and their image instead of their integrity.

When problems surfaced at Enron, WorldCom, Arthur Andersen, Tyco, and dozens of other companies, the severity of the leadership crisis became painfully apparent, creating a widespread erosion of trust in business leaders. This may surprise you, but I am not so concerned with people who broke the law, such as Jeff Skilling, Bernie Ebbers, Richard Scrushy, and Dennis Koslowski. Our legal system has proven quite effective in dealing with them.

What concerns me are the many powerful business leaders who bowed to stock market pressure in return for personal gain. They lost sight of their True North and put their companies at risk by focusing on the trappings and spoils of leadership instead of building their organizations for the long term. Many of those who failed walked away with enormous financial settlements.

The result was a severing of trust with employees, customers, and shareholders, as public trust in business leaders fell to its lowest level in fifty years. In business, trust is everything, because success depends upon customers' trust in products they buy, employees' trust in their leaders, investors' trust in those who invest for them, and the public's trust in capitalism.

Learning from Authentic Leaders

In large part the leadership vacuum has resulted from a misunderstanding of what constitutes an effective leader. During the past fifty years, leadership scholars have conducted more than one thousand studies in the attempt to determine the definitive leadership styles, characteristics, or personality traits of great leaders. None of these studies has produced a clear profile of the ideal leader. Thank goodness. If scholars had produced a cookie-cutter leadership style, people would be forever trying to emulate it. That alone would make them into personas, and others would see through them immediately.

The reality is that *no one can be authentic by trying to be like someone else*. There is no doubt you can learn from their experiences, but there is no way you can be successful trying to be *like* them. People trust you when you are genuine and authentic, not an imitation. As Dr. Reatha Clark King of General Mills said, "If you're aiming to be like somebody else, you're being a copycat because you think that's what people want you to do. You'll never be a star with that kind of thinking. But you might be a star—unreplicatable—by following your passion."

Amgen Chairman and CEO Kevin Sharer, who gained priceless experience working as Jack Welch's assistant in the 1980s, saw the downside of GE's cult of personality in those days. "Everyone wanted to be like Jack," he explained. "Leadership has many voices. You need to be who you are, not try to emulate somebody else."

Since turning over the reins of Medtronic to my successor in 2001, I have focused on this leadership crisis by helping develop the next generation of business leaders through teaching, mentoring, writing, and speaking. In 2003 I wrote *Authentic Leadership* to challenge the new generation of leaders—from new CEOs to young leaders just embarking on their careers—to lead authentically.

The feedback I received from readers of *Authentic Leadership*, including many CEOs, was that they had a tremendous desire to be authentic leaders. Many people asked: "How can I become an authentic leader?" Author Jim Collins raised a similar question in

Good to Great, asking, "Can you learn to become a Level 5 leader?" His conclusion: "I still don't know the answer."

With the assistance of coauthor Peter Sims and my colleagues Diana Mayer and Andrew McLean, I set out to get definitive answers to the question. We interviewed 125 authentic leaders to learn the secrets of their development as leaders. They were open and honest about how they developed their leadership and candidly shared their life stories, including their greatest personal struggles, failures, and triumphs. Many said they had never granted such a personal interview before. These interviews constitute the largest in-depth study ever undertaken about how business leaders develop.

The leaders we interviewed ranged in age from twenty-three to ninety-three, with no fewer than fifteen per decade. They were chosen based on their reputations for being authentic and our personal knowledge of them. We also solicited recommendations from other leaders and academics. After the interviews, we assessed each leader against the dimensions of authentic leadership described in this book.

Our interviewees are a diverse group of women and men from an array of racial, religious, and socioeconomic backgrounds and nationalities. Among them are Dick Kovacevich of Wells Fargo, Andrea Jung of Avon Products, Chuck Schwab, founder of Charles Schwab & Co., and Narayana Murthy, founder of Infosys. Half of them are CEOs, and the other half includes a broad range of nonprofit leaders, midcareer leaders, and young leaders just starting on their journeys. (For more on our research methodology, see Appendix A. A complete list of the interviewees is shown in Appendix B.)

After interviewing these leaders, we believe we understand *why* academic studies have not produced the profile of an ideal leader. *Leaders are highly complex human beings, people who have distinctive qualities that cannot be sufficiently described by lists of traits or characteristics.* Leaders are defined by their unique life stories and the way they frame their stories to discover their passions and the purpose of their leadership.

Reading through three thousand pages of transcripts, our team was startled to see that these leaders did not identify any universal characteristics, traits, skills, or styles that led to their success. Rather, their leadership emerged from their life stories. By constantly testing themselves through real-world experiences and by reframing their life stories to understand who they are, these leaders unleashed their passions and discovered the purpose of their leadership.

Rather than waiting to get to the top to become leaders, they looked for every opportunity to lead and to develop themselves. Every one of them faced trials, some of them severe. Many cited these experiences, along with the people who helped them develop, as the primary reasons for their success. Without exception, these leaders believed being authentic made them more effective and successful. Their experience in becoming authentic leaders parallels my personal experience: *successful leadership takes conscious development and requires being true to your life story.*

True North is written for anyone who wants to be an authentic leader. It is for leaders at all stages of their lives, from those at the top of organizations to students preparing to become leaders to lifelong leaders looking for new opportunities. You are never too young, or too old, to take on leadership challenges and to lead authentically. It is grounded in the hundreds of years of experience of the 125 authentic leaders we interviewed as well as my own forty years in leadership roles. For you, the reader, it is an opportunity to learn from authentic leaders about how they developed and to create your own development plan to become an authentic leader.

The bottom line is this: *You can discover your authentic leadership right now.*

- You do not have to be born with the characteristics or traits of a leader.
- You do not have to wait for a tap on the shoulder.
- You do not have to be at the top of your organization.
- You can step up and lead at any point in your life.

As Young & Rubicam CEO Ann Fudge said, "All of us have the spark of leadership in us, whether it is in business, in government, or as a nonprofit volunteer. The challenge is to understand ourselves well enough to discover where we can use our leadership gifts to serve others. We're here for something. Life is about giving and living fully."

So why hold back? Why not lead now?

In considering whether to step up and lead authentically, ask yourself these two questions: *If not me, then who? If not now, then when?*

Wendy Kopp: Stepping Up at Twenty-One. Many people feel that in order to lead they must have the power that comes with authority. For twenty-one-year-old Wendy Kopp, all that was required was finding her passion. As a senior at Princeton University, Kopp was uncertain about what to do after graduation. Burning with desire to change the world, she did not want to pursue the typical corporate training track her classmates were following. To address her interest in reforming education to reduce disparities, she organized a conference of students and business leaders to examine ways to improve the nation's K–12 education system.

During the conference an idea came to her: "Why doesn't this country have a national teacher corps of recent college graduates who commit two years to teach in public schools?" Her rhetorical question inspired her to found Teach For America, the most successful secondary educational program in the past twenty-five years.

Kopp grew up in a middle-class family in an affluent area of Dallas. Looking back, she said her community was "extraordinarily isolated from reality and the disparities in educational opportunity." At Princeton she was deeply involved in leading the Foundation for Student Communications. Not sure what to do after graduation, Kopp went into "a deep funk" during her senior year. As she explored teaching in public schools, she realized there were many like her who believed that depriving kids of an excellent education was a national tragedy.

Seeing the need for more committed teachers in the public schools across America, Kopp created Teach For America to recruit thousands of graduating students to teach in public school systems. Passionate about Teach For America's purpose, she also recognized the challenges her teachers faced in closing the achievement gap. "Corps members care deeply about their students," she said. "Our biggest challenge is figuring out how they can stay centered, strong, and healthy, and reenergize themselves around our mission when they're pressured by so many other challenges."

It wasn't easy. Lacking management experience and a permanent funding base, Teach For America lurched from one crisis to the next. The organization was constantly short of cash. Time and again, Kopp threw herself into fundraising as she restructured budgets and financing to cover deficits. Her passion for the mission kept her going and inspired others to stay with the organization through its trials and tribulations.

Fifteen years after the founding of Teach For America, Wendy Kopp's tireless efforts and passionate leadership are paying off. Today the program has ten thousand graduates, 60 percent of whom have remained in teaching. Kopp's organization continues to attract exceptional college graduates to join its teacher corps and has established a sustainable funding base to support its programs. In 2006 Kopp was named one of "America's Best Leaders" by *US News & World Report*. Kopp's experience at such a young age captures the essence of authentic leadership: *find something you are passionate about and then inspire others to join the cause*.

The Authentic Leader

A dramatic shift is taking place today in the caliber and character of new leaders. Led by General Electric's Jeff Immelt, IBM's Sam Palmisano, Xerox's Anne Mulcahy, and Procter & Gamble's A.G. Lafley, these leaders recognize that leadership is *not* about their success or about getting loyal subordinates to follow them. They know the key to a successful organization is having empowered leaders at all levels, including those that have no direct reports.

Authentic leaders not only inspire those around them, they empower them to step up and lead. Thus, we offer the new definition of leadership: *The authentic leader brings people together around a shared purpose and empowers them to step up and lead authentically in order to create value for all stakeholders.*

In *Authentic Leadership*, I described authentic leaders as genuine people who are true to themselves and to what they believe in. They engender trust and develop genuine connections with others. Because people trust them, they are able to motivate others to high levels of performance. Rather than letting the expectations of other people guide them, they are prepared to be their own person and go their own way. As they develop as authentic leaders, they are more concerned about serving others than they are about their own success or recognition.

This is not to say that authentic leaders are perfect. Far from it. Every leader has weaknesses, and all are subject to human frailties and mistakes. Yet by acknowledging their shortcomings and admitting their errors, they connect with people and empower them.

Figure I.1 summarizes the five dimensions of an authentic leader:

- Pursuing purpose with passion
- Practicing solid values
- Leading with heart
- Establishing enduring relationships
- Demonstrating self-discipline

Pursuing Purpose with Passion

Most people struggle to understand the purpose of their leadership. In order to find their purpose, authentic leaders must first understand themselves and their passions. In turn, their passions show the way

Figure I.1 Dimensions of Authentic Leadership

Purpose

Heart

The
Authentic
Leader

Values

Self-Discipline

Relationships

to the purpose of their leadership. Without a real sense of purpose, leaders are at the mercy of their egos and narcissistic vulnerabilities.

Practicing Solid Values

Leaders are defined by their values, and values are personal—they cannot be determined by anyone else. Integrity, however, is the one value required of every authentic leader. If you do not have integrity, no one will trust you, nor should they. The values of authentic leaders are shaped by their personal beliefs and developed through study, introspection, consultation with others, and years of experience. The test of authentic leaders' values is not what they say but the values they practice under pressure. If leaders are not true to the values they profess, people quickly lose confidence in their leadership.

Leading with Heart

Authentic leaders lead with their hearts as well as their heads. To some, leading with the heart may sound soft, as though authentic leaders cannot make tough choices involving pain and loss. Leading with the heart is anything but soft. It means having passion for your work, compassion for the people you serve, empathy for the people you work with, and the courage to make difficult decisions. Courage is an especially important quality for leaders as they navigate through unpredictable terrain.

Establishing Enduring Relationships

The ability to develop enduring relationships is an essential mark of authentic leaders. People today demand personal relationships with their leaders before they will give themselves fully to their jobs. They insist on access to their leaders, knowing that trust and commitment are built on the openness and depth of relationship with their leaders. In return, people will demonstrate great commitment to their work and loyalty to the company.

Demonstrating Self-Discipline

Authentic leaders know competing successfully takes a consistently high level of self-discipline in order to produce results. They set high standards for themselves and expect the same from others. This requires accepting full responsibility for outcomes and holding others accountable for their performance. When leaders fall short, it is equally important to admit their mistakes and initiate immediate corrective action. Self-discipline should be reflected in their personal lives as well, because without personal self-discipline it is not possible to sustain self-discipline at work.

Discovering Your Authentic Leadership

Becoming an authentic leader is not easy. First, you have to understand yourself, because *the hardest person you will ever have to lead is yourself*. Once you have an understanding of your authentic self, you will find that leading others is much easier.

Second, to be an effective leader, *you must take responsibility for your own development*. Like musicians or athletes born with great abilities, you must devote yourself to a lifetime of development in order to become a great leader. That sounds logical, but often you don't know how. That is the purpose of this book—to show how you can discover your authentic leadership.

Kroger CEO David Dillon says that most people he has seen develop as good leaders were self-taught. "The advice I give to individuals in our company is not to expect the company to hand you a development plan that will take care of everything. You need to take responsibility for developing yourself." To assist in this process, in Appendix C, you will find a series of exercises corresponding to each chapter that you can use to build your own leadership development plan.

Part One of *True North* examines the journey to authentic leadership. It begins with the leaders' life stories, which are unique to them and more powerful than any set of characteristics or leadership skills they possess. Next, the three phases of the leader's journey are dissected, looking at the key steps in each phase of the journey. During their journeys, many leaders lose their way and end up derailed. To understand how this happens, five types of leaders who see themselves as heroes of their own journeys are described. Finally, by exploring the life-changing experiences leaders have had, we see how they made the transformation from "I" to "We" and learned the importance of empowering others to lead.

On your journey, you will need the True North of your internal compass to stay focused and to get back on track when you are at risk of being derailed. Part Two provides you with that compass and the development plan to stay true to who you are while you confront the challenges in the world around you. (See Figure I.2.) It includes five key areas of your development as a leader: self-awareness at the center of your compass, and at the four points, your values and principles, your motivations, your support team, and the integration of your life.

Part Three describes how you can follow your passions to discover the purpose of your leadership. It illustrates how to empower other people to step up and lead by inspiring them around a shared

Figure I.2 A Compass for the Journey

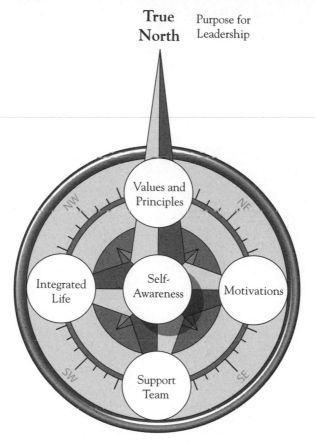

purpose. Finally, it addresses how you can achieve superior results through your organization by optimizing your leadership effectiveness. In the Epilogue I share my thoughts on how fulfilling leadership can be.

By dedicating yourself to your development, you *will* discover your authentic leadership.

Note to the reader: Before going on to Chapter One, you may want to complete the Introduction Exercise found in Appendix C.

Part One

Leadership Is a Journey

There is no such thing as the instant leader. Your journey to authentic leadership will take you through many peaks and valleys as you encounter the world's trials, rewards, and seductions. Becoming an authentic leader takes dedication to your development and growth, as there will be many temptations to pull you off the course of your True North. Maintaining your authenticity along the way may be the greatest challenge you ever face.

In interviewing authentic leaders about their journeys and their development, what stood out was the passion they felt about their life stories and the motivation these stories gave them to become leaders. Begin by asking yourself: What is my life story? In understanding and framing your story, you will find the calling to lead authentically, and you will maintain fidelity to your True North.

1

THE JOURNEY TO AUTHENTIC LEADERSHIP

Leadership is a journey, not a destination.
It is a marathon, not a sprint.
It is a process, not an outcome.
—John Donahoe, president of eBay

Starbucks founder Howard Schultz is a leader who used his life story to define his leadership. In the winter of 1961, seven-year-old Schultz was throwing snowballs with friends outside his family's apartment building in the federally subsidized Bayview Housing Projects in Brooklyn, New York. His mother yelled down from their seventh-floor apartment, "Howard, come inside. Dad had an accident." What followed would shape him for the rest of his life.

He found his father in a full-leg cast, sprawled on the living room couch. While working as a delivery driver, Schultz's father had fallen on a sheet of ice and broken his ankle. As a result, he lost his job—and the family's health care benefits. Workers' compensation did not yet exist, and Schultz's mother could not go to work because she was seven months pregnant. The family had nothing to fall back on. Many evenings, Schultz listened as his parents argued at the dinner table about how much money they needed to borrow and from whom. If the telephone rang, his mother asked him to answer it and tell the bill collectors his parents were not at home.

Schultz vowed he would do it differently when he had the opportunity. He dreamed of building a company that treated its employees well and provided health care benefits. Little did he realize that one day he would be responsible for 140,000 employees working in eleven thousand stores worldwide. Schultz was motivated by his life's experiences to found Starbucks and build it into the world's leading coffeehouse. After being CEO for thirteen years, he has turned the reins over to his successors but remains as chairman.

Memories of his father's lack of health care led Schultz to make Starbucks the first American company to provide access to health coverage for qualified employees who work as few as twenty hours per week. "My inspiration comes from seeing my father broken from the thirty terrible blue-collar jobs he had over his life, where an uneducated person just did not have a shot," Schultz said.

> That event is directly linked to the culture and the values of Starbucks. I wanted to build the kind of company my father never had a chance to work for, where you would be valued and respected, no matter where you came from, the color of your skin, or your level of education. Offering health care was a transforming event in the equity of the Starbucks brand that created unbelievable trust with our people. We wanted to build a company that linked shareholder value to the cultural values we create with our people.

Unlike some who rise from humble beginnings to create great personal wealth, Schultz is not ashamed of his roots. He credits his life story with giving him the motivation to create one of the great business successes of the last twenty-five years. But understanding the meaning of his story took deep thought because, like nearly everyone, he had to confront fears and ghosts from his past.

Brooklyn is burned into Schultz. When he took his daughter to the housing projects where he grew up, she surveyed the blight and said with amazement, "I don't know how you are normal." Yet his experience growing up in Brooklyn is precisely what enables Schultz to be so normal that he can connect with anyone. He speaks with a slight Brooklyn accent, relishes an Italian meal at a familiar restaurant, dresses comfortably in jeans, and respects all types of people. He never forgets where he came from or lets his wealth go to his head: "I was surrounded by people who were working hand-to-mouth trying to pay the bills, who felt like there was no hope, and they just couldn't get a break. That's something that never leaves you—never."

His mother told him that he could do anything he wanted in America. "From my earliest memories, I remember her saying that over and over again. It was her mantra." His father had the opposite effect. As a truck driver, cab driver, and factory worker, he often worked two or three jobs at a time to make ends meet but never earned more than $20,000 a year. Schultz watched his father break down while complaining bitterly about not having opportunities or respect from others.

As a teenager, Schultz felt the stigma of his father's failures, as the two clashed often. "I was bitter about his underachievement and lack of responsibility," he recalled. "I thought he could have accomplished so much more if he had tried." Schultz was determined to escape that fate. "Part of what has always driven me is fear of failure. I know all too well the face of self-defeat."

Feeling like an underdog, Schultz developed a deep determination to succeed. Sports became his early calling, because "I wasn't labeled a poor kid on the playing field." As star quarterback of his high school football team, he received a scholarship to Northern Michigan University—and became the first person in his family to earn a college degree. His fierce competitiveness never faded: it just shifted from football to business.

Schultz started his career at Xerox but felt the environment was too bureaucratic and rigid for him to flourish. While others thrived in the Xerox culture, Schultz yearned to go his own way. "I had to find a place where I could be myself," he said.

> I could not settle for anything less. You must have the courage to follow an unconventional path. You can't value or measure your life experience in the moment, because you never know when you're going to find the true path that enables you to find your voice. The reservoir of all my life experiences shaped me as a person and a leader.

Schultz then got involved in selling coffee filters, where he encountered Starbucks Coffee during a sales call at Pike Place

Market in Seattle. "I felt I had discovered a whole new continent," he said. He actively campaigned to join the company, becoming its director of operations and marketing.

On a buying trip to Italy, Schultz noticed the unique community experience that Milanese espresso bars played in their customers' daily lives. He dreamed of creating a similar sense of community in the United States, using coffee as the vehicle. Upon his return, Schultz decided to launch the new business on his own and opened three coffeehouses in Seattle. Learning he could acquire Starbucks from its founders, Schultz quickly rounded up financing from private investors.

As he was finalizing the purchase, Schultz faced the greatest challenge of his business career when one of his investors proposed to buy the company himself. "I feared all my influential backers would defect to this investor," he recalled. "I asked Bill Gates Sr., father of the founder of Microsoft, to help me stand up to one of the titans of Seattle because I needed his stature and confidence."

Schultz had a searing meeting with the investor, who told him, "If you don't go along with my deal, you'll never work in this town again. You'll never raise another dollar. You'll be dog meat." On leaving the meeting, Schultz was overcome with tears. For two frenzied weeks, he prepared an alternative plan that met his $3.8 million financing goal and staved off the alternate investor.

> If I had agreed to the terms the investor demanded, he would have taken away my dream. He could have fired me at whim and dictated the atmosphere and values of Starbucks. The passion, commitment, and dedication would have all disappeared.

The saddest day of Schultz's life was when his father died. When he shared with a friend the conflicts he felt in his relationship with his father, his friend remarked, "If he had been successful, you wouldn't have the drive you have now."

After his father's death, Schultz reframed his image of his father, recognizing strengths such as honesty, work ethic, and commitment to family. Instead of seeing his father as a failure, he came to believe the system had crushed him. "After he died, I realized I had judged him unfairly. He never had the opportunity to find fulfillment and dignity from meaningful work."

Schultz channeled his drive into building a company where his father would have been proud to work. By paying more than minimum wage, offering substantial benefits, and granting stock options to all its workers, Starbucks offers its employees what Schultz's father never received. Schultz uses these incentives to attract and retain people whose values are consistent with the company's values. As a result, Starbucks employee turnover is less than half that of other retailers.

Among Schultz's greatest talents is his ability to connect with people from diverse backgrounds. He tells his story and the Starbucks story at special events and visits two dozen Starbucks stores per week. Each day he gets up at 5:30 A.M. to speak by phone with Starbucks personnel around the world. He says Starbucks gave him "the canvas to paint on."

> Starbucks is the quintessential people-based business, where everything we do is about humanity. The culture and values of the company are its signature and its competitive difference. We have created a worldwide appeal for our customers because people are hungry for human connection and authenticity. Whether you're Chinese, Japanese, Spanish, or Greek, coffee is just the catalyst for that connection. I don't know if I was drawn to this business because of my background, or whether it gave me the opportunity to connect the dots, but it has come full circle for me.

Schultz's experience is instructive in the way he consciously used his life experiences to envision the kind of company he wanted to create in Starbucks and then made it happen. His example is one of dozens from authentic leaders who traced their success and inspiration directly to their life stories.

Your Life Story Defines Your Leadership

Asked what motivates them to lead, authentic leaders consistently say they find their motivation through understanding their own stories. Their stories enable them to know who they are and to stay focused on their True North.

The stories of authentic leaders cover the full spectrum of life's experiences. They include the impact of parents, teachers, coaches, and mentors who recognized their potential; the impact of their communities; and their leadership in team sports, scouting, student government, and early employment. Many leaders find their motivation comes from a difficult experience in their lives: personal illness or the illness of a family member; death of a parent or a sibling; or feelings of being excluded, discriminated against, or rejected by peers.

What emerges from these stories is that virtually all the leaders interviewed found their passion to lead through the uniqueness of their life stories.

Not by being born as leaders.

Not by believing they had the characteristics, traits, or style of a leader.

Not by trying to emulate great leaders.

Some outstanding leaders like former Merck CEO Roy Vagelos said they did not see themselves as leaders at all. Instead, they viewed themselves as people who wanted to make a difference and inspired others to join with them in pursuing common goals. If that isn't leadership, what is?

Let's focus on the life stories of three more leaders. As you read these stories, think about the ways your life story inspires you and defines your leadership.

Dick Kovacevich: From Athletic Field to Premier Banker. During the past twenty years, Dick Kovacevich, chairman and CEO of Wells Fargo Bank in San Francisco, has compiled one of the most successful track records of any commercial banker. In his interview, he did not focus on his professional success but talked instead about how his experiences growing up in a small town in western Washington shaped his leadership philosophy.

Kovacevich was raised in a working-class family and interacted with people of all income and education levels. The dairy farmers, loggers, and workers at the local Weyerhaeuser sawmill that he knew were intelligent people who worked hard and had high ethical standards but lacked a college education. His teachers had a tremendous influence on him, encouraging him to do well academically and go to college.

From the age of eleven through high school, Kovacevich worked in a local grocery store, which stimulated his interest in business. He would go to school, play sports from 3 to 5:30 P.M., run home and eat, and then be at work from 6 to 9 P.M. Eventually, he ran the produce department in the summer when the produce manager went on vacation. He did the displays, pricing, and ordering and learned he enjoyed business. Those experiences taught Kovacevich disciplines that stayed with him ever since: "I developed the intuition and leadership skills needed in business, more so than in business school where there weren't any leadership courses."

Athletics had a significant impact on Kovacevich's development as a leader. From the age of four, he played a team sport several hours every day, becoming the team's leader as captain in baseball or quarterback in football. "On the athletic field I learned that a group of people can perform so much better as a team than as the sum of their individual talents. Through my early leadership experiences, I learned skills by trial and error that I could apply in business."

> If you were quarterback of a team of quarterbacks, you would lose every game. Just as quarterbacks are overrated, CEOs are too. You can't be an all-star quarterback unless you have some great linemen, outstanding receivers, and a good running game. Diversity of skills is an important element of any effective team. I am amazed at leaders who surround themselves with people just like themselves. There is no way they can be

effective. We need to recognize our weaknesses, but don't want to amplify them. You need to surround yourself with people whose strengths complement your weaknesses.

Dick Kovacevich has made good use of that principle throughout his business career, from Citibank to Norwest Bank to Wells Fargo. He has surrounded himself with talented executives who build the bank's individual businesses, giving them the authority and latitude to lead in their own way while continuing to act as quarterback of the team.

His life experience of growing up in a small town has profoundly shaped his banking philosophy. While other banks were using computers to eliminate customer-service personnel, Kovacevich endeavored to make Wells Fargo the most client-friendly bank in every community where it operates by having its employees adopt an attitude of helping their clients meet their financial needs. For example, when you approach Wells Fargo for a mortgage on your home, the loan officer is likely to ask you about setting up a savings account for your daughter's college fund or an individual retirement account. Because Kovacevich has surrounded himself with highly talented executives and has remained so deeply engaged in the business, Wells Fargo has been able to sustain the highest growth in earnings over the past two decades of any commercial bank.

Ellen Breyer: Recapturing Her Passion. Ellen Breyer, CEO of Hazelden Foundation, the leading chemical dependency treatment organization, relies on passion to guide her leadership. As a college student in New York in the late 1960s, she was an activist involved in many causes. She protested the Vietnam War, organized civil rights marches in Washington, and led voter registration drives in her hometown of New Rochelle, New York.

Breyer did not know the federal government was taking notice of her activities, or that it considered them subversive. Then one day she was notified that her federal student loans had been withdrawn. "The government was taking pictures at rallies, looking at petitions, and identifying college students. I was one of four people in my class who had their student loans pulled as a result," she explained.

> *There were some borderline activities, but I wasn't part of them. The anti-war movement was a long continuum, and we played within the law. We had strong feelings, passions, beliefs, and a solid rationale for what we were doing. It was remarkable that you could put your energies into something and make significant change. I loved it.*

Breyer married after graduation and went into business, rising to head of corporate marketing for Godiva Chocolate. After her three sons were born, she cut back on her work schedule to spend time raising them. As a result of her husband's promotions at American Express, the Breyers moved to London, back to New York, and then to Minneapolis. Each time Ellen took a new position in the corporate world. When her youngest son graduated from high school, she decided to take a sabbatical. "It is interesting how my life came full circle," she reflected.

> *I was spending a lot of time on nonprofit volunteer activities and enjoying that more than my day job. I went skiing in Aspen for a season and thought about what I wanted to do with the rest of my life. I asked myself, how can I make the transition from the for-profit environment to working in a nonprofit?*

While serving on the board of Hazelden Foundation, Breyer was made interim CEO as the board conducted a national search. Seven months later she became permanent CEO, enabling her to fulfill her desire to help people with dependency issues.

> *This experience has reconnected me with my passions. I feel strongly about helping people recover from alcohol and drug addiction. On a personal level, my father died of alcoholism. There is a direct link to what I did*

before I was thirty and what I am doing now, in terms of connecting your
work life with your passions, and the belief that you can change things in
a dramatic way.

Breyer's ability to recapture the passions of her early years and link them to her current work is impressive. She has reframed her life story by taking experiences from her past to define and empower her present. As a result, her passion for leading has a remarkable impact on those around her.

Reatha Clark King: From Cotton Fields to the Boardroom. Reatha Clark King's roots trace to a rural community, where she was encouraged by many to become a leader. King acknowledges, "I didn't get here on my own. I am standing on the shoulders of the giants in my life who reached out and helped me get launched, and all those who helped me along the way."

King grew up in Georgia in the 1940s as the daughter of farm laborers. Her father left the family when she was young, so her mother worked as a maid to support her three children. Her family was so poor that she often had to leave school to work in the cotton fields for $3 per day so her mother could pay the bills. "Those were bitter moments in my experience, because white children didn't have to leave school," she recalled. "That contrast was so clear and so wrong."

The young King found her church a haven amid the constant poverty and discrimination. "I have fond memories of going to church every Sunday morning at eleven and being there until two o'clock. I can still close my eyes and see my grandmother praying." The older women of the church, known as "sisters," identified her special abilities, noticing her intellectual potential, initiative, work ethic, and dependability. "The sisters, my teachers, and people in the community kept an eye on me, and encouraged me to overcome unjust barriers against black people."

King credited two mentors with influencing her development the most: her grade school teacher for seven years and the school librarian. They encouraged her to go to Clark University in Atlanta, where she won a tuition scholarship and worked in the library for 35 cents an hour to pay for room and board.

While studying at Clark, King was mentored by the chair of the chemistry department, who stimulated her interest in becoming a research chemist. She applied to the University of Chicago's doctoral program, a bold step for a young woman from Georgia. After earning her Ph.D. in physical chemistry, she worked at the National Bureau of Standards and then taught at York College in New York. Even there, things were not easy. "One black faculty member called me an Uncle Tom for trying to resolve issues," she recalled. "That was one of the most hurtful moments of my life."

She got her first opportunity to lead when she became president of Metropolitan State University in Minneapolis. But she did not yet see herself as a leader.

> *Others thought of me as a leader, but I saw myself as someone doing what needed to be done. My reasons for leading were not centered on my needs but on the needs of my people, of women, and of my community. I saw compelling challenges to be met. If no one else is willing to lead, or capable of leading, then it is my obligation to step up to the challenge.*

King found her gender represented another barrier to opportunity. "You had to reach down deep to reinforce your courage in order to overcome both race and gender. To find inspiration, I would think back on the sisters and teachers along the way who had such great influence on my life."

While at Metro State, she was recruited by the CEO of General Mills to be president of the General Mills Foundation. Using this platform, she pioneered programs to help young people of color. Since King retired from General Mills, she has devoted her energies to corporate boards. Her reputation grew as she was elected to the boards of directors of ExxonMobil and Wells Fargo Bank, as well as Minnesota Mutual, Department 56, and H. B. Fuller. In 2004 the National Association of Corporate Directors named her Director of the Year. "I enjoy opportunities to serve on corporate boards because diversity should be at that table. Not everybody likes being the only one there, but I feel comfortable," she said.

King often thinks back to what her parents did with what they had and wonders if she is doing enough. "The question is, what do people lead toward? I'm leading toward a cause: to get more opportunities for people. It is in my blood to remove unjust barriers and to help people appreciate themselves and be who they are."

Throughout her life, King has used the inspiration of her life story to stay on course to her True North. She reaches out and helps others as she quietly walks past barriers of racial and gender discrimination, without ever expressing discomfort or anger. She is as comfortable in the boardrooms of the world's largest corporations as she is in creating opportunities for the poor.

What's Your Life Story?

What can be learned from the stories of Howard Schultz, Dick Kovacevich, Ellen Breyer, and Reatha Clark King? All of them, like other leaders interviewed, take their passion and inspiration to lead from their life stories. By understanding the formative experiences of their early lives, they have been able to reframe their life stories and their leadership around fulfilling their passions and following their True North.

At this point you may be wondering, doesn't everyone have a life story? What makes leaders' stories different from everyone else's?

Many people with painful stories see themselves as victims, feeling the world has dealt them a bad hand. Or they lack the introspection to see the connection between their life experiences and the goals they are pursuing now. Some get so caught up in chasing the world's esteem that they never become genuine leaders.

The difference with authentic leaders lies in the way they *frame* their stories. Their life stories provide the context for their lives, and through them they find their passion and inspiration to make an impact in the world. Novelist John Barth once said, "The story of your life is not your life. It is your story." In other words, it is your story that matters, not the facts of your life. Our life stories are like permanent tapes playing in our heads. Over and over, we replay the events and interactions with people that are important to our lives, attempting to make sense of them and using them to find our place in the world.

Reframing our stories enables us to recognize that we are not victims at all but people shaped by experiences that provide the impetus for us to become leaders. Our life stories evolve constantly as we shape the meaning of our past, present, and future. Warren Bennis says, "You are the author of your life." He advocates using our stories to provide the inspiration to create our futures.

As the author of your story, can you connect the dots between your past and your future to find your inspiration to lead authentically? What people or experiences have shaped you? What have been the key turning points in your life? Where do you find your passion to lead in your life story?

The Journey to Authentic Leadership

Having considered how our life stories provide the basis for our leadership, we are ready to embark on the journey to authentic leadership.

When I graduated from college, I had the naive notion that the journey to leadership was a straight line to the top of an organization. I learned the hard way that leadership is not a simple destination of becoming CEO. Rather, it is a marathon journey that progresses through many stages until you reach your peak leadership. I was not alone. *Of all the leaders over forty we interviewed, none wound up where they thought they would.*

Vanguard CEO Jack Brennan believes that the worst thing people can do is to manage their careers with a career map: "The dissatisfied people I have known and those who experienced ethical or legal failures all had a clear career plan." Brennan recommends being flexible and venturesome in stepping up to unexpected opportunities. "If all you're interested in is advancing your career, you'll be dissatisfied at the end of the day."

Fifty years ago, business leaders chose their careers in their early twenties when they joined a company after college or military service, worked there diligently for forty years, retired to a warm climate, and often died before seventy. In interviewing leaders at all phases of their leadership journeys, it became clear that an entirely new leadership development path is emerging, as illustrated by Figure 1.1.

As the lifeline indicates, your development as a leader is not a straight line to the top (dashed line) but a journey filled with many ups and downs as you progress to peak leadership and continue leading through the final stage (solid line). These days your journey is more likely to follow a winding path than it is to be a race to the top.

As eBay's John Donahoe said, "Everything in life is a cycle."

When things are up, the only thing you know is that they are going to go down. On the down slope the only thing you know is that things will turn up. You don't recognize the upward slope as the lows are higher than your highs used to be. That's life as a process, an opportunity to learn and grow. Make a movie of your life, not just snapshots along the way.

Figure 1.1 The Journey to Authentic Leadership

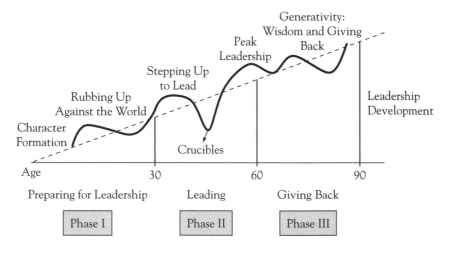

Because many people are living well into their nineties these days, the leader's journey follows the new span of life and subdivides into three periods, each of roughly thirty years. Each stage of the journey opens up a myriad of opportunities for leadership. In their first thirty years, leaders develop through education and studying, as well as extracurricular and early work experiences. Phase I is labeled "Preparing for Leadership." Phase II, from thirty to sixty years of age, is the "Leading" phase in which leaders take on successive roles until they complete their peak leadership experience.

Finally, Phase III is for "Giving Back," a stage of human development that psychologist Erik Erikson called "generativity." It begins around age sixty, when leaders have completed their principal career leadership roles, and continues for the rest of their lives. In this phase, authentic leaders look for opportunities to spread their knowledge and wisdom across many people and organizations, even as they continue their own active learning process.

Phase I: Preparing for Leadership

The first thirty years is the time to prepare for leadership, when character is formed and people become individual contributors or lead teams for the first time. As Randy Komisar, former CEO of LucasArts, says, "This is your opportunity to rub up against the world."

Very few leaders these days are making career commitments in their twenties. Instead, they use the time following college to gain valuable work experience. Typically changing jobs every eighteen to twenty-four months to diversify their experience, many young leaders have an eye on gaining admission to graduate school in business, law, or government. Even some who complete their master's degrees prefer individual contributor roles in consulting or finance before committing to a specific company or industry.

Stanford Business School professor Joel Peterson, former managing partner of real estate developer Trammell Crow, offers a challenging view of this phase:

You're in a self-absorbed decade, asking yourself, "What are my strengths and weaknesses, how can I get ahead, how can I impact the world?" It's all about you. But once you get out there and start to do things that matter and develop relationships with people, you find that you're no longer just managing your résumé.

This self-absorption is a natural phase of development, as the measures of success in your teens and twenties are based primarily on what you accomplish as an individual. Your performance determines what schools you are admitted to and how well you do in your initial jobs. Here's how Randy Komisar described what comes next:

We begin life on a linear path where success is based on having a clear target. Life gets complicated when the targets aren't clear anymore, and you have to set your own targets. By rubbing up against the world, you get to know yourself. Either do that, or you're going to spend your life serving the interests and expectations of others.

He acknowledges that the start of the journey is particularly hard for young people. He tells his students that life is not in their control. "They look at me and say, 'Hey, man. All I want to do is get a good job, buy a car, have a house, get married, and have kids. Just get out of my way.'" Komisar says he wishes life were so simple. He tells them:

Let me just plant this seed. Keep it alive and come back to it in ten years, but don't flush it. I'm not asking you to follow my path. I'm only challenging you to ask yourself the question from time to time, "What do you want out of your life?" At some point it's going to be relevant, and I want to empower you for that time.

Jonathan Doochin: Pay It Forward. At twenty-three, Jonathan Doochin was the youngest leader we interviewed. In his senior year of college he created Harvard's Leadership Institute as an umbrella organization for the more than two hundred student organizations on the campus. As the founder, he organized programs to facilitate the development of young leaders.

Doochin traces his passion to help others to an experience he had in third grade, when he could not spell "surprise" during a spelling bee. "The kids made fun of me. I felt like a total failure." After he was diagnosed with dyslexia, his parents worked with him on homework three to five hours every night, while his fifth-grade teacher mentored him daily. "Miss Jackson's interest made me believe I could do anything," he explained. "Without her faith and my parents' dedication, I would have never gone to Harvard."

As a result of this experience, Doochin developed a personal philosophy of "pay it forward" that guides his leadership today. He believes those he affects directly will pay it forward to a handful of others, and over time the cycle will compound to help countless people. "I can never directly repay all those along the way who helped me, but I can have a positive impact on those coming behind," he said. "You don't have to be CEO to make an impact. You can do it every day, starting with your next-door neighbor. Leadership happens at every stage of your life."

Ian Chan: Creating a Scientific Revolution. Ian Chan is another young leader who discovered his passion to lead at an early age. As his college graduation approached, he knew he wanted "an opportunity that would get me excited to jump out of bed every day and go to work." After uninspiring experiences in investment banking and private equity, he and his younger brother got excited about the human genome revolution.

Starting a cutting-edge company that could revolutionize medicine, the Chan brothers founded U.S. Genomics to deliver personalized genomics on a broad scale. As their advisers, they attracted noted scientists like Craig Venter, who originally mapped the human genome, and Bob Langer, a renowned technologist. Starting with a $100,000 credit card loan, they subsequently raised $52 million from venture capitalists, several of whom joined their board of directors as the Chan brothers gave up more than half their ownership.

Over the next five years the company's work attracted attention in the scientific community and venture capital world and became the pioneer in its field. When the founders presented the company's exceptional performance in December 2001, the board gave them a standing ovation. Four months later, the Chan brothers were shocked when the board told them that they were being replaced by a new CEO. "Even to this day, I have no idea why this happened when things were going so well," he said.

> *You put your heart and soul into it for many years and then boom, it's all gone. It was gut-wrenching to have something you created, believed in deeply, and made incredible sacrifices for, taken away from you. You still have some shares, but you're not part of the enterprise anymore with its mission you believe in. At first, I was in denial and wanted to continue fighting the battle, but I felt helpless.*
>
> *In hindsight, it was a very rich experience for five years that I can build on for the next journey. I had been working crazy hours and was very tired. I didn't have a personal life and needed a more balanced approach. To regroup, I spent two years getting my MBA. That provided time for self-reflection and opportunities to interact with some of the world's top business leaders. I realized I was still fortunate to have my health, family, and the privilege of living in a free country. These should never be taken for granted.*
>
> *I recognized my heart is still in entrepreneurship and biotechnology. There are so many untreatable diseases today that provide the opportunity to make a broad impact. That's why I'm now starting another company that can improve health care through technology and innovation.*

Ian Chan appears to be a victim of his own success. As the potential of U.S. Genomics became apparent to the venture capitalists that funded the venture, they decided they needed a more experienced executive to lead it. Yet for all the heartache and pain,

Chan had an invaluable experience that will be formative to him on his leadership journey. Unfortunately, fear of failure keeps many young leaders from jumping into opportunities like he did. Young & Rubicam CEO Ann Fudge offered a different point of view, noting, "Struggle and tough experiences ultimately fashion you."

Don't worry about the challenges. Embrace them. Go through them even if they hurt. Tell yourself, there is something to be learned from this experience. I may not fully understand it now, but I will later. It's all part of life, and life is a process of learning. Every challenging experience develops your core of inner strength, which gets you through those storms. Nothing worth doing in life is going to be easy.

Phase II: Leading

The second phase of your leadership journey begins with a rapid accumulation of leadership experiences and it culminates in the fifties, when leaders typically reach their peak leadership. In between, most leaders go through a crucible, a difficult period at work or at home that tests them to the core. The result is a transformation of their understanding of what their leadership is all about, followed by a rapid acceleration of their development.

Many leaders express a strong drive to gain experience in leading early in their careers. In contrast to many business school classmates who started as consultants or investment bankers, Wells Fargo's Kovacevich just wanted to run something when he got out of school: "My goal was to find a company that would give me the opportunity to run a business as quickly as possible."

Dan Schulman, Virgin Mobile USA's CEO, compared accumulating experiences to the weight lifting he did when he played high school football. "Leading a company is like doing multiple repetitions of three-hundred-pound weights. No one can lift three hundred pounds unless they start much lower and work their way up," he says. "If they don't have their muscles in shape through a variety of experiences, they will be crushed by it."

In Schulman's view, every experience prior to becoming CEO helped him build muscle. "I never viewed them as a steppingstone to the next rung on the ladder," he said.

> *You need those early experiences to learn the lessons that will help prepare you for challenges later in your career. Those who move up the ladder too quickly find themselves in a precarious place. They think they are heroes, but when real challenges and the realities of failure hit them, they're unprepared to deal with them.*

Martha Goldberg Aronson: Taking on Added Responsibility. After several successful experiences, emerging leaders are often identified as having the talent to lead across a much wider business spectrum, and their companies test them in more challenging settings.

In her early years at Medtronic, Martha Goldberg Aronson developed a reputation as a high-potential leader. She joined the company's acquisitions group and was selected two years later as a Medtronic Fellow to attend business school. Rejoining Medtronic as a product manager, she was soon promoted to run a start-up venture.

When management consolidated Aronson's venture with an existing business, she became general manager of the business. As her business flourished, Aronson's career prospects brightened. One day she was home alone with her two children when the phone rang. Medtronic's head of human resources asked her, "What would you think about an international assignment?" Aronson recalled, "I hemmed and hawed and told her this wasn't the best day to talk about a move."

Aronson was skeptical about whether an international move was right for her career or her personal life. Being far from the support of her parents and older siblings with a baby and a toddler was not part of her game plan. She also balked at walking away from her current job before it was done and worried about the impact on her husband's career. After discussing the European opportunity with her mentors and her husband, she decided to take the job because she realized it was a special opportunity to work overseas and broaden her understanding of how business is done there.

Aronson flourished in the European environment. She gained significantly from the daily exposure to the wide range of cultures in her region, and she led her multi-country team to produce significant results. She took the risk when an opportunity came, willing to learn more about leading in a complex geographic environment without knowing the next step in her career. After three years, she was recalled to Medtronic headquarters to head investor relations, just as she was having her third child.

Jeff Immelt: Hitting the Wall. Many leaders go through a crucible when they have an experience at work that dramatically tests their sense of self, their values, or their assumptions about their future or career. I call this "hitting the wall," because the experience resembles a fast-moving race car hitting the wall of the track, something most rising leaders experience at least once in their careers.

General Electric CEO Jeff Immelt was a fast-rising star in his mid-thirties when he faced his toughest challenge. Asked to return to GE's plastics business as head of world sales and marketing, he had reservations about accepting the move because it was not a promotion. Jack Welch told him, "I know this isn't what you want to do, but this is a time when you serve the company."

Facing stiff competition, the division had entered into several long-term, fixed-price contracts with key customers, including U.S. automakers, when a spike of inflation sent the division's costs soaring. Immelt's operation missed its operating profit target by $30 million, or 30 percent of its budget. He tried to increase prices, but progress was slow, as Immelt's actions caused its crucial relationship with General Motors to deteriorate.

This only intensified the pressure on Immelt to produce results and forced Welch to resolve the issues by talking to GM CEO Roger Smith. Welch did not hesitate to reach down to pepper

Immelt with questions by phone. Immelt recalled the year as a remarkably difficult one until he and his team could start to turn the business around.

> *Nobody wants to be around somebody going through a low period. In times like that you've got to be able to draw from within. Leadership is one of these great journeys into your own soul.*

Jeff Immelt was under enormous pressure to deliver immediate results, but he withstood the pressure to compromise and took the long-term course of getting the business back on track. Immelt's success in leading this turnaround prepared him to become Welch's successor, where he has faced much greater pressure but has stayed the course of his True North to build GE for the next decade.

These journeys illustrate that reaching your peak leadership these days is anything but a straight line to the top. In truth, it is the difficult experiences that prepare you to lead your organization through the challenges you will face.

Phase III: Giving Back

Two thousand years ago Roman statesman Marcus Cicero declared that "old age is to be resisted." Today the last thirty years of a leader's journey can be the most productive and rewarding of all. Many leaders are bypassing retirement to share their experience with multiple organizations. They serve on for-profit or nonprofit boards, mentor young leaders, take up teaching, or coach newly appointed CEOs.

Lord John Browne, who has led British Petroleum to new heights in his eleven years at the helm, agrees with this assessment. In announcing he would step down as CEO at the age of sixty, Browne said, "I don't believe in retirement. The idea seems a touch out of date." He suggested he would be looking for an interesting new position with a purpose. "I'm hooked on business," he concluded.

Ninety-three-year-old Zyg Nagorski was the senior leader interviewed for our study. After running the Aspen Institute's Executive

Programs for a decade, Nagorski stepped aside at seventy-five. Then he and his wife started the Center for International Leadership to conduct values and ethics seminars for executives. Nagorski's probing style caused many leaders to rethink their values and how they would respond in complex situations. Eighteen years later, he is still going strong.

Exploring Leadership After CEO: My Story

Along with Warren Bennis, Nagorski is one of my role models for Phase III. Early in life I adopted the philosophy that "you only go around once in life," so I wanted to have as many meaningful experiences as I could. I observed many CEOs who stayed too long, never groomed a successor, and retired without anything to do. My goal was to lead a major organization doing important work, turn it over to my successor, and then move on.

Elected CEO of Medtronic in 1991, I told the board that I should not serve more than ten years, because that was sufficient time to accomplish the organization's goals and develop a well-qualified successor. I was fortunate to have Art Collins to lead Medtronic when I stepped aside in 2001 at age fifty-eight. Not having a clear vision of what I wanted to do next, I spent the first six months exploring wide-ranging opportunities in government, education, health care policy, and international relations. Each field was interesting, but none seemed just right.

Meanwhile, I stayed active in the business community by serving on the boards of Goldman Sachs, Novartis, and Target and now ExxonMobil. Viewing these corporations from the board's vantage point has been a superb education into leaders in the vital industries of financial services, health care, retail, and energy and the challenges they face.

In 2002 Penny and I moved to Switzerland for a "working sabbatical," as I had a joint appointment to teach leadership at two leading Swiss universities. We found living in Switzerland was very stimulating, although it was hard for Penny to be so far from her work. I vividly recall my first day in the classroom, when I met ninety MBA students from thirty-five countries. It was a scary feeling to stand in front of these very bright and demanding students. Talking about Medtronic was easy, but leading a case discussion on Intel that engaged all ninety students was an enormous challenge. But I found I loved teaching and also enjoyed counseling students and hearing their dreams, hopes, and fears.

While in Switzerland, I began writing *Authentic Leadership*, an experience that was difficult but rewarding. Returning from Switzerland, I became a full-time professor of management practice at Harvard Business School, following a four-month stint at Yale School of Management. At Harvard I teach "Leadership and Corporate Accountability," the new required MBA course, and an elective I created, "Authentic Leadership Development," whose content is a forerunner of this book.

At this stage of my journey I feel fortunate to have these opportunities for continued growth and interaction with outstanding leaders at all stages of their journeys. And I have discovered a new purpose for my leadership: to help develop the next generation of authentic leaders.

Regardless of where you are in your journey—at the top of your organization, just getting started, or looking for a new challenge— *every leadership experience you have will enable you to grow and to discover your authentic leadership*. Just as you conclude one portion of your journey, another opportunity will emerge to take your learning from previous experiences and apply it to a new situation. If you embrace your story, your leadership journey never ends. Yet along the way many leaders stumble and get derailed. This is a risk that all leaders face. Before exploring how you become an authentic leader, let's explore why some leaders lose their way.

Note to the reader: Before going on to Chapter Two, you may want to complete the Chapter One Exercise found in Appendix C.

2

WHY LEADERS
LOSE THEIR WAY

During the course of their leadership journeys many leaders lose sight of their True North and get derailed. This is a risk all leaders face. Before describing how to become an authentic leader, let's explore what causes some leaders to lose their way. Why do people with excellent potential get derailed just as they appear to be hitting the peak of their leadership? Can they recover from failures and still become authentic leaders?

These questions trouble everyone who wants to lead, because people who lose their way are not necessarily bad leaders. They have the potential to become good leaders, even great leaders, but somewhere along the way they get pulled off course. Little by little, bit by bit, they get caught up in their own success. Just as they are receiving more acclaim from the external world and the rewards that go with it, they are at greatest risk of deviating from their True North.

A recent example of a high-profile leader who lost sight of his True North is Philip Purcell, the former CEO of Morgan Stanley. Purcell accomplished a great deal in his career and did nothing illegal or unethical, but he lost his way.

Throughout his career Purcell was a star, from finishing at the head of his class at Chicago Graduate School of Business to his successes at McKinsey, Sears, and Dean Witter. When he led the merger of Dean Witter with Morgan Stanley and wound up as its CEO, he appeared to be on top of the world.

His primary challenge at Morgan Stanley was to create a financial services powerhouse by integrating the investment bank with the brokerage business. Instead of spending time with the money managers and traders, who were the big earners in his firm, and with his new customers in this most client-centric of all businesses, he focused on building his power base by maneuvering the merged board.

Purcell also pushed out many capable executives who challenged his leadership. The criterion for promotion shifted from Morgan Stanley's performance-based meritocracy to loyalty to Purcell. He reportedly reneged on his promise to turn over the CEO position after three years to Morgan Stanley's former CEO, John Mack. As frustration with his leadership grew, so did the departures of talented people.

In 2005 things got so bad that former Morgan Stanley executives formed the "Gang of Eight" to lobby the board for Purcell's removal. As the departures accelerated and pressure for action from Wall Street mounted, the board finally recognized it had to choose between saving Purcell's job and saving the firm. It chose the firm, and Purcell was forced to resign. The board persuaded Mack to return as CEO to restore Morgan Stanley, and he is moving rapidly to do just that. Purcell has retired to his Utah ranch.

What Causes Leaders to Lose Their Way?

Purcell is not at all unique. He is just one of several dozen well-known leaders who lost their way in recent years. Let's look deeper into the reasons *why* leaders lose their way.

Before people take on leadership roles, they should first ask themselves two fundamental questions: "What motivates me to lead?" and "What is the purpose of my leadership?" If honest answers to the first question are simply power, prestige, and money, leaders risk being trapped by external gratification as the source of their fulfillment. There is nothing wrong with desiring these outward symbols *as long as they are combined with a deeper desire to serve something greater than oneself.*

Leaders whose goal is gaining power over others, maximizing wealth, or becoming famous tend to look to other people for satisfaction and acknowledgment of their status. In public and in private, they display a high degree of narcissism. As leaders of institutions, they ultimately believe that the institution cannot survive without them because in their mind they *are* the institution. A tragic example of this was Richard Grasso in his closing days as CEO of the New York Stock Exchange. Grasso got so caught up in his power and celebrity that he lost touch with the negative reaction to a public servant receiving a $130 million compensation package and was forced to resign by his board.

In contrast, Xerox CEO Anne Mulcahy deflects most media attention, in spite of her success in turning the company around. She told us about receiving a telephone call from her mentor, former CEO David Kearns, when she was in the darkest hours of trying to keep the company out of bankruptcy and fending off an SEC investigation. "Mulcahy, do you believe all that bull they are writing about you in the newspapers?" Kearns asked over the phone. "No, David," Mulcahy replied calmly. "Good," responded Kearns. "Then don't believe it when they start writing about you as the savior of Xerox."

Losing Touch with Reality

Leaders who focus on external gratification instead of inner satisfaction find it difficult to stay grounded. They reject the honest critic who holds a mirror to their face and speaks the truth. Instead, they surround themselves with supporters telling them what they want to hear. Over time, they lose the capacity for honest dialogue, and people learn not to confront them.

Fearing Failure

Underlying these tendencies may be a fear of failure. Many leaders advance by imposing their will on others. By the time they reach the top, they may be paranoid that someone is waiting in the wings to knock them off their pedestal. Underneath their bravado lies uncertainty that they may not be suitable for such powerful leadership roles, and any day someone is going to unmask them.

To overcome their fears, they drive so hard for perfection that they are incapable of acknowledging either failures or weaknesses. When confronted with their failures, they try to cover them up or to create a rationale that convinces others these problems are not their fault. Often they look for scapegoats on whom to blame their problems, either within their organization or outside. Through the combination of power, charisma, and communications skills, they convince others to accept these distortions, causing entire organizations to lose touch with reality. In the end, it is their organizations that suffer.

. . . and Craving Success

The other side of the fear of failure is an insatiable craving for success. Most leaders want to do a good job for their organizations and to be recognized and rewarded accordingly. When they achieve success, they are given added power and enjoy the prestige that goes with it. Along the way, success can go to their heads, and they develop a sense of entitlement. At the height of their power, their success creates a deep desire to keep it going. They are prone to pushing the limits and thinking that they can get away with it.

Novartis CEO Daniel Vasella described this process in a 2002 *Fortune* magazine interview:

> Once you get under the domination of making the quarter—even unwittingly . . . you'll begin to sacrifice things that are important and may be vital for your company over the long term. The culprit that drives this cycle isn't the fear of failure so much as it is the craving for success. . . . For many of us the idea of being a successful manager is an intoxicating one. It is a pattern of celebration leading to belief, leading to distortion. When you achieve good results, you are typically celebrated, and you begin to

believe that the figure at the center of all that champagne toasting is your-
self. You are idealized by the outside world, and there is a natural tendency
to believe that what is written is true.

Turning Failures into Successes

While many leaders have a deep-seated fear of failure, the irony is
that they learn the most from their failures. David Pottruck, former
CEO of Charles Schwab, relishes the opportunity to learn from
every experience: "You don't have to be perfect," he said. "You can
start off on a bad path and recover. You can turn most failures into
successes if you ask yourself, what can I learn from this so that I can
do better the next time?" Pottruck believes that the key to learning
from failure is to avoid denial and be honest with yourself. "If you're
open, you can learn a lot more from failure than success," he says.

> *When you're successful, you take it for granted and move on to the next*
> *thing. Failure forces you to reflect. What went wrong? How could I have*
> *done this better? It's an opportunity for you to take responsibility. The path*
> *of least resistance is to blame it on someone else. I failed many times but*
> *learned from each experience and usually managed to come back stronger.*
> *I kept plugging away and eventually was successful.*

Mike Baker, CEO of Arthrocare, tells the story of the mental
and physical pressures he felt at West Point. "I remember taking my
first advanced statistics exam and absolutely failing. That was serious business at West Point. If you failed a class, you were out. There
was no margin for error," he said.

> *I'm suspicious of somebody who's never failed, because you don't know*
> *how they're going to react when they do. Everyone is born to fail. Every-*
> *one is going to break down. What matters is not how often you have*
> *been on the canvas, but whether you get up, how you get up, and what*
> *you learn from it.*

In contrast to Pottruck and Baker, some rising leaders have such a fear of failing that they avoid risks. When they reach the top, they are not prepared to cope with the greater challenges they face there.

The Loneliness Within

It is lonely at the top. Leaders know they are ultimately responsible and that the well-being of so many rests in their hands. If they fail, many people will get hurt. Some leaders simply run faster to ignore the mounting pressures.

Who can they share their worries with? It can be difficult to talk with subordinates or their boards of directors about their biggest problems and deepest fears. Friends outside the organization may not understand the challenges they are facing, and sharing their doubts openly may set off rumors. Sometimes it is even difficult to share these concerns with your spouse or mentor.

As a result of this loneliness, many leaders deny their fears. They shut down their inner voice because it is too uncomfortable to hear. Instead, they start listening to the external voices pressuring them, thinking that all will be well if they can satisfy them. But the advice of outsiders is often conflicting or too painful to face, so they choose to listen only to people who reinforce their views.

Meanwhile, their work lives and personal lives grow more unbalanced. Fearing failure, they favor their work life, even saying, "My work *is* my life." Eventually, they lose touch with those closest to them—their spouses, children, and best friends—or they co-opt them to their point of view. Over time, little mistakes turn into major ones. No amount of hard work can correct them. Instead of seeking wise counsel at this point, they dig a deeper hole. When the collapse comes, there is no avoiding it.

Who are "they"? They could be one of those executives facing prosecution for their actions. Or a former CEO or organization head forced to resign "for personal reasons." *But "they" could also be you, me, or any one of us.* We may not face a plight as severe as these leaders, but we can all lose our way.

Derailment: Losing Sight of Your True North

In observing leaders who have derailed, we identified five types who lose sight of their True North. Their shortcomings link directly to the failure to develop themselves: *Imposters*, who lack self-awareness and self-esteem; *Rationalizers*, who deviate from their values; *Glory Seekers*, who are motivated by seeking the world's acclaim; *Loners*, who fail to build personal support structures; and *Shooting Stars*, who lack the grounding of an integrated life.

Can you see yourself in any of these archetypes? Could these characteristics cause you to derail?

Imposters

Imposters rise through the organizational ranks with a combination of cunning and aggression. They understand the politics of getting ahead and let no one stand in their way. They are often unabashed students of Machiavelli, determining every angle to advance as they execute their game plan. They are the ultimate political animals, adept at figuring out who their competitors are and then eliminating them one by one. They have little appetite for self-reflection or for developing self-awareness.

Abraham Lincoln once said, "If you want to test a man, give him absolute power." Having acquired power, Imposters may not be confident about how to use it. They are beset with doubts about handling the responsibilities of leadership. Because their greatest strength is besting internal opponents, they are often paranoid that underlings are out to get them.

Paralyzed by doubt, they are unable to act decisively. Their inaction leads to poor results and external challenges, so they attack their critics and cut themselves off from internal feedback. Their most competent subordinates see their lack of influence on their leader and move on to greener pastures or else slip into paralytic submission. Meanwhile, people remaining in the organization do not feel empowered, so they sit back and wait for their leaders to make decisions.

Rationalizers

To people outside their organizations, Rationalizers always appear on top of the issues. When things don't go their way, they blame external forces or subordinates or offer facile answers to their problems. They rarely step up and take responsibility themselves.

As they advance and find themselves facing greater challenges, they transmit pressure to their subordinates instead of modulating it. When pressuring subordinates fails to produce the numbers, they cut funding for research, growth initiatives, or organization building in the effort to hit immediate goals. Eventually, these short-term actions catch up with them. Then they borrow from the future to make today's numbers look good, or stretch accounting rules, rationalizing that they can make it up in the future.

Unfortunately, their actions only make the future worse. So they turn to more aggressive schemes, such as reporting future revenue streams in quarterly sales or filling customer warehouses with inventory. When these short-term actions fail to stem the tide, they resort to even more desperate measures. Ultimately, they become victims of their own rationalizations, as do their depleted organizations.

The misdeeds of Rationalizers have become all too apparent in recent years. The high stock prices of the 1990s, based on ever-higher expectations of revenue growth, led many executives to play the game of meeting stock market expectations while sacrificing the long-term value of their companies. Even years later, many Rationalizers cling to denial, unwilling to take responsibility for problems they caused. As Warren Bennis says, *"Denial and projection are the enemies of reality."*

Glory Seekers

Glory Seekers define themselves by acclaim of the external world. Money, fame, glory, and power are their goals, as they pursue visible signs of success. Often it seems more important to them to appear on lists of the most powerful business leaders than it does to build organizations of lasting value.

Their thirst for fame is unquenchable. There are always people with more money, more accolades, and more power, so no achievement is sufficient. Inside, these people feel empty. Sometimes the emptiness creates envy of those who have more, a quality that is hard for outsiders to comprehend from someone who seems to have it all.

Loners

Loners avoid forming close relationships, seeking out mentors, or creating support networks. They believe they can and must make it on their own. Not to be confused with introverts, Loners often have a myriad of superficial relationships and acolytes, but they do not listen to them. They reject honest feedback, even from those who care about them.

Without wise counsel, Loners are prone to make major mistakes. When results elude them and criticism of their leadership grows, they circle the wagons. They become rigid in pursuing their objectives, not recognizing it is their behavior that makes it impossible for them to reach their goals. Meanwhile, their organizations unravel.

Shooting Stars

The lives of Shooting Stars center entirely on their careers. To observers, they are perpetual motion machines, always on the go, traveling incessantly to get ahead. They rarely make time for family, friendships, their communities, or even themselves. Much-needed sleep and exercise routines are expendable. As they run ever faster, their stress mounts.

They move up so rapidly in their careers that they never have time to learn from their mistakes. A year or two into any job, they are ready to move on, before they have had to confront the results of their decisions. When they see problems of their making coming back to haunt them, their anxiety rises and so does the urgency to move to a new position. If their employer doesn't promote them, they are off to another organization. One day they find themselves at the top, overwhelmed by an intractable set of problems. At this point, they are prone to irrational decisions.

Heroes of Their Own Journeys

All five archetypal leaders described here—Imposters, Rationalizers, Glory Seekers, Loners, and Shooting Stars—frame their life stories in the model of an all-conquering hero. This approach may work well for musicians, actors, or athletes who excel as solo performers. It fails utterly when one leads a team, precisely because being a hero is *not* empowering to teammates or subordinates.

The role of leaders is not to get other people to follow them but to empower others to lead. They cannot elicit the best performance from their teams if they are in the game primarily for themselves. In the end, their self-centeredness keeps other people from leading. Why should they, when it is for the leader's glory and not the team's success?

Kevin Sharer: Getting Back on Track. Many leaders ask whether you can rebound after losing your way. Let's look at the story of a talented leader who worked hard at becoming authentic, almost lost his way, and then got back on track.

Amgen's chairman and CEO, Kevin Sharer, is one of the most successful CEOs in the United States today, but in 1989 he faced the most difficult situation of his life. Having succeeded at everything he had done, Sharer was facing failure for the first time. A rising star at General Electric, he was eager to get to the top and thought he could succeed at any leadership challenge. He jumped ship from GE to join the telecommunications company MCI because he thought he had a shot at the top job within two years.

"MCI was a crucible for me," Sharer observed later. "I learned that whether you are right or not, there is a price to be paid for arrogance." He also realized his style did not suit MCI's hypercompetitive culture. "People were personally competitive in a way that was not consistent with my values," he explained.

> The internal competition was mean-spirited and at your throat. It was eating me up as I was becoming less effective and less committed to the company. If your values are not consistent with the people you're working with, you should not be there.

Desperate to escape from the MCI environment, Sharer telephoned Jack Welch about returning to GE. Welch wasn't happy with the sudden way Sharer had bailed out of GE after he had opened up so many opportunities. "Hey, Kevin, forget you ever worked here," Welch replied. "At that moment," Sharer recalled, "I knew I had been cast adrift in a lifeboat."

> I realized I had to make a go of this big operating job. I couldn't just bail out. It was a gut-wrenching two years for me, the most challenging and unhappy time of my professional life. I'm not a good knife fighter, and I was getting outmaneuvered. At first I went into denial. Then I became defeatist and cynical.

Finally, Sharer said to himself, "I'm not going to play these games. I'm not going to be a sharp-elbowed, mean-spirited guy."

> It was grinding me down, and I began to retreat emotionally. My wife could not understand what I was going through because she had no corporate experience. She feared I would be fired, which only added to my feeling of isolation. Without question, it was the toughest time of my life.

Kevin Sharer's story of discovering his True North parallels the difficulties that many leaders face. They are pulled by the challenges and their egos into ever more complex situations, where they have to learn to confront their weaknesses and their failures. If they have self-awareness and insight, they readjust their compass to get back on the track of their True North.

Sharer's dream as a boy had been to follow in his father's footsteps as a naval aviator. He attended the U.S. Naval Academy, but
shortly before graduation his dream was shattered when he failed
the eyesight exam. Bouncing back quickly, he applied for admission
to the navy's prestigious nuclear submarine program. Just two weeks
later, he was interviewed by the program's famous creator, Admiral
Hyman Rickover, and was admitted.

After sailing under the waters of the world for five years as chief
engineer on a nuclear submarine, Sharer joined McKinsey, where
his role model became founder Marvin Bower. Two years later, he
had the opportunity to join GE as Welch's assistant.

In his interview Welch immediately put Sharer on the spot,
asking "Why should I hire you? You never took a risk in your life."
He took the bait, telling Welch, "I took a nuclear submarine off the
coast of Russia at age twenty-six." Then he decided to challenge
Welch, asking him, "What risk did you ever take, except with your
company's money?" That got him the job.

His experiences with the navy and McKinsey prepared Sharer
for the bare-knuckle intensity of the GE environment. His success
at GE led to his first general-management opportunity while he
was still in his mid-thirties. Looking back on his time at GE,
Sharer said, "I gained priceless experience by observing Welch's
leadership."

By age forty, Sharer ran GE's satellite business, was elected a
corporate officer, and hit the company's list of its top one hundred
executives. This would be heady stuff for anyone, but especially for
someone as ambitious as Kevin. When the headhunters came looking for a new head of sales and marketing for MCI, he seized the
opportunity to leapfrog his career.

"The CEO race is wide open," MCI's vice chairman assured
Sharer. Once again, Sharer took the bait. This time, however,
things did not go his way. Upon joining the company, Sharer
learned that the chief operating officer was in line for the top slot
and didn't welcome competition from the ambitious young hotshot
from GE.

Sharer wasted no time in developing his strategy to transform MCI and position himself. Within six weeks, he concluded that the company's geographic marketing organization was improperly structured. "I was at the zenith of my arrogance at that time," Sharer said. "I marched into the chairman's office and proposed a restructuring of MCI's sales organization." His proposal was threatening to senior executives who had spent their careers building MCI. Lacking telecommunications experience, Sharer found he had little credibility within the organization.

Sharer's crucible at MCI proved invaluable to him. It humbled him, forced him to control his ego and recognize there is more to life than just grabbing the next promotion. Caught up in the glamour of being a rising star, Sharer was brought down to reality by MCI.

Two years after joining MCI, Sharer received a letter asking if he knew anyone who could be president of Amgen. Never having heard of the company, he went to the public library to learn about it. He decided to nominate himself for the job and was offered the position, under the tutelage of CEO Gordon Binder.

Having learned a painful lesson at MCI about being perceived as a "know-it-all," he recognized he knew nothing about the biotechnology business. "If I hadn't had that chastening experience at MCI, I could easily have blown up at Amgen," he said.

> My last brush with health care had been ninth-grade biology, so I asked one of our scientists to teach me biology. By being patient, I became an insider before I started making changes. I learned the business from the ground up, made calls with sales representatives, and showed my desire to learn.

In contrast to his earlier experiences, Sharer was unusually patient for seven years while understudying Binder. This time around he avoided the seduction of the headhunters, telling them being number two at a rapidly growing company like Amgen was "better than anything else that was on the plate." A year before

Binder's retirement, the board told Sharer, "Look, Kevin, you've got the job. For the next year spend your time learning R&D." Sharer studied the Amgen research process from the ground up, working in its labs, being tutored by scientists, and visiting competitors' research facilities.

When the board announced that Sharer would become CEO, he met individually with the top 150 people in the company. Listening to their feedback gave Sharer a thorough picture of what the company's top leaders wanted.

> These interviews were the single most important thing I did upon becoming CEO. They gave me the mandate to create a shared reality for the company. That enabled people to align around the new vision and strategy for building Amgen for the next ten years.

Kevin Sharer's searing experience enabled him to return to his True North. By being introspective about his role in the MCI debacle, he recognized changes he needed to make. Landing at the top of Amgen, he did not fail to learn the lessons of his earlier experience. He focused on learning the business before taking charge, listened to the wisdom and experience of his colleagues, and was patient in reaching his goal.

So far his efforts to become an authentic leader have paid off for Sharer and for Amgen. In Sharer's first six years as CEO, Amgen's revenues grew at a 25 percent clip, with earnings and market capitalization increasing rapidly. The company has been transformed from a two-drug firm to a highly innovative organization that continues to produce breakthrough drugs from its labs.

Contemplating his MCI experience fifteen years later, Sharer reflected, "We are the mosaic of all of our experiences."

> In retrospect, the MCI experience wasn't all bad. I learned what a truly competitive company can do, and I learned about entrepreneurship and innovation. A tough experience like that gives you genuine empathy for other people.

Contrasting his experiences at MCI and Amgen, Sharer commented, "It is vitally important that you love what you do because if you don't, you won't do your best."

> It is powerful when you connect with a product. When I was at MCI, I never had an emotional connection with low-priced long distance. If somebody walks up to you and says "your product saved my life," the power of that connection is enormous.

Sharer's story illustrates that leaders who temporarily lose their way can indeed get back on track if they learn that leadership is not about them but about empowering others to lead. That is the transformation from "I" to "We" that we'll explore in the next chapter.

Note to the reader: Before going on to Chapter Three, you may want to complete the Chapter Two Exercise found in Appendix C.

3

TRANSFORMATION FROM "I" TO "WE"

When you become a leader, your challenge is to inspire
others, develop them, and create change through them.
You've got to flip that switch and understand that
it's about serving the folks on your team.
—*Jaime Irick, General Electric*

What enables leaders like Kevin Sharer to avoid derailment and make the transition from being heroes of their own journeys to become authentic leaders who empower other leaders? Most of the leaders we interviewed had transformative experiences on their journeys that enabled them to recognize that leading was not about their success but the success they could create by empowering others to lead.

In his best-selling novel, *The Alchemist,* Paulo Coelho tells the story of Santiago, a shepherd boy who travels to the desert in search of a treasure. We, too, start out on our journeys in search of our treasure, whether it is material or spiritual. As we enter the world of work, we envision ourselves in the image of a hero who can change the world for the better.

This is a perfectly natural embarkation point for leaders. After all, so much of our early success in life depends upon our individual efforts, from the grades we earn in school to our performance in individual sports to our initial jobs. Admissions offices and employers examine those achievements most closely and use them to make comparisons. Early leadership opportunities are often limited to team sports, student government, and school organizations.

As we are promoted from individual roles to management, we start to believe we are being recognized for our ability to get others to follow us. But if we believe that leadership is just about getting others to follow us and do *our* bidding as we climb the organization ladder, we risk being derailed.

You may reach the point in your journey when your way forward is blocked or your worldview is turned upside down by events, and you have to rethink what your life and leadership are all about. You start to question yourself: "Am I good enough?" "Why can't I get this team to achieve the goals I have set forth?" Or you may have a personal experience that causes you to realize that there is more to life than getting to the top.

Transformation: The Vital Step on Your Journey

To become authentic leaders, we must discard the myth that leadership means having legions of supporters following our direction as we ascend to the pinnacles of power. Only then can we realize that authentic leadership is about empowering others on their journeys.

This shift is the transformation from "I" to "We." It is the most important process leaders go through in becoming authentic. How else can they unleash the power of their organizations unless they motivate people to reach their full potential? If our supporters are merely following our lead, then their efforts are limited to our vision and our directions about what needs to be done.

Jaime Irick, a graduate of West Point and rising star at General Electric, offered an insight into this process. "You have to realize that it's not about you," he explained.

> We spend our early years trying to be the best. To get into West Point or General Electric, you have to be the best. That is defined by what you can do on your own—your ability to be a phenomenal analyst or consultant or do well on a standardized test. When you become a leader, your challenge is to inspire others, develop them, and create change through them. If you want to be a leader, you've got to flip that switch and understand

Figure 3.1 The Transformation from "I" to "We"

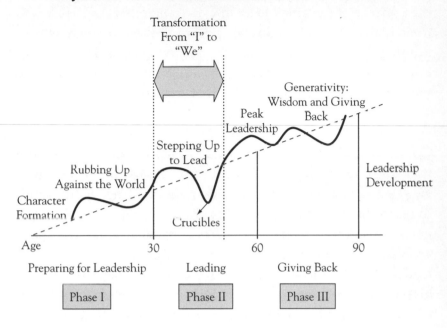

that it's about serving the folks on your team. This is a very simple concept, but one many people overlook. The sooner people realize it, the faster they will become leaders.

Only when leaders stop focusing on their personal ego needs are they able to develop other leaders. They feel less competitive with talented peers and subordinates and are more open to other points of view, enabling them to make better decisions. As they overcome their need to control everything, they learn that people are more interested in working with them. A lightbulb goes on as they recognize the unlimited potential of empowered leaders working together toward a shared purpose.

A transformative experience may come at any point in your life. It could result from the positive experience of having a wise mentor or having a unique opportunity at a young age. But as much as we all want positive experiences like these, transformations for many leaders result from going through a crucible.

In *Geeks and Geezers*, Warren Bennis and Robert Thomas describe the concept of the crucible as an experience that tests leaders to their limits. A crucible can be triggered by events such as confronting a difficult situation at work, receiving critical feedback, or losing your job. Or it may result from a painful personal experience such as divorce, illness, or the death of a loved one.

Dan Vasella: The Long Journey to Transformation. Novartis Chairman and CEO Daniel Vasella followed a path to leadership that was one of the most difficult and unusual of all our interviewees. Vasella's emergence from extreme challenges in his youth to reach the pinnacle of the global pharmaceutical industry illustrates the transformation many leaders go through on their journeys.

Vasella was born in 1953 in a modest family in Fribourg, Switzerland. His early years were filled with medical problems that stoked his passion to become a physician. His first recollections of a hospital date from age four when he had food poisoning. Since his family had no car, the physician came to his home, packed him in a blanket, and drove him to the hospital, leaving him with positive memories.

Suffering from asthma at age five, he was sent alone to the mountains of eastern Switzerland for two summers. There he lived on a farm with three brothers and their niece. Everyone in the area spoke Romanisch, a language young Dan could not understand. He found the four-month separations from his parents especially difficult because the niece had an alcohol problem and was insensitive to him. One day the niece caught him with coins stolen from the Postal Service office. The shame of having to give the coins back had a strong impact on Dan, as did the kindness of one of the brothers who felt sorry for him and put one coin in his empty purse.

At age eight, he had tuberculosis followed by meningitis and was sent for a year to a sanatorium. He suffered a great deal that year from being lonely and homesick, as his parents very rarely visited him. He still remembers the pain and fear of the lumbar punctures as the nurses held him down so that he would not move.

One day a new physician arrived and took time to explain each step of the procedure. Vasella asked the physician if he could hold the nurse's hand rather than being held down. "The amazing thing is that this time the procedure didn't hurt. Afterward, he asked me, 'How was that?' I reached up and gave him a big hug." Vasella recalled, "These very human gestures of forgiveness, caring, and compassion made a deep impression on me and on the kind of person I wanted to become."

In his early years, Vasella's life never settled. When he was ten, his eighteen-year-old sister passed away after suffering from cancer for two years. Three years later, his father died in surgery. To support the family, his mother went to work in a distant town and came home only once every three weeks. Left to himself, he and his friends had beer parties and got into frequent fights. This lasted for three years until he met his first girlfriend, whose affection changed his attitude.

At twenty Vasella entered medical school at the University of Fribourg. "I decided to become a physician so I could understand health, and gain more control over my own life after disease had impacted my family so much," he explained. "Memories of the compassionate doctor at the sanatorium and others who helped me became role models for the kind of physician I wanted to be."

During medical school, Vasella sought out psychoanalysis so he could come to terms with his early experiences. "I wanted to understand myself and not feel like a victim," he said. "I learned eventually that I did not have to be in control all the time." Through analysis, he reframed his life story and realized he did not want to be just an individual practitioner but wanted to have an impact on the lives of many more people by running an organization that helped restore people to fuller health. Graduating with honors from medical school, Vasella did his residency at the Universities of Bern and Zurich, eventually becoming chief resident. Upon completion, he applied to become chief physician at the University of Zurich hospital; however, the search committee considered him too young for the position.

Disappointed but not surprised, Vasella decided he wanted to use his leadership to broaden his impact on medicine. At that time, he had a growing fascination with finance and business. He talked to his wife's uncle, Marc Moret, who was CEO of Sandoz, one of Switzerland's leading chemical companies, about his interest in getting into business. Moret advised him, "Believe me, I know how unpleasant it can be leading a firm. You don't want to go into business."

Moret's discouraging words only piqued Vasella's interest. Eventually he met with the head of the pharmaceutical division, who offered him the opportunity to join Sandoz's U.S. affiliate as a sales representative and later a product manager. Vasella hesitated, but his wife, Anne-Laurence, told him, "Daniel, do it; otherwise, you will turn fifty, look back in regret, and be unhappy." In his five years in the United States, he flourished in the stimulating environment and advanced rapidly through the Sandoz marketing organization.

Returning to Switzerland as assistant to the chief operating officer of Sandoz's pharmaceutical business, Vasella was forced to take a step back. As he languished without responsibilities in a cubicle outside his boss's office, he became frustrated in his new role. "My pay was cut by 40 percent, and I wrote minutes and did my boss's mail."

Soon he was asked to lead a team to redesign the R&D process, giving him intimate knowledge of drug discovery and development. His next steps led him to head of marketing and then global drug development. When both his bosses left in a political battle, he became CEO of the pharmaceutical division. Vasella loved his new position because he now had full responsibility for moving the pharmaceutical business forward.

Within two years negotiations began to merge Sandoz with Ciba-Geigy, its crosstown rival in Basel. It was a natural fit, facilitated because neither company had a successor to its powerful CEO. In spite of Vasella's youth and limited experience, Moret nominated him to be CEO of the merged companies. Ciba-Geigy leadership agreed, as their CEO became chairman of the board of the new company: Novartis.

Once in the CEO's role, Vasella blossomed as a leader. He envisioned the opportunity to build a great global health care company that could help people through lifesaving new drugs. Drawing on the physician role models of his youth, he created an entirely new Novartis culture built around compassion, competence, and competition. He went beyond integrating the two organizations by empowering new leaders throughout the new organization.

One of these new drugs was Gleevec, which Vasella found languishing in the Novartis research labs. Stunned by positive results in preliminary clinical trials for patients with chronic myelogenous leukemia, Vasella was upset to learn that the drug was being given low priority due to modest market projections. He convinced his team that the drug had to get to market within two years, breaking all records for FDA approvals. Characteristic of his passion for helping patients, Vasella had personal contact with many Gleevec users.

Gleevec is just one of a continuing stream of lifesaving drugs emerging from Novartis research labs as Vasella dramatically expanded the company's research budget and moved its research headquarters to Massachusetts. These moves established Novartis as one of the global health care giants and Vasella as a compassionate leader in the industry.

Dan Vasella says his greatest satisfaction comes when his organization is fulfilling its mission. "My childhood illnesses, the deaths of my father and my sister, and the experience of patients' dying all had a very powerful impact on my life."

> As CEO, I have the leverage to impact the lives of many more people. I can do what I believe is right, based on my moral compass. At the end of the day the only thing that matters is what we do or omit to do for other people.

Vasella is a rare leader who can address the most difficult business challenges in an engaged and thoughtful manner yet maintain his deep compassion for the patients Novartis serves. By increasing his self-awareness and reframing his life story through psychoanalysis, Vasella accelerated his transformation from "I" to "We," recognizing he wanted to go beyond being a compassionate physician and instead use his leadership to help millions of people suffering from life-threatening disease.

Oprah Winfrey: Reframing Her Story at Thirty-Six. Often it takes a triggering experience before you can realize the essential purpose of your leadership. Oprah Winfrey was in the middle of an interview on her show with a woman named Trudy Chase who had been sexually abused as a child. Hearing Chase's story, Oprah was overcome with emotion. "I thought I was going to have a breakdown on television. I said, 'Stop! Stop! You've got to stop the cameras!'" But the cameras kept rolling as feelings roiled inside her. Chase's story triggered many traumatic memories from her own childhood. "That was the first day I recognized that I was not to blame," she said.

Her demons had haunted her without explanation until that day. "I became sexually promiscuous as a teenager and got myself into a lot of trouble. I believed I was responsible for it. It wasn't until I was thirty-six years old that I realized, 'Oh that's why I was that way.' I always blamed myself."

Born out of wedlock, Winfrey grew up in poverty in rural Mississippi. When she was very young, her mother moved north to find work. "I was left with my grandmother. It probably saved my life. It is the reason why I am where I am today." Yet even as a young child, she had a vision that she could make something of her life. She recalled standing outside on the back porch when she was four, watching her grandmother boiling the laundry in a large cauldron. "I remember thinking, 'My life won't be like this. It will be better,'" she said. "It wasn't from a place of arrogance; it was just a place of knowing that things could be different for me somehow."

Winfrey credits her illiterate grandmother for teaching her to read. "Reading opened the door to all kinds of possibilities for me. I loved books so much as a child, as they were my outlet to the world." She recited biblical verses in church from the age of three, which endowed her with a reservoir of self-confidence. "All the sisters sitting in the front row would fan themselves and turn to my grandmother and say, 'Ida Mae, this child is gifted.' I heard that enough that I started to believe it. I didn't even know what 'gifted' meant. I just thought it meant I was special."

Relocating to Milwaukee to be with her mother when she was nine, Oprah recalled the trauma of being raped by her cousin. She was molested several more times by family members or friends of the family during the five years she lived with her mother. "It was an ongoing, continuous thing, so much so that I started to think, 'This is the way life is.'" At age fourteen, she gave premature birth to a child who lived only two weeks.

Like most of us, Winfrey started out trying to make it in the world as an individual contributor. She went to college, and while there she had her first opportunity in broadcasting. "It was very uncomfortable for me at first," she explained. "I was pretending to be Barbara Walters, looking nothing like her. I had to take the heat from my college classmates calling me a token. I used to say, 'Yeah, but I'm a paid token.'"

Today Winfrey has built a media empire that is one of the most respected in the world that includes her own production company, named Harpo (Oprah spelled backwards). But it was not until the Trudy Chase interview that she realized her broader mission. Ever since the traumatic experiences of her youth, she had felt the need to please people and could never say no. That day she finally understood why. Since then, her mission has gone far beyond pursuing personal success to empowering people all around the world, especially young women.

"I was always searching for love, affection, and attention, and somebody to say, 'Yes, you are worthy.' The greatest lesson of my life has been to recognize that I am solely responsible for my life—not living to please other people, but doing what my heart says." Asked about her show's theme, Winfrey replies, "The message has always been the same: you are responsible for your own life. I hope the work I do on the show and in speaking around the country can help young people get the lesson sooner than I did."

Winfrey's story illustrates the kind of transformative events most authentic leaders experience in their lives. It is naive to think that you can go through life without difficulties, or spend your entire life trying to avoid them. Life is not always fair. It is often during the hard times in your life that you realize that authentic leadership is not about advancing yourself and your personal interests. Rather, it is the capacity to inspire others to bring out their best.

Like many others, I saw Oprah as a celebrity and missed the real impact of her leadership and its effect on the lives of her viewers. When I talked with her for three hours at the 2004 Nobel Peace Prize dinner in Oslo, Norway, I heard firsthand just how passionate she is to influence millions of people and embolden them to take responsibility for their lives. From Oslo, Winfrey was on her way to Africa with a planeload of books and supplies to help people and to launch a new school to empower young women, where she has personally invested $30 million.

Given the abuse and poverty she experienced earlier in her life, it would have been easy for Winfrey to get caught up in feelings of victimhood. Yet she rose above them by reframing her story in positive terms: first about taking responsibility for her life and then in recognizing her mission to empower others to take responsibility for theirs. Her transformation did not occur until her mid-thirties. Often the gestation takes that long because we need real experiences to see where we fit in the world and help us understand the meaning of those difficult experiences for our personal missions.

Jim Thompson: The Power of a Mentor. When people find a mentor they deeply respect, the relationship can have a transformative effect and open up their vision of what they can become as leaders. Jim Thompson, executive director of the Positive Coaching Alliance, struggled for many years to find his True North until he met John Gardner, who served in President Lyndon Johnson's cabinet.

Growing up in South Dakota, Thompson was a good athlete and student but never saw himself as a leader who could have a national impact. In his early years, he tried teaching and government service but struggled to find his place. After attending Stanford's business school, he returned to run its public-management program. It was there that he met Gardner, who helped him see himself as someone with a larger role to play. From their first conversation, Gardner treated Thompson as an equal and told him it had taken him many years to find his own calling.

Through coaching his son, Thompson decided that the "win at all costs" mentality of youth sports was destroying kids' fun and learning. Gardner encouraged him to pursue his passion with vigor. He helped him get appointed to a national task force on building character through sports and supported him in writing a book. Thompson's *Positive Coaching* outlined the ways coaches could teach kids lessons about character, team building, and life. Sharing his experience in building Common Cause into a national organization, Gardner prodded Thompson to launch a national movement to transform the culture of youth sports.

Thompson credits Gardner's influence with helping him transform his view of himself, his capabilities, and his purpose so that he could help others. In 1998 Thompson founded the Positive Coaching Alliance, building it into a national organization that has run youth coaching workshops for more than 100,000 coaches across the United States, in large part due to John Gardner's encouragement and mentoring.

Doug Baker: Getting Tough Feedback. One of the hardest things to do is to see ourselves as others see us. When we receive unexpected critical feedback, we tend initially to be defensive—to challenge the validity of the criticism or the critics themselves. If we can get past those feelings and process the criticism objectively, however, constructive feedback can trigger a fundamental reappraisal of our leadership.

That's what Doug Baker Jr. learned when he was rising through the ranks of Minnesota-based Ecolab. After working in marketing in Germany for three years, Baker moved to North Carolina as deputy head of a newly acquired company. To integrate his team, Baker hired a coach to conduct 360-degree assessments and facilitate group sessions. "I elected to be first to go through the high-impact leader-ship program."

At thirty-four, Baker saw himself as a fast-rising star, moving rapidly from one leadership role to the next. "I had become, frankly, fairly arrogant and was pushing my own agenda." Then he got the results from the 360-degree process, in which his colleagues told him all this and more. "It was a cathartic experience. I got a major dose of criticism I didn't expect," he said.

> As part of this process, I went away for five days with a dozen strangers from different companies and shared my feedback with them. Since I had been so understanding in this session, I expected people to say, "How could your team possibly give you that feedback?" Instead, I got the same critical feedback from this new group.
>
> It was as if someone flashed a mirror in front of me at my absolute worst. What I saw was horrifying, but it was also a great lesson. After that, I did a lot of soul-searching about what kind of leader I was going to be. I talked to everyone on my Ecolab team about what I had learned, telling them, "Let's have a conversation. I need your help."

Meanwhile, Baker's division was challenged by a larger com-petitor who threatened to take away its business with McDonald's, which accounted for the bulk of its revenues. When he forecast a significant shortfall from his financial plan, the corporate CEO trav-eled to North Carolina to find out what was going on. Asked by the CEO to commit to saving the McDonald's business and getting back on plan, Baker refused to give him any assurances. This raised the CEO's ire, but Baker held his ground. Reflecting on his candor in confronting his powerful leader, Baker commented, "I'd rather have a bad meeting than a bad life."

> If we had lost McDonald's, it would be embarrassing for me, but it was all these folks in the plant who were really going to be hurt. There was unemployment all over North Carolina as many factories were shutting down. If they don't have a job here, they don't have a job, period. Sud-denly, you find the cause is a call to the heart. Saving the McDonald's

account created a lot of energy and fortunately, we retained the business. It was a traumatic time, but ultimately a great learning experience for me.

Doug Baker's critical feedback came at just the right time. On the verge of becoming overly self-confident and thinking that leadership was about his success, the criticism brought him back to earth. It enabled him to realize that his role as a leader was to unite the people in his organization around a common purpose, and the challenge of saving the McDonald's account provided a rallying point for that unity. Under pressure from the CEO to deliver short-term numbers, Baker kept his organization focused on the long-term objective of building the business. This experience paved the way for him to become CEO of Ecolab.

Gail McGovern: "It's Not Fair." Gail McGovern, a former telecommunications executive who is currently a business school professor, told of struggling with her own leadership. "Within one month I went from being the best programmer to the worst supervisor that Bell of Pennsylvania had," she said.

It's unbelievable how bad I was. I didn't know how to delegate. When somebody would have a question about something they were working on, I'd pick it up and do it. My group was not accomplishing anything because I was on the critical path of everything. My boss and mentor saw that we were imploding and did an amazing thing. He gave me every new project that came in. It was unreal. At 4:30 my team would leave, and I'd be working day and night trying to dig through this stuff.

Finally, I couldn't take it any longer. I went into his office and stamped my foot like a five-year-old. "It's not fair. I have the work of ten people."

He said calmly, "Look out there. You've got ten people. Put them to work." It was such a startling revelation. I said sheepishly, "I get it."

Have you ever had a difficult time absorbing constructive criticism? Hard as it is to take in, feedback provides the opportunity to make the transformation from focusing on ourselves to understanding how we can be effective motivators and leaders of others, just as Baker and McGovern did. This requires letting go and trusting others.

Steve Rothschild: Finding His Calling. Steve Rothschild had been on the move at General Mills. He created the Yoplait yogurt business in the United States and put it on course to become a $1 billion business. Promoted to executive vice president while still in his thirties, he faced many new challenges, but after eight years in this role he became restless. He felt like a man in the middle, missing the satisfaction of leading his own team. He also disagreed with the company's direction, judging it had to become more global. His frustration came to a head when he was asked to present the company's international business strategy to its board of directors. "My conclusion was that we ought to be doing more internationally, because we couldn't rely on domestic growth forever," he explained.

While in Spain on business, he got a frantic phone call from the company president, who told him the CEO wanted to change the recommendation to expand internationally. Rothschild replied, "I can't do that because I don't believe it." He explained, "The CEO wanted me to heel, but never talked to me directly." Shortly after that incident, Rothschild faced up to the reality that he was marching to a different drummer and wasn't enjoying his work. After some reflection, he decided it was time to leave General Mills. "I was stuck in a job I no longer enjoyed. I needed to feel alive again," he said.

After a year of spending more time with his working wife and one of their three children still at home, Rothschild decided against rejoining the corporate world. He realized his passions were in helping poor, underprivileged people become financially self-sufficient and develop stronger families. Using his own money, he founded Twin Cities RISE! Its mission is to provide employers with skilled workers by training unemployed and underemployed adults, especially African American men, for skilled jobs that pay a wage of at least $20,000 per year with benefits.

Leaving General Mills was a godsend for me. It allowed me to explore things that were underneath my skin and in my soul and gave me the opportunity to refocus on my marriage and family. Since leaving, my relationships with my family have become much closer and deeper. Making this move has made me a more complete person, more fulfilled and happier.

Leaders react to "hitting the wall" in one of two ways. The experience can be sobering—as it was for Jeff Immelt—when they realize they are not superhuman and have to face difficult trials like everyone else. This enables them to be more empathic and empowering to the people around them. Or they may decide, as Steve Rothschild did, that fundamental changes are required in their lives and wind up pursuing different career directions. In either case, such a crucible provides the basis for the transformation from "I" to "We."

Mike Sweeney: Dealing with Personal Illness. Mike Sweeney, CEO of the private equity firm of Goldner Hawn, was only twenty-eight when he discovered he had testicular cancer. "That was the first time I realized I wasn't immortal," he said.

In some ways I'd recommend it to everyone. If you're going to get cancer, testicular cancer is the one to get because it is curable in most cases. Cancer caused me to think very differently about my life.

Sweeney described an experience he had after all the treatments were done:

I woke up one morning and literally couldn't get up off the sofa. I got hit by a wave of depression that I had never experienced before. It wasn't a matter of will. I just could not get up. While I was fighting cancer, my work was to heal. When that stopped, the room got really quiet, and all of a sudden I realized, holy cow, I could die. At that age the thought of death never occurs to you.

The experience changed the way Sweeney thought and propelled him on a path of understanding himself better and rethinking his life and his career.

The shock of not being able to get up off the sofa scared me. I spent a lot of time thinking about what I want to do, what is meaningful in my life, and who do I want to do it with. I saw a psychiatrist and talked about having cancer not as a physical matter, but an emotional one. Cancer gave me clarity about those things.

His father told him that now his cancer problem was solved, he should shake it off and get back to work. "I thought there was more involved than that," Sweeney says.

I started asking myself what is important to me in business and in life. I wouldn't say I was less ambitious. I just wanted different kinds of things out of life. I wanted to create and build businesses where everyone involved did as well as I did.

When you face your own mortality, as Mike Sweeney did, your priorities and your True North become crystal clear. The same is true when someone close to you passes away.

Losing a Loved One. When you meet Carlson Companies' CEO Marilyn Carlson Nelson for the first time, you are struck by her warmth, her zest for life, and her optimism that any problem can be solved by inspiring people to step up and lead. Yet hers is a more complex story. As if it were yesterday, she vividly recalls learning the news of her daughter's death. "My husband and I heard one morning that our beautiful nineteen-year-old Juliet had been killed in an automobile accident."

That's the most profound test we've ever had, a test of our faith and our personal relationship. I lost my faith at the time and felt angry with God. But God didn't abandon me and didn't let me go. I discovered how valuable every day is and how valuable each person is. I decided to make whatever time I had left meaningful so that the time that Juliet didn't have would be well spent. My husband and I vowed to use every tool at hand as an opportunity to give back or a way to make life better for people. They are all human beings with one short time on Earth.

Soon after her daughter's death, Nelson joined Carlson Companies full time, where she has devoted herself to empowering the organization's 150,000 employees to serve its customers in a highly personalized manner. Twenty years later she remains dedicated to the vow she made to make life better for people. In 2006 she was named one of "America's Best Leaders" by *US News & World Report*.

Virgin Mobile USA CEO Dan Schulman described how his sister's death transformed his attitudes toward leadership. "Before my sister died, I was focused on moving up in AT&T," he said. "I was upwardly oriented and insecure. Often I took credit that wasn't mine to claim."

> *My sister's death was the first time I had been dealt a giant blow. I loved her immensely. When death happens so young and cuts a life short, a lot of things you thought were important aren't important at all. When she died, I decided, "I am going to be who I am." I wanted to spend more time with my folks and my brother, rather than moving up the corporate ladder.*
>
> *At that point I didn't care if I got credit for anything and became quick to credit everyone else. As team leader, I focused only on getting the job done in the best way. As a result, our teams became much more functional than they were before. All of a sudden, my career started to shoot up.*

Both Nelson and Schulman used the trauma of the death of their loved ones to rethink what their lives and leadership were about. With a newfound sense of mission, they transformed their leadership into focusing on others.

My Life as a Series of Crucibles. In my case, I experienced a series of crucibles that ultimately transformed my approach to leadership. From my earliest days my father encouraged me to become a leader, in part to make up for his perceived failures. Hard as I tried, however, none of my peers wanted to follow me. When I wasn't chosen for high school leadership roles, I ran for elected office and was disappointed not to win.

Discouraged, I went off to Georgia Tech so I could have a fresh start where no one knew me. As mindfulness meditation expert Jon Kabat Zinn has written, "Wherever you go, there you are." I learned the hard way that I couldn't escape my past unless I changed myself in the present. I ran for office in my college fraternity six times and lost every time. Clearly, I had not learned why others did not want to follow me.

At this point a group of seniors took me under their wing and gave me some sound advice. "Bill, you have a lot of ability, but you come across as more interested in getting ahead than you are in helping other people. No wonder no one wants to follow your lead." Although devastated by this feedback, I took their advice to heart. I talked to my peers about what I was doing wrong and how I could change. Eventually, the changes took hold, and I was chosen for more leadership positions than I could take on. Most rewarding of all was being selected as fraternity president by the same people who had rejected me earlier.

In my mid-twenties I experienced the most significant crucibles of my life. An only child, I was extremely close to my mother, who gave me unconditional love. When she died suddenly of cancer and a heart attack, I went into a period of deep reflection about the purpose of my life. Eighteen months later, as I was only three weeks away from being married, my fiancée died suddenly from a malignant brain tumor. Her death came as an incredible shock. Once again, I felt all alone in the world. Had it not been for the power of prayer and the support of my friends, I might not have recovered.

Not long after that, I had the blessing of meeting my future wife, Penny. She was very empathetic about my experiences, and a year later we were married. I can honestly say that she has been the best thing that ever happened to me. In addition to being a great wife and mother, Penny is an outstanding counselor to me.

Even so, I still wasn't out of the woods. I saw myself on an unbroken sprint to the top of a major corporation. By age thirty, I was president of Litton Microwave, the pioneer and leader in the emerging U.S. consumer microwave oven industry. For the next five years I led our team in creating the field of consumer microwave cooking. Toward the end of that time, the board of directors of our parent company, Litton Industries, visited our rapidly growing division. I was proud to explain how we had grown at 55 percent per year and had become the largest profit contributor in the corporation.

Sailing high, I was pulled aside after the meeting by the corporate CEO, who offered some stern advice. "Young man, you're still in the honeymoon phase here. You don't have a clue what business is all about. Wait until you have to turn around failing businesses."

His advice really angered me. I thought he was the one who didn't have a clue about how to create growth businesses. Was I ever wrong. A year later I left Litton and joined Honeywell, with the opportunity to lead a global corporation. As I was asked to turn around one business after another, I recognized that Litton's CEO had been absolutely right. During my fourth major turnaround, I finally looked at myself in the mirror and admitted this was not how I wanted to spend my life.

I was in the midst of a severe crucible but had been too busy to recognize it. I finally faced the reality that my unhappiness at work was harming my marriage, my relationship to our sons, and my close friendships. Maybe my destiny was not to be CEO of Honeywell after all, or maybe I would not enjoy the job if I got it.

At that point I talked with my wife, my best friend, and a group of men I met with each week and asked them all for candid feedback. They had seen what was happening and were pleased I was finally facing it. I was so focused on becoming CEO that I had lost sight of the purpose of my leadership—to benefit the lives of others. For all my earlier work, I had not fully made the transition from "I" to "We."

Three times I had turned down the opportunity to become president and COO of Medtronic, the creator of the pacemaker, because I did not believe the company suited my ambition to lead a large company. Back then, it was only one-third the size of the sector I was leading at Honeywell. Facing up to my need for a renewed sense of purpose, I called Medtronic back to find out if the position was still open.

Several months later, after conversations about the Medtronic mission with founder Earl Bakken, I joined Medtronic as president. My thirteen years there became the best professional experience of my life. By embracing the Medtronic mission of restoring people to full life and health, and discovering the purpose of my leadership in serving patients and empowering 30,000 employees, I was finally on the right side of the transformation from "I" to "We."

Nelson Mandela: Seeking Reconciliation, not Retribution. Have you ever felt unfairly treated? How about the time you missed an important promotion, or someone less capable got a larger bonus than you did or was recognized for contributions you made? The next time you feel sorry for yourself, think of the example of Nelson Mandela, who led protests against the unjust apartheid policies of his South African government. Of all the leaders I have met, his journey of transformation is the most dramatic.

In his younger years, Mandela organized boycotts and demonstrations against the apartheid government that often erupted in violence. In 1956 his government arrested him for high treason in causing violence. He endured a four-year-long trial and was eventually declared not guilty. Not satisfied, the government had him arrested for political crimes. A magistrate sentenced him to five years in prison without possibility of parole.

Mandela spent the next twenty-seven years of his life in prison, doing hard labor in spite of his advancing age. As global pressure mounted on his government and many global companies boycotted his country, Mandela was finally released from prison in 1990 at the age of seventy-one.

If ever a person had a right to be bitter toward his captors and the injustice done to him, it was Mandela. How then could he find it in his heart to honor the prison guards who looked after him and to forgive the judge who had sentenced him many years before? How was he able to negotiate with the leader of a minority government that repeatedly ordered his people beaten and killed to keep itself in power? When Mandela was elected president four years later, how was he able to cast aside calls for revenge and instead offer reconciliation to his oppressors?

To know the real answers to these questions, one would have to walk in Mandela's shoes or look into his soul. Here was a person who rose above discrimination, injustice, and hatred. Through his years in prison, Mandela realized that his greater purpose was to save his nation from civil war and to reunite the people of his country. The day of his release, he told the massive crowds who greeted his freedom:

> *I stand here before you not as a prophet but as a humble servant of you, the people. Your tireless and heroic sacrifices have made it possible for me to be here today. I therefore place the remaining years of my life in your hands.*

During those long years in prison, Nelson Mandela realized that his leadership was not about the "I" of getting people to follow him but the "We" of reconciliation. He saw his role as bringing people from diverse backgrounds together around a common vision for the new South Africa, centered on the values of social justice and opportunity for all.

What can we learn from Nelson Mandela?

- He inspires people around the cause of restoring South Africa for *all* its people.
- He makes decisions based on who he is, not what has happened to him.
- He credits his people for freeing him.
- He is driven to make life better for all people.

His leadership transformation inspires us to abandon our image as heroes of our own journey in order to lead others in a greater calling. Not many of us can be liberators of an oppressed people, but all of us can make a difference in the world around us.

Note to the reader: Before going on to Chapter Four, you may want to complete the Chapter Three Exercise found in Appendix C.

Part Two

Discover Your
Authentic Leadership

How do you develop as an authentic leader?

Discovering our authentic leadership requires us to test ourselves, our values, and our beliefs through real-world experiences. This is not an easy process as we are constantly buffeted by the demands of the external world, the model of success that others hold out for us, and our search to discover our truth.

Because there is no map or direct path between where you are now and where you will go on your leadership journey, you need a compass to keep you focused on your True North and get back on track when you are pulled off by external forces or are at risk of being derailed.

The compass is a dynamic tool that you can update and calibrate after every experience to ensure that each step you take on your leadership journey is consistent with how you want to lead your life. Because your circumstances, opportunities, and the world around you are always changing, you will never stop calibrating your compass. When each part of your compass is well developed, you will be pointed toward your True North. The chapters that follow address the five major areas of your personal development as a leader: self-awareness, values and principles, motivations, support team, and the integrated life. As you consider each of these areas, ask yourself these fundamental questions:

- *Self-Awareness:* What is my story? What are my strengths and developmental needs?
- *Values:* What are my most deeply held values? What principles guide my leadership?
- *Motivations:* What motivates me? How do I balance external and internal motivations?
- *Support Team:* Who are the people I can count on to guide and support me along the way?
- *Integrated Life:* How can I integrate all aspects of my life and find fulfillment?

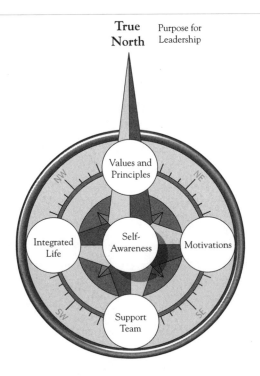

4

KNOWING YOUR AUTHENTIC SELF

Know Thyself
—*Inscribed at the temple wall at Delphi
in Greece during the sixth century* B.C.

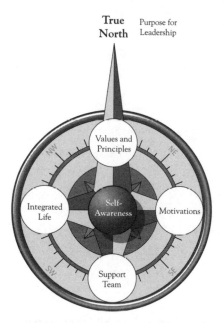

The advice to know yourself is thousands of years old. But knowing ourselves at the deepest level is not easy, as we are complex human beings with many aspects to our character. We are constantly evolving, as we test ourselves in the world, are influenced by it, and adapt to our environment—all in an attempt to find our unique place.

In their interviews, leaders said that gaining self-awareness was central to becoming authentic leaders. For this reason it is at the center of your compass. When you know yourself, you can find the passion that motivates you and the purpose of your leadership. Nancy Barry, CEO of Women's World Banking and one of "America's Best Leaders," tells young leaders to "take the time to get to know yourself and find your passion. Look inside, to find your power, your purpose. If you find and go with this flow, you will make a difference in our world—and you will find joy in the journey."

FirstMark CEO Lynn Forester de Rothschild urges leaders to remember Shakespeare's admonition, "To thine own self be true."

> Being true to yourself is the most important thing. If you're ambitious, that's great; if not, that's also fine. Just be true to what you want. Not everyone can be at the top of the class. If they try to be, they may not get there. If they did get there, they might not be happy. Know who you are, and you can achieve anything in life. You can overcome almost any obstacles, unless you are the obstacle.

The task of discovering your authentic self becomes more complicated as you are confronted by a myriad of options in the broader world. These opportunities can provide new openings to develop yourself, or they can be seductions that take you away from your true self. At the same time, you will be confronted by people who threaten you, do not like you, or reject you. To protect yourself from harm, you may develop a false self by building protective layers and, in so doing, become less authentic.

Your Emotional Intelligence

Self-awareness is the first element of emotional intelligence, or EQ, that psychologist Daniel Goleman, author of *Emotional Intelligence*, uses in describing the leader's role. While intellectual intelligence, or IQ, has long been thought of as an essential characteristic for managers, EQ may be more important for authentic leaders. Too many leaders believe that by being the smartest person in the room, they can use their intellect to carry the day. As a result, they overpower less forceful voices that may have the vital ideas, insights, and answers they need to succeed.

As a leader, I am certainly not immune from this criticism. I recall the advice from Medtronic's general counsel not to be so forceful in meetings because I was shutting down people who had something to contribute. That was also keeping me from gaining their support for the eventual conclusion.

Wells Fargo's Dick Kovacevich argues that high IQ can actually be an impediment to leadership. "Above the 99th percentile of intelligence, there is an inverse correlation between leadership and intelligence," he says.

Leaders with an exceptionally high IQ get too intellectually involved and have trouble being tolerant of others. You have to have a certain level of intelligence at the top; maybe it is the 90th or 95th percentile, but it isn't the 99th. Above that level, you need leadership skill, interpersonal skills, and teamwork more than you need a few extra points of IQ. Dirk Jager, the former CEO of Procter & Gamble, is an example of a leader failing to impose his intellect on others. Jager was a brilliant strategist who had excellent ideas about the strategic and cultural changes needed at P&G, but his style was so abrasive he threatened the essence of P&G's culture. As a result, his management team rebelled, and the board asked him to step down in less than two years, as A.G. Lafley, a longtime P&G executive, took his place. Using a combination of wisdom, humility, and personal engagement with employees, Lafley is transforming P&G into one of the great success stories of the twenty-first century. As one of the most successful business leaders of our era, in 2006 he was named "CEO of the Year" by *Chief Executive* magazine and one of "America's Best Leaders" by *US News & World Report*.

Why Knowing Yourself Is So Important

When the seventy-five members of the Stanford Graduate School of Business Advisory Council were asked to recommend the most important capability for leaders to develop, their answer was nearly unanimous: self-awareness.

Big Brothers Big Sisters CEO Judy Vredenburgh confirmed its importance. "Having self-awareness early in life is very important. You need to understand the cultures you thrive in, the roles you are best in, your natural strengths, and your natural interests. Then put yourself in a place where you can shine." Other leaders stressed several reasons why self-awareness is so important:

Finding the Right Role. Whether you're in a start-up, a turn-around situation, or a growth opportunity, the better you know yourself, the more likely you are to choose the right role for yourself. Former Medco CEO Per Lofberg is an organization builder who has thrived in growth enterprises. He joined Medco, a pharmacy-benefit-management company, early in its development and built it to $30 billion in revenue and 15,000 employees. He commented, "I could never be like 'Chainsaw Al' Dunlap (former CEO of Sunbeam) in cutting everything in sight. Likewise, someone like Dunlap would be terrible in building businesses."

Increasing Self-Confidence. When leaders know themselves well, they become comfortable in their own skin. Adobe CEO Bruce Chizen once felt insecure about working in the technology industry because he was not an engineer. When he recognized his strong business and product-marketing skills and his ability to learn about engineering, a switch flipped in Chizen's mind. After that, he became increasingly self-confident: "I understood myself well enough to know what I didn't know, but also knew enough to feel comfortable. That awareness helped me find real self-confidence."

Being Consistent. By being aware of their actions and intentions, leaders act consistently in different situations and gain the trust of others. Former American Airlines CEO Don Carty reasoned, "You cannot motivate people unless you talk and walk in the same way. How can you expect an employee to be pleasant with a customer if you're not pleasant with the employee?"

Connecting with Others. Most leaders see the process of gaining self-awareness as crucial to their ability to build strong relationships. Debra Dunn, former senior vice president at HP, stresses, "If someone is self-aware, you can have a more authentic interaction with them." Those who are comfortable with themselves tend to be more open and transparent—which includes sharing their vulnerabilities.

Complementary Skills. Leaders who know their strengths and weaknesses can fill their skill gaps with colleagues that complement them. Ned Barnholt, Agilent's former CEO, said, "You understand your strengths and shortcomings and try to build a strong team around you. I didn't grow up as an accountant so I surround myself with excellent financial people. That's a lot better than trying to be somebody you're not."

Becoming Self-Aware

Without self-awareness, it is easy to get caught up in chasing external symbols of success rather than becoming the person you want to be. It is difficult to regulate your emotions, control your fears, and avoid impulsive outbursts when you feel threatened or rejected. Without being aware of your vulnerabilities, fears, and longings, it is hard to empathize with others who are experiencing similar feelings.

Many leaders, especially those early in their careers, are trying so hard to establish themselves in this world that they leave little time for self-exploration. Nor do they focus on becoming more self-aware. As they age, they may find something is missing in their lives or realize something is holding them back from being the person they want to be. They may encounter a life-changing event, as Dan Schulman did in his sister's death, that causes them to reflect deeply on what they want out of their lives.

For other leaders, memories of childhood are so painful that they shut themselves off from their feelings. Anxious to bury these memories altogether, they drive extremely hard to achieve success in the tangible ways that are recognized in the external world—money, fame, power, status, or a rising stock price. Often their drive enables them to be successful, at least for a while, but it may leave them highly vulnerable to being derailed, as their lack of self-awareness can lead to major mistakes and errors in judgment.

Dave Pottruck: Journey to Self-Awareness. Of all the leaders interviewed, David Pottruck, former CEO of Charles Schwab, had one of the most courageous journeys to discovering his authentic self. Pottruck grew up in modest circumstances: his father was a Grumman Aircraft machinist, and his mother was a nurse. He was an all-league high school football player who was offered a full scholarship to play linebacker at the University of Pennsylvania. He noted, "I tried to inspire the team to rise to the occasion and do their best on game day. I wound up MVP of my college team."

Disappointed not to be recruited for professional football, he went to Wharton for his MBA, then joined Citigroup, and later went to Charles Schwab as head of marketing, moving from New York to San Francisco. He was an extremely hard worker, and he could not understand why his new colleagues resented his long hours and aggressiveness in pushing for results. "I thought my accomplishments would speak for themselves," he recalled.

> *It never occurred to me that my level of energy would intimidate and offend other people, because in my mind I was trying to help the company. My peers resented the fact that I worked fourteen hours a day and they only wanted to work nine, but Chuck Schwab appreciated my level of intensity.*

One of the most difficult things in becoming self-aware is seeing ourselves as others see us. Although it can be difficult to hear, leaders need accurate feedback to identify their blind spots. Pottruck was shocked when his boss gave him a low rating on trustworthiness and told him, "Dave, your colleagues do not trust you." As he recalled, "That feedback was like a dagger to my heart."

I was in denial, as I didn't see myself as others saw me. I became a light-
ning rod for friction, but I had no idea how self-serving I looked to other
people. But somewhere in my inner core the feedback resonated as true.
At first I thought about finding another job. Chuck Schwab heard rumors
I was looking around and asked me to stay and work out my differences
with the rest of his team. Finally, I faced the fact that I could not succeed
the way I was and had to change.

Pottruck found that changing himself was a very hard process. "The more stress you are under, the more you revert to your old patterns."

Much like Alcoholics Anonymous, I went back to my colleagues and said,
"I'm Dave Pottruck, and I have some broken leadership skills. I'm going
to try to be a different person. I need your help, and ask you to be open to
the possibility that I can change."

Pottruck worked with a coach and developed a cadre of advisers to use as a sounding board. His coach taught him about authenticity and the power of storytelling. In his speeches, Dave began telling stories that revealed his life, fears, ambitions, and failures and found that people were inspired.

After his second divorce, Pottruck realized he still had large blind spots. "When my first marriage ended, I was convinced that it was all her fault. After my second marriage fell apart, I thought I had a wife-selection problem." Then he worked with a counselor who told him, "I have good news and bad news. The good news is you do not have a wife-selection problem; the bad news is you have a husband-behavior problem."

After another long period of denial, Pottruck made a determined effort to change. "I was like a guy who has had three heart attacks and finally realizes he has to quit smoking and lose some weight."

Denial is the biggest challenge we face. The only way to overcome it
is to be honest with yourself and not make up excuses. This has

helped me accept criticism, listen to it, and take it seriously, as painful
as it may be.

These days Pottruck is happily remarried and listens carefully
when his wife, Emily, offers constructive feedback. He acknowledges that he falls back on his old habits at times, particularly during moments of high stress, but he has developed ways of coping
with it. "My wife's advice makes me a better person and a better
husband," he noted.

We all want to be stroked, admired, and complimented, but we have to be
willing to listen to feedback we don't want to hear. That requires a strong
sense of yourself and a solid foundation. I have had enough success in life
to have that foundation of self-respect, so I can take the criticism and not
deny it. I have finally learned to tolerate my failures and disappointments
and not beat myself up.

We must get outside our egos and listen to feedback we don't
want to hear. Young people often have not developed the self-
esteem to see their mistakes and take accountability for them.
When you can do that and be open to new ways of doing things,
the change you can accomplish is almost unlimited. The discovery
process never ends.

Pottruck's hard work in becoming self-aware paid off. He won
the support of his colleagues, and his dynamic leadership produced
outstanding results for the firm. As a result, Schwab promoted him
to president in 1992. Six years later he was named co-CEO along
with Schwab. During his fourteen years at or near the helm of
Schwab, Pottruck substantially broadened Schwab's business base,
as it became one of the most admired companies in America and
was named to *Fortune*'s "100 Best Places to Work."

In 2003 Pottruck was named sole CEO, with Schwab continuing as board chair. These were difficult times for the firm, as the brokerage business turned down after the stock market decline of
2001–02. Pottruck and his colleagues, still in a growth mode, did

not understand the depth of permanent change occurring in their markets, thinking the business was just in a down cycle. "I didn't see the sea change," he said.

> I hated firing people, so I did the minimum I had to do to make the company right. I was so connected to the people that I didn't have the resolve to steel myself emotionally to get rid of people that I had affection for. Now I realize you have to cut constantly.

Only fourteen months after his appointment as sole CEO, Pottruck was forced to resign by the board as Schwab returned as CEO. His first reaction was one of shock and disbelief. The day after the public announcement, Pottruck attended an Intel board meeting, where Andy Grove, Intel's longtime leader, pulled him aside and offered some sage advice, "When you got promoted to CEO, did that make you a better man? Well, then, do you think because you're no longer CEO of Schwab, you're not a better man? Hold your head high. You're as good as you were last week."

Along with Grove's timely counsel, letters and e-mails poured in with messages of gratitude for his leadership and friendship. These messages helped snap Pottruck out of his depression, as his wife helped him confront his new reality. These days Pottruck is devoting his time to helping others develop their leadership and self-awareness by teaching at the Wharton School. He recently became CEO of start-up Eos Airlines when the former CEO floundered.

"All of us have an innate ability to become better," Pottruck concluded.

> If I can help people believe they can improve, I can motivate them to make this journey of discovery, of honest self-appraisal, and of hard work toward fundamental change. None of us is born perfect. We all have things that we do wrong and get in our way. You have a choice of letting them get in your way your whole life, or fixing them. Why wouldn't you want to do that? It's illogical to me.

Dave Pottruck readily acknowledges his imperfections and still tries to improve his leadership abilities. Perfection is not the goal of authentic leadership. Rather, it is to be true to who you are while continuing to develop yourself into a more effective leader. That requires the kind of deep introspection, feedback, and support illustrated by Pottruck's story.

Peeling Back the Onion

Knowing yourself can be compared to peeling back the layers of an onion as you search for your true self. The outer layers of the onion are the visible ways you present yourself to the world—how you look, your facial expressions, your body language, your attire, and the way you express yourself. Often these layers are rough and hardened in order to protect you from the assaults of the world around you.

Understanding your outer layers is a necessary first step to going deeper into what lies beneath, because they provide the access to your inner core. Beneath those outer layers resides your understanding of your strengths and weaknesses and what you need and desire from the world around you. Once I asked a teenage mentee of mine, who was getting ready to go out with his friends, why he spent so much time in front of the mirror. His reply was telling: "I need to look good on the outside, because I feel so much pain on the inside."

Peeling the onion further, you gain an understanding of your values and the ways in which experiences often put you in conflict with your values. Digging still deeper, you learn what is driving and motivating you. Underneath these layers of your proverbial onion lies your understanding of your life story and of the way in which your experiences build your story and create a mosaic of your life. As you approach the deepest layers surrounding your inner core, you find your blind spots and your vulnerabilities. At the core of your being is what you believe and how you envision your place on earth.

Figure 4.1 Peeling Back the Onion

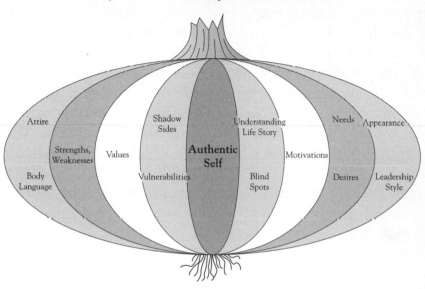

As you explore who you are, you peel back one layer only to discover a deeper and often more interesting layer underneath it. As you get nearer to your core, you find that the inner layers feel quite tender and vulnerable because they have not been exposed to the assaults of the outside world. When you do not feel in a safe place, you cover your core self to protect it from exposure and harm, and you develop a false self. At the same time you are continually growing, adding new layers of complexity, as you develop ways of interfacing effectively with the world while preserving the integrity of your core self.

Confronting Your Blind Spots

There are several ways you can peel back your onion and uncover your blind spots. One of the best means of learning more about yourself is getting feedback from others. Stanford's Joel Peterson calls feedback "the breakfast of champions." Verizon's Judy Haberkorn says, "They called me the feedback queen. The best thing you can get in this world is honest feedback from someone who cares about your success and well-being. Some are of us more self-aware than others, but few of us see the world as it sees us."

Kroger CEO Dave Dillon discovered the value of feedback during college, after he lost an important election in his fraternity. His first reaction was to get defensive and think, "I'm better than that guy. Why didn't they choose me?" After considerable introspection, he realized that "My point of view wasn't the relevant one. The important one was what others thought." Through feedback, he learned he had a number of traits that needed improvement. As a result, he went on to become president of the student body and his fraternity, the first steps in a life of successful leadership. Dillon says, "Feedback helps you take the blinders off, face reality, and see yourself as you really are."

Dillon continues to ask his colleagues at Kroger for feedback, which sometimes hits so close to home he feels defensive. "When I get defensive, I go back to the individual and apologize. I tell him, 'My reaction was against me, not you. My defensiveness is a mechanism to help me cope with unpleasant personal news. I assure you I hold you in higher regard because you shared that with me.'"

Reflection and Introspection

Next in the process of gaining self-awareness is taking time for personal reflection or introspection. Reflecting on your life story and your experiences can help you understand them at a deeper level— and so you can reframe your life story in a more coherent way as your future direction becomes congruent with the knowledge of who you are and the kind of person you want to become.

Former LucasArts CEO Randy Komisar went through a period of deep reflection to figure out what he wanted out of life. At LucasArts he clashed frequently with founder George Lucas. Frustrated by his lack of independence, he became CEO of a rival, Crystal Dynamics. It turned out to be the worst decision he ever made.

Komisar soon realized the business did not stir his passions. "I couldn't find my reason for being there. The business floundered and ultimately succeeded, but I failed. First, I had to admit my mistakes. Then I had to face tough issues like what was I going to do with my life? I could have made Crystal work, but at what cost? I hadn't asked myself that question before."

He resigned after a year and began a meditation practice to gain clarity, with a Buddhist monk as his teacher. "That was a point in my life where it was time to just be. My Buddhist practice became a formative part of the next phase of my life."

After reflection, Komisar realized there was a war going on inside him that traced back to the two most influential people in his life: his father and grandmother. His father was a contract salesman for countless companies who was fiercely independent. He craved material success and gambled constantly. "When he lost money, we became very nervous that we would not be able to pay our college tuition. I worried that I would not graduate." The elder Komisar encouraged his son to attain financial success: "Insecurity about money was built into me as a child."

Komisar was very close to his grandmother, who died when he was ten. "We bonded in a way that I never bonded with anyone else," he said. "Her death devastated me, as she had an incredible influence on my life. She was generous, interested in people, and had great character. She loved people and they loved her."

Komisar recognized he needed to release himself from his image of success and embrace his own qualities.

> I was on a fast track, but it wasn't my track. There was a war inside me between the need to be fulfilled versus the desire to be successful in my father's eyes and of society. It was time to let go of the notion I was climbing the ladder of success and accept the fact that I was on a long and winding journey.

When leaders accept who they are and release the need to be on someone else's fast track, they can be comfortable in their own skin. "The ability to face reality and acknowledge that you can fail and still feel good about yourself is an important turning point in your self-awareness," said Komisar.

He joined the venture capital firm of Kleiner Perkins, helping leaders of the firm's portfolio companies develop themselves, their strategies, and their self-awareness. "Now I get to spend all my time on the part of the CEO's role that energizes me—strategizing, building relationships, making deals, and mentoring teams," he concluded.

Tad Piper: Being Vulnerable Under Pressure. One fear all of us have to confront is whether others will accept us if we show our vulnerability. We fear being rejected if we admit our mistakes. Will others take advantage of our weaknesses? Will they think less of us? As hard as we try to deny them, these questions continually nag when we are feeling most vulnerable.

Tad Piper, Piper Jaffray's former chairman and CEO, went through a difficult ordeal when his firm faced a financial and legal crisis because of the actions of a bond trader who lost money for some of the firm's major clients. After the bond fund increased by a cumulative 90 percent in five years, the fund manager took increasing risks with complex new derivative instruments to sustain its unusually high returns. When interest rates turned down in 1994, the fund declined by 25 percent.

Investors cried foul, and their lawyers went on the attack. Suit after suit was filed, charging Piper Jaffray with failing to inform clients of the fund's risks and with falsely designating the fund as "conservative." Piper tried working with the clients to resolve the issues, but doing so became increasingly difficult. "When you get into problems," he pointed out, "you find out quickly how strong your relationships are, which people are real and which aren't, and who will abandon relationships for money. A lot of very sophisticated people got dumb and naive very quickly. Nevertheless, we were responsible for the problem."

By the spring of 1994, Piper knew he had a momentous problem on his hands. "The future of our entire company was in jeopardy," he recalled. "We had to deal with it as best we could." Asked if he thought about bailing out, Piper said bluntly: "Absolutely. The problems were overwhelming, and the temptation to walk away was overpowering. But I knew I couldn't do that. It was my problem to resolve, with God's help. Ultimately, we could have gone out of business, but I was going to give it my best shot."

Piper felt that his leadership of the company during this period had never been stronger. The experience helped him solve business problems by developing inner strength. He admitted his uncertainties openly, even at their height, and was willing to be vulnerable. "One of the most important things we did was to bring together our leaders and their spouses from our branch offices around the country," he explained.

> My wife and I decided to be completely honest with them and totally vulnerable. We showed them we were real people, feeling just like they were. We stood in front of them and told them we were scared. I also talked about my chemical dependency and about my faith. That was the most powerful thing we have ever done. People never forgot that day because we showed our vulnerability. All of a sudden everybody on our team trusted us, even the skeptics.

Piper said he never would have opened up like that had he not found himself in the middle of a crisis. "As a result, I've learned the power of being vulnerable. Most leaders are afraid to be vulnerable. They think, 'I'm supposed to be strong and have all the answers.' "

Piper eventually recognized that he had to settle the lawsuits to get the issue resolved. With the issue behind him, he and his colleagues were able to focus all their energies on building the business once again.

What is remarkable about Piper's story is his openness in struggling to resolve the issues and his willingness to share his vulnerabilities with his teammates. Many leaders would simply hunker down and try to fix the problems without reaching out for help. Piper's approach takes courage but is ultimately much more successful because it is so empowering to teammates who genuinely want to help the organization succeed. Above all, leadership is a human undertaking. When leaders reveal their vulnerabilities, they develop trusting human connections with others that motivate and empower those they engage.

Accepting Yourself

Self-awareness is only half of the challenge. You still have to accept yourself. But with self-awareness, accepting your authentic self becomes much easier. You see yourself clearly and accurately, and you know what you truly believe.

The key to self-acceptance is to love yourself unconditionally. It is easy to love our strengths and bask in our successes. Even Narcissus could do that. To love ourselves unconditionally, we have to learn to accept ourselves as we are, with all our warts and our flaws, rather than wish we were different. Reatha Clark King captured this feeling when she said, "I feel good in my skin. I get along well with myself and have learned to accept myself race-wise and gender-wise."

Loving yourself unconditionally requires self-compassion. In "The Poetry of Self-Compassion," poet David Whyte talks about dealing with your weaknesses and shadow sides so that you can accept the things you like least about yourself. That requires digging into experiences you have hidden for years and finding the innocent child inside you waiting to reemerge. Whyte also addresses this challenge in his poem, "The Well of Grief."

THE WELL OF GRIEF

> *Those who will not slip beneath*
> *the still surface on the well of grief*
> *turning downward through its black water*
> *to the place we cannot breathe*
> *will never know the source from which we drink,*
> *the secret water, cold and clear,*

> *nor find in the darkness glimmering*
> *the small round coins*
> *thrown by those who wished for something else.*

David Whyte
from *Where Many Rivers Meet*
Many Rivers Press, © 1990

Whyte says you cannot wall yourself off from the pain of past experiences. Like David Pottruck and Tad Piper, you have to confront them directly, accept yourself unconditionally, and learn to love your weaknesses as much as you revel in your strengths. That level of self-compassion enables you to get to the source of your True North and to accept yourself as you are.

Once armed with a high level of self-awareness and self-acceptance, it is much easier to regulate yourself and your feelings. Your anger and emotional outbursts usually result when someone penetrates to the core of what you do not like about yourself or still cannot accept. By accepting yourself just as you are, you are no longer vulnerable to these hurts and are prepared to interact authentically with others who come into your life—your family, friends, coworkers, even complete strangers. Free of having to pretend to be someone you are not, you can focus on pursuing your passions and fulfilling your dreams.

With the center of your compass solidly grounded in self-awareness and supported by self-acceptance, you are ready to focus on your values and principles.

Note to the reader: Before going on to Chapter Five, you may want to complete the Chapter Four Exercise found in Appendix C.

5

PRACTICING YOUR VALUES AND PRINCIPLES

Leaders with principles are less likely to get bullied or pushed around because they can draw clear lines in the sand. . . . The softest pillow is a clear conscience.
—*Narayana Murthy, founder and former CEO, Infosys*

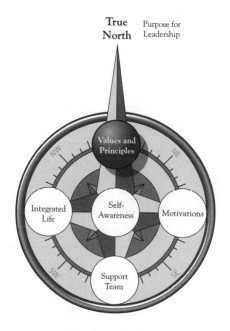

In gaining a clear awareness of who you are, you must understand your values and the principles that guide your leadership. Several leaders referred to their values as their moral compass. Novartis's Dan

Vasella observed, "Most people have some kind of moral compass that tells them in which direction to go." Former Johnson & Johnson chairman and CEO Jim Burke, who made the courageous decision to recall Tylenol in 1982, said, "Without a moral center, you will swim in chaos."

Staying centered on your values is not easy. You can easily drift off course as the temptations and pressures of the outside world pull you away from your moral center. But if you are centered through a high level of self-awareness, your compass can help you get back on track.

Values, Leadership Principles, and Ethical Boundaries

The values that form the basis for your True North are derived from your beliefs and convictions. In defining your values, you must decide what is most important in your life. Is it maintaining your integrity, making a difference, helping other people, or devoting yourself to your family? There is no one right set of values. Only you can decide the question of your values. When you do, you will be better positioned to align with people and organizations that share similar values.

When you have a clear understanding of your values and their relative importance, you can establish the principles by which you intend to lead. *Leadership principles are values translated into action.* They are like navigational instruments sailors use to get their bearings at sea, as they fix the direction of their travel with respect to the north. Principles enable leaders to prioritize their values and demonstrate which ones trump others.

After defining your leadership principles, you need a clear understanding of your ethical boundaries. These are the limits you place on your actions, based on your values and your standards. Where do you draw the line between the actions that are acceptable and those that are not? Exhibit 5.1 sketches the relationship.

Exhibit 5.1 Defining Your Values, Principles, and Ethical Boundaries

Values:	The relative importance of the things that matter in your life.
Leadership Principles:	A set of standards used in leading others, derived from your values. Principles are values translated into action.
Ethical Boundaries:	The limits placed on your actions, based on your standards of ethical behavior.

Perhaps you have engaged in exercises in which you list your values and force-rank them in order from the most important to the least. While these exercises are helpful in clarifying what is important, you do not know what your true values are until they are tested under pressure. It is relatively easy to list your values and to live by them when things are going well.

It is under pressure—when your success, your career, or your life hangs in the balance—that you must decide what your values are. When you are forced to make trade-offs between your values under difficult circumstances, you learn what is most important in your life and what you are prepared to sacrifice for. Those who develop a clear sense of their values *before* they get into a crisis are better prepared to keep their bearings and navigate through difficult decisions and dilemmas when the pressure mounts.

Sara Lee CEO Brenda Barnes said, "I attribute my success to values that were instilled in me in my upbringing, things like honesty, integrity, and treating people with respect. You can't fake your values. You have to live by them. You are who you are."

David Gergen: Discovering His True North. David Gergen wanted to lead a life that was consistent with the values he learned from his family and the Durham community where he grew up. He became the first person to serve as White House adviser to four presidents of the United States: Richard Nixon, Gerald Ford, Ronald Reagan, and Bill Clinton. Gergen served in the Nixon White House during the aftermath of the 1972 break-in at the Watergate headquarters of the Democratic National Committee. That experience convinced him to follow a basic leadership principle—"act transparently"—that has helped him stay true to his values.

Gergen was twenty-eight when he was hired as a White House speechwriter during Nixon's first term. He had a ringside seat for history as it was being made. "When I first arrived, the power, glamour, and status went to my head," he said. He would later come to realize how naive and unprepared he was for the events of the next few years.

His ambition helped him become a rising star in the Nixon administration. He recalled, "I was grasping for the brass ring and was as ambitious as everybody else, probably more so." After Nixon's 1972 reelection, Gergen was named head of the president's speechwriting and research team, with responsibility for supervising fifty people. "It was tempting to fall into the trap of thinking I was important, instead of recognizing that people think you're important only because of where you're standing. I had some of the arrogance that other people in that administration had," he confessed.

When stories about the Watergate cover-up began to emerge in early 1973, Gergen did not believe the allegations were true. "We were continuously reassured that neither Nixon nor anyone high up in the White House staff had done anything wrong," he explained. "Nixon told us that directly, and Haldeman and others confirmed it in the most adamant terms." As public focus on Watergate intensified throughout 1973 and 1974, an increasing number of staff members resigned, including some of his own team, but Gergen did not feel he could leave. "My resignation would have made a public statement about my lack of belief in President Nixon's integrity. So I stayed and kept hoping against hope he was innocent."

Gergen learned of Nixon's guilt only two days before the news broke in August 1974. Even then, he did not feel he could leave, lest he be viewed as "a rat leaving the sinking ship," especially when President Nixon asked him to write his resignation letter. As he watched Nixon leave the White House for the last time in his helicopter, Gergen thought his own career in public life was over. He recalled the infamous 1919 Chicago Black Sox World Series team, whose players were accused of cheating and banned from baseball for life. "I thought I'd never play again," he said.

> *Watergate was an epiphany for me. It shattered my notion that, because you are in a position of power and glamour, you can rise above being challenged. You can't.*

Almost immediately, Gergen's phone stopped ringing. "Suddenly, you're not as glamorous as you were. You realize just how fast it all comes and goes." During the lonely and depressing days that followed, Gergen was most impressed by the people who stood by him—primarily his old friends from Durham and his college classmates.

> *When you're in trouble and all your defenses get stripped away, you realize what matters and who matters. That's when you need to get back to your roots and to your values.*
>
> *The people who were innocent have come back to outstanding careers. Jon Huntsman, the founder and chairman of Huntsman Corporation, was one who did that. Hank Paulson is another person who came through it and had an extraordinary career as CEO of Goldman Sachs and now as Secretary of the Treasury.*

"Since that searing experience with Watergate," Gergen concluded, "I have always favored transparency."

> *I have frequently disagreed with those I worked for, because the Watergate lessons were so vivid in my mind. They remind you that you have*

to stay true to your values. Nixon did not have a moral compass, and everything went off track.

David Gergen's Watergate experience was formative in his development as an authentic leader. He recognized he had been seduced by the glamour and prestige of being at the center of the world's power and needed to return to his authentic roots and the people who were there for him when his world was collapsing. This early experience improved his ability to advise Presidents Ford, Reagan, and Clinton and to become a wise teacher of future leaders as director of Harvard's Center for Public Leadership.

Keith Krach: When Values Conflict. You may not know for certain what your values are until you find yourself under the pressure of having your values in conflict, or you find the values of the people with whom you work differ from your own.

That was the situation former Ariba CEO Keith Krach faced in his early thirties following a successful experience at General Motors (GM), where he was the youngest vice president ever. Krach left GM to become COO of a Silicon Valley start-up named Qronos Technology with the promise of becoming CEO within a year. "My career was like running the hundred-yard dash and getting smacked in the face with a two-by-four," he said.

> *The company didn't have the same values I had. The CEO used to say, "Let's hide this from the board." After a few months, it was crystal clear to me I had made a mistake. With its values, the company was never going to survive. Although I had never resigned from anything in my life, I realized that if I stayed there much longer, I wouldn't be able to look myself in the mirror.*

Krach prided himself on being loyal and having integrity, so these two core values were in conflict inside him. Although the situation was difficult, he did not want to give up, but he did not feel that he was being true to himself. His best friend told him, "You don't look good. If you have your attitude and enthusiasm, you're an A-plus performer. But you've lost it. You're like a D-minus. There is no in-between for you. You should quit."

The moment of reckoning came when his wife was giving birth to their first child. Krach was at her side during labor, yet the CEO kept calling, demanding that he come to work. "We have a big partner meeting with IBM," the CEO told him. Krach responded, "That's anatomically impossible. I'm going to see my son born." After a few minutes, Krach's values clicked in, and he reached clarity in his mind. He called his boss back and said simply, "I quit."

> That was a big moment in my life. I immediately felt a sense of relief. I learned more at Qronos than in any year in my life about what's important in terms of values, trust, and integrity. It was like a process of tempering steel that made me much more resolved about my values.

Jon Huntsman: Testing Values Under Pressure. In preparing for a day when your values conflict with those of your organization and with each other, you need to decide what you want to stand for in your life. How will your obituary read? What do you want people to say at your funeral?

The life of Jon Huntsman, founder and chairman of Huntsman Corporation, a $13 billion chemical company, offers an interesting example of the way one person answered these questions. To the outside observer, Huntsman seems to lead an idyllic life, one marked by integrity, clarity of values, a large and successful family, and material success. Yet Huntsman has been tested at least three major times in the most severe ways. Each time he was forced to look deep inside himself to determine what he stood for.

Huntsman has strong views about his values and the importance of values in the lives of others. When he asserts, "There is no such thing as a moral agnostic," Huntsman's clarity forces you to reflect on your own values.

Each of us possesses a moral GPS, a compass or conscience programmed
by parents, teachers, coaches, grandparents, clergy, friends, and peers.
The compass is an integral part of our being. It continues to differentiate
between proper and improper behavior until the day we die.

Huntsman, who was born in a humble family in rural Idaho, says his values and leadership are inextricably linked to his family roots. Although he was close to his mother, he never developed a close relationship with his father, who was a stern disciplinarian. "My mother was a sweet, loving person who never said a negative word about anyone. Because of her, my heart has always been soft." He observed, "I was taught to play by the rules: be tough, be competitive, but do it fairly."

The principles we learned as children were simple and fair. With moral
compasses programmed in the sandboxes of long ago, we can navigate
career courses with values that guarantee successful lives, a path that is
good for one's mental and moral well-being, and the opportunity for long-
term material success.

Huntsman's leadership abilities were evident from a young age. He garnered his first leadership opportunity when he was elected president of his sixth-grade class—and the seventh-grade class, the eighth-grade class, and the ninth-grade class. Then he moved to Palo Alto High School and became president of the eleventh-grade class.

At the University of Pennsylvania Huntsman was elected president of the senior class and his fraternity and was selected as the outstanding undergraduate by the fraternity's international organization. He had a mission for each of his leadership roles and worked to get all the people associated with him to buy into that mission.

When he was just out of college, his mother developed breast cancer and died in her fifties. "She suffered so much that it broke my heart," he said. Nor was her suffering the family's only brush with cancer. His father died of prostate cancer, and his stepmother died from ovarian cancer. Like a dark cloud hanging over the family, cancer struck Huntsman himself twice, but he overcame it.

Emerging from the sadness he felt over his mother's struggle and death, he was determined someday to create a cancer research institute. His dream came true decades later when he and his wife, Karen, founded the Huntsman Cancer Institute in 1995. As of 2007 the Huntsmans have donated and raised over $350 million to make it one of the most respected cancer institutes in the world. Huntsman's own experience with cancer convinced him that the best therapy was knowing how much others cared about him. Behind his desk, he has a sign that reads, "The greatest exercise for the human heart is to reach down and lift another up." "That," he says, "is exactly what life is all about."

Like David Gergen's, Jon Huntsman's moral compass also was tested when he went to work for the Nixon administration in 1972, shortly before the Watergate incident. After founding his own company, he was hired by Elliot Richardson, secretary of Health, Education and Welfare (HEW), as associate administrator of social services. His success in installing a management by objectives program that saved $100 million in its first six months brought him to the attention of the White House. Shortly thereafter, he was hired by Bob Haldeman, President Nixon's powerful chief of staff. He found the experience of taking marching orders from Haldeman "very mixed."

> I had been CEO of a company and then was running a big division at HEW. I wasn't geared to take orders, irrespective of whether they were ethically or morally right. We had a few clashes, as plenty of things that Haldeman wanted to do were questionable. An amoral atmosphere permeated the White House.

One day Haldeman asked Huntsman to help him entrap a California congressman who had been opposing a White House initiative. The congressman partially owned a plant that reportedly employed undocumented workers, and Haldeman wanted to gather information that could be used to embarrass him. Huntsman's task was to place some Latino employees from his Huntsman facility on an undercover operation. He said, "I was under the gun from Haldeman to call my plant manager."

> *There are times when we react too quickly and fail to realize immediately what is right and wrong. This was one of those times when I didn't think it through. I knew instinctively it was wrong, but it took a few minutes for the notion to percolate. After fifteen minutes, my inner moral compass made itself noticed and enabled me to recognize this wasn't the right thing to do. Values that had accompanied me since childhood kicked in. Halfway through my conversation with our plant manager, I said to him, "Let's not do this. I don't want to play this game. Forget that I called."*
>
> *I informed Haldeman that I would not have my employees spy. Here I was saying no to the second most powerful person in the country. He didn't appreciate responses like that, as he viewed them as signs of disloyalty. I might as well have been saying farewell. So be it. I left within the next six months.*

As one can see from the photo of the seventy-three family members that graces his annual Christmas card, Huntsman is extremely proud of his large family. Just a year after resigning from the White House staff, he and Karen faced a big test when their youngest son, Mark, was born with severe mental limitations. Mark's doctor told his parents that their son would not be able to read, write, or go to school, because his mental capacity would never go beyond that of a four-year-old. The doctor recommended that Mark be committed to an institution. The doctor's proposal to institutionalize Mark represented an impossible values conflict for the Huntsmans. Family was everything to them, and Mark was just as much a part of their family as their other children. They decided that, whatever it took, Mark would live at home.

When Penny and I visited the Huntsmans for a tour of their cancer institute and hospital in 2002, Jon proudly introduced us to Mark, who greeted us with a friendly smile and a big hug. "Mark doesn't know what people do for a living, and can't tell a custodian from a CEO," Huntsman told us. "He judges people only by the goodness of their heart. He sizes up individuals quickly and spots phonies immediately. If their heart is good, he gives them a big hug. Every day I learn from watching him. He has been the role model and anvil of our family."

In 2001 Huntsman faced the biggest challenge of his career. His company was on the verge of bankruptcy. The company's desperate condition was less a function of its own missteps than the deep recession in its chemical and packaging markets. Prices and profit margins were falling rapidly as competitors continued to produce far more than the shrinking demand. To make matters worse, energy costs and raw material prices were spiraling out of control. As a consequence, Huntsman's high-yield bonds were trading at 25 cents on the dollar.

Although he had made his son Peter the CEO, Huntsman was still chairman of the board, founder, and the company's largest shareholder. On a somber day, financial experts, lawyers, representatives of his eighty-seven lenders, and bankruptcy experts from New York and Los Angeles gathered in Salt Lake City and presented him with their unanimous opinion. Huntsman had but one choice: seek a court-supervised Chapter 11 bankruptcy or sit helplessly by as creditors shut the company down altogether by refusing to ship vital raw materials.

Listening patiently to their analyses and entreaties, he thought to himself, "I will not let this company be seized by corporate lawyers, bankers, and highly paid consultants. Not one of them can comprehend my notions of character and integrity." Huntsman answered in a single word: "No." To him, bankruptcy was not an option. His name was on the door—and on the debt. He believed his integrity was at stake.

There are times when the consultants and lawyers and outside advisers would like to tell us how to run our lives. Are we men and women of character, integrity, kindness, and charity, or are we going to be

motivated by what somebody else says? At the end of our life, we have to
determine what we want said at our funeral.

Huntsman called his team together day after day in the darkest
of hours and told them, "We are going to make it. Our name is on
the door. We will go to every one of our bankers, all eighty-seven of
them, and carve out deals that we can live with. We will bring in
our bonds and redeem them for equity."

The company went through three years of turmoil, as Huntsman refused to give in. The only person standing with him throughout this crisis was his wife. As he observed, "Karen was a great
cheerleader and supporter."

You have to have someone next to you who is tremendously sympathetic.
My bankers and close associates abandoned me, so for years Karen was
the only one there for me. That's because she knew me best. She knew
how critical it was to me to maintain my integrity. If one person lost one
penny anywhere along the line, I would have lost my character as a man.

During the process Huntsman had a heart attack and con-
tracted Addison's disease as a result of his run-down immune system. However, he said with pride, "I repaid every single debt."

As of today, the bondholders have been paid 100 cents on the dollar.
Huntsman's creditors have been paid in full and have extended us more
credit. Huntsman stock is listed on the New York Stock Exchange and is
doing well. Our earnings are the highest in history.

Reflecting on his brush with bankruptcy, Huntsman commented,
"At the end of the day, the creditors were our salvation. Building
good will, being honest and kind, and paying your bills along life's
pathway come back to serve you when you're down and out."

There are times in our lives when we have to ask ourselves, are we going
to let this erosion of our life happen, or are we going to step up and change

it? Your life speaks for itself. If I had tried to cheat somebody during my lifetime or did not play by rules, they would have exercised their natural rights when I got in trouble. The human heart and the human soul have an enormous amount of capacity to change direction in a positive way if we just keep outsiders from influencing what we're doing.

Again and again, Huntsman's True North was tested in the most severe ways. Yet he remained true to his values, without deviating. It is highly unlikely he could have done so without a high level of self-awareness and clarity about what he believed.

Do you know how you will respond in similar situations? What are you going to stand for in your life? Once you know that, it is essential to be true to what you believe. The only way to prepare for crises like these is to understand your values and then determine your leadership principles.

Principles are values translated into action. Having a solid base of values and testing them under pressure enables you to develop the principles you will use in leading. For example, a value such as "concern for others" might be translated into a leadership principle such as "create a work environment where people are respected for their contributions, provided job security, and allowed to fulfill their potential."

All leaders operate with principles, even if they do so subconsciously. Take the basic question, "What motivates people?" Some leaders believe that people are motivated to do as little work as possible. They lead by a principle that establishes strict rules of conduct and behavior and enforces them rigidly in order to force people to work. In response to the same question, other leaders believe that people genuinely want to do good work and find significance through their work. They operate with a principle of empowerment that gives people freedom to do their work, encourages them to excel, and trusts them to monitor themselves.

Narayana Murthy: Leading with Principles. Narayana Murthy is a successful entrepreneur who founded Infosys on a clear set of guiding principles from which he has never deviated.

Murthy grew up in lower-middle-class surroundings in southern India. His father was a civil servant who prided himself on his ethical standards and who taught his children a clear sense of values. In his youth Murthy was influenced by the teachings of Mahatma Gandhi and was involved with socialist youth organizations. He became a strong believer in the redistribution of wealth as a method of alleviating India's massive poverty.

After Murthy's graduation from his university, his professor nominated him to go to Paris to install a logistics and baggage-handling system at Charles de Gaulle Airport. Murthy was fascinated by the intellectuals he met at Parisian cafés in the late 1960s. Describing his time there, he said, "As a twenty-three-year-old Indian, I grew up on a heavy diet of Nehru's socialist philosophy. In Paris I got the inspiration for compassionate capitalism. I learned how French people put the interest of community ahead of their own interest."

In the process, Murthy imbibed an atmosphere of action and inquiry that gave rise to four guiding principles. First, the only way to remove poverty is to create new jobs and more wealth. Second, there are only a few people who can lead the creation of these enterprises and create jobs and wealth. Third, these people need incentives to create wealth in a fair manner. And, finally, it is not the responsibility of the government to create jobs or wealth; the government's task is to create an environment where a fair incentive system encourages people to create more jobs and more wealth. Murthy explained,

> As I look back on the idealism of my youth, I realize that people need opportunities, incentives, and competition in order to better themselves. This is the essence of capitalism. If you combine the spirit of capitalism with fairness, decency, transparency, and honesty, the result is compassionate capitalism.

Returning to India, Murthy and a group of younger colleagues founded Infosys Technologies in 1982 and built it into India's leading IT outsourcing company. Infosys gave Murthy the platform to translate his values into his business principles and to be clear about his ethical boundaries. "Our dream was to demonstrate that you could run a business in India without corruption and create wealth, legally and ethically," he explained.

From the outset, Murthy and his colleagues wanted to create India's most respected company. Despite the difficulties of starting the business, Murthy and his team adhered to a principled approach. "It was a crisis throughout," he recalled. "We were forced to finance growth out of our earnings, but that instilled discipline."

Because Murthy refused to pay bribes, Infosys had to wait a year for installation of a telephone line. "What drains your energy or enthusiasm is not the fiscal problem, but violating your value system. Leaders with principles are less likely to get bullied or pushed around because they can draw clear lines in the sand. We always believed that the softest pillow is a clear conscience. I feel fortunate that we have never had a situation where we lost sleep because we did something wrong." Eventually, the demands for bribes ceased. "If you refuse to buckle on the first couple of transactions," said Murthy, "they will go trouble someone else."

> Compliance with the value system creates an environment that enables people to have high aspirations, self-esteem, confidence in the future, and the enthusiasm to take on very difficult tasks. Leaders have to "walk the talk" and demonstrate their commitment to the value system. There is a direct correlation between the value system of our company and the success we have had over the last twenty-four years. I hope this is justification for our people to accept our values and run with them.

I have rarely met a business leader who is as intentional about knowing his values and establishing his leadership principles as Narayana Murthy. His experience living in France had a formative impact on his thinking about his principles and led to the growth and success of Infosys. Murthy has had the courage to stick to his values, going contrary to many cultural norms in India, and he has adhered to his principles throughout his career.

Judy Haberkorn: Acknowledging Mistakes. Verizon's Judy Haberkorn operated with a clear principle in dealing with customers: "Always be open and transparent." That principle was tested when one of her people made a significant mistake, one for which Haberkorn thought she might be fired. In attempting to save money, an employee decided to send consumers their telephone PIN numbers in unsealed envelopes. The envelopes wound up in building lobbies below the mailboxes where anyone could steal the name, phone number, and PIN. When she took the issue and her concerns to her boss, Haberkorn was told not to worry. "It will die down," he said. Frustrated, she responded, "This is a test of how to handle a disaster versus how not to handle it, much like Johnson & Johnson Tylenol."

> If you don't want to do this the Tylenol way, then fire me right now and put somebody else in this job. As long as I'm in charge, we're going the Tylenol route. I am sending a telegram to every one of our customers explaining what happened. We will pay for any calls made inappropriately as a result of this disaster, and immediately give customers a new calling-card number and PIN. I will be on the local news shows tonight to explain what happened and what Verizon will do.

As a result, the issue went away. Reflecting on her experience, Haberkorn noted,

> It cost us some money, but there was no doubt in anybody's mind that we did the right thing. A mistake happened, and it was costly. To have our customers feeling we didn't care about their security and were careless with their privacy would have been a far greater disaster.

It isn't easy to take on your boss. Most people would feel they would be protected if their boss told them to do nothing. For Haberkorn, her principles of how to treat customers were worth challenging her boss and taking the corrective action anyway. Her actions took a lot of courage, a mark of an authentic leader.

Setting Ethical Boundaries

Your ethical boundaries set clear limits on what you will do when you are tempted or are under pressure or when you start rationalizing a series of marginal decisions. If you establish clear boundaries early in life, your moral compass will kick in when you reach your limits and tell you it is time to pull back, even if the personal sacrifices may be significant. That's what Enron leaders Ken Lay and Jeff Skilling lacked as they lurched from deal making into dishonesty and destroyed their company.

One of my MBA students, who had just returned from a tour of duty in Iraq as a counterintelligence officer in the U.S. Marine Corps, told a poignant story of how he used ethical boundaries to set limits on his behavior. Before he left for Iraq, he made a list of the things he would not do, even under the most extreme circumstances. He put the list in an envelope and kept it with him. When he came under pressure in Iraq, he frequently pulled it out as a reminder of the ethical boundaries he had established for himself.

One way leaders understand their ethical boundaries is to use the *New York Times* test. Before proceeding with any action, ask yourself, "How would I feel if this entire situation, including transcripts of our discussions, was printed on the first page of the *New York Times?*" If your answers are negative, then it is time to rethink your actions; if they are positive, you should feel comfortable proceeding, even if others criticize your actions later.

Leading by Values

Many companies these days are shifting from management by objectives to leading by values. IBM CEO Sam Palmisano is using this approach to unite IBM employees as a powerful global force in information systems. When he took over from Lou Gerstner, his iconic predecessor, Palmisano did not create new values or merely reiterate the values professed by founder Thomas Watson. Instead, he employed a company-wide online process in which all employees around the globe had the opportunity to participate for three days in determining what IBM's values should be. Palmisano is using the values emerging from this process to integrate IBM's 350,000 employees into a global integrated network.

Medtronic founder Earl Bakken first exposed me to leading by values when I joined the company in 1989. For the next thirteen years we used the company's values to unify employees around a common purpose and philosophy of doing business. At first, we had some employees, concentrated in the international division, who did not take us seriously and continued to do business according to their local practices. Internal audit reports turned up repeated violations of company standards in these countries.

I decided we had no choice but to make significant management changes. Rather than focusing on lower-level employees, we started by replacing the heads of international, Europe, Asia, and Latin America with leaders who were committed to leading by values. When violations were uncovered, we made a public statement about what had happened and what actions the company was taking. The new international leaders gave us the confidence that we could expand the business rapidly without constantly worrying about ethical violations. When the company went through a rapid growth phase in the mid- to late 1990s, the leading by values philosophy became an invaluable tool for rapidly introducing new employees to the company's culture.

As we search for our True North, it is important to acknowledge how easy it is to get pulled off course. The pressures to perform, the ingrained fear of failure, and the rewards for success can cause us to deviate from our values. By knowing our ethical boundaries and testing our values under pressure, we are able to get back on track.

Note to the reader: Before going on to Chapter Six, you may want to complete the Chapter Five Exercise found in Appendix C.

6

WHAT MOTIVATES YOU
TO BE A LEADER?

If you're just chasing the rabbit around the course,
you're not running toward anything meaningful.
                                    —Alice Woodwark, McKinsey

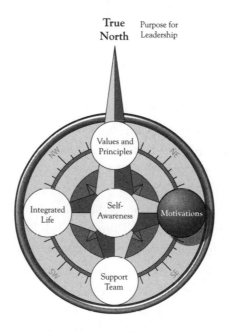

Charles "Chuck" Schwab went through some very low moments in his mid-thirties. Recently divorced, he experienced a period of deep uncertainty about what to do professionally. He enrolled in law school at night in an attempt to follow in the footsteps of his father and grandfather. After just three weeks, he realized he lacked the required reading and writing skills and dropped out.

Schwab had struggled with reading all his life, but it was not until his early forties that he learned he was dyslexic. Although dyslexia had caused him difficult times in school, he always knew he was good at math. So he began working part-time for an investment firm and discovered his interest in investments and knack for investment research.

Like many leaders, Schwab needed time and experience to determine what motivated him. Eventually, he turned his passion for investments into building a company that would democratize the entire brokerage industry. Schwab's motivations and capabilities finally came together when he was thirty-seven, and he founded Charles Schwab & Company.

Schwab traces his motivations to his upbringing in the post-Depression era. Times were tough in the small farming community of Woodland, California, where he grew up during the 1940s. His family used ration stamps during World War II to buy food and bartered for its business transactions. Schwab's parents struggled their entire lives to be financially independent. "We were still suffering from the hangover of the Depression years," he recalled.

He began his entrepreneurial pursuits as a boy. At age ten, he recruited a friend to help him pick up empty Coca-Cola bottles at Woodland High School football games, collecting a nickel for each. During the hot summer days he sold ice cream and raised chickens. He was one of the first Avon kids, riding his bike around Woodland delivering cosmetic orders. "My father taught me the importance of being independent," he explained. "I was motivated to be financially successful because I didn't want to have my life limited by resources."

When the SEC deregulated brokerage services in the early 1970s, Schwab saw his opportunity to start a company. Prior to that time, stock market transactions went through large brokerage firms that charged fixed fees. Without competitive rates, many Americans could not afford to participate in the stock market. In 1974 Charles Schwab & Company entered the market, reducing brokerage commissions by 75 percent. Before long, individual accounts like 401(k)s and IRAs were commonplace. "If you knew what you wanted to buy or sell, we could do it very efficiently. We'd complete the trade for a small commission without the interference of some hotshot broker."

In his interview Schwab spoke calmly about his early years. But when he began talking about how Wall Street brokers neglected the average American investor, his face reddened and his hand gestures fired. Leaning forward in his chair, he exclaimed, "Let me tell you, it was a den of thieves. Whatever the dealers wanted, they got!"

The unfairness of brokerage industry practices that existed prior to deregulation touched a nerve deep inside him. "I always put the customer on top of a stool whose four corners are value, customer service, technology, and the best price," he explained. "Wall Street flips the stool over, sitting on top of the stool with the client underneath."

> In a capitalist society, financial independence is fundamental. We are blessed in America with tremendous economic freedom and freedom of choice. I wanted to make Schwab a fully democratic place where people could come to us, disclose what they wanted, and get the best package available at the lowest cost, all without the conflicts of interest so prevalent in the brokerage industry. Wall Street should be like your doctor, focusing on your interest, not its interest.

Schwab's strengths, talents, and motivations all came together when he founded Charles Schwab. He combined his investment research skills with the persistence and resilience learned from years of suffering with dyslexia. His upbringing instilled an enormous respect for individuals who want to achieve financial independence. Building a company with a cause in which he passionately believed, he has helped millions become more independent while achieving financial independence himself. His company is an American icon, with fourteen thousand employees and a market capitalization of $20 billion.

Schwab's case exemplifies the importance of discovering your motivations: you need to know what motivates you and have a realistic understanding of your strengths and weaknesses so you can put your strongest capabilities to work. When you do so, you will discover the *sweet spot* of your motivated capabilities.

Intrinsic and Extrinsic Motivations

Because authentic leaders need to sustain high levels of motivation and keep their motivations in balance, it is critically important to understand what motivates them. This may take many years, even if their formative experiences occurred when they were much younger.

There are two types of motivations—extrinsic and intrinsic. *Extrinsic motivations*, such as getting good grades, winning athletic competitions, or making money, are measured by the external world. Nearly every leader has had a strong achievement orientation since childhood. Most competed in athletics in their youth and worked to excel in school. After graduating, many young leaders want to obtain a job with a prestigious organization. Eventually, their extrinsic motivations take the form of monetary accumulation, power, title, elevated social status, and prestige.

Although they are reluctant to admit it, many leaders are motivated by achieving success against the parameters measured by the outside world. They enjoy the feelings of success, recognition, and status that come with promotions and financial rewards.

Intrinsic motivations, on the other hand, are derived from your sense of the meaning of your life—your True North. They are closely linked to your life story and the way you frame it. Examples include personal growth, helping other people develop, taking on social causes, and making a difference in the world. Chuck Schwab's passion for helping Americans achieve financial independence is an intrinsic motivation, even if the end result made him wealthy. Exhibit 6.1 highlights the differences between extrinsic and intrinsic motivations.

Exhibit 6.1 Extrinsic and Intrinsic Motivations

Extrinsic Motivations	Intrinsic Motivations
• Monetary compensation	• Personal growth
• Having power	• Satisfaction of doing a good job
• Having a title	• Helping others develop
• Public recognition	• Finding meaning from efforts
• Social status	• Being true to one's beliefs
• Winning over others	• Making a difference in the world

Discovering Your Intrinsic Motivations

Intrinsic motivations come from within you and are congruent with your True North. They are more subtle than extrinsic motivations. Don Carty, former CEO of American Airlines, noted, "What motivated me was the notion that you can have a far greater societal impact in large corporations than you can in a small enterprise." John Thain, CEO of the New York Stock Exchange, said, "I am motivated by doing a really good job at whatever I am doing, but I prefer to multiply my impact on society through a group of people."

Ann Moore, now CEO of Time, Inc., said, "I love magazines and the publishing world. I came here twenty-five years ago solely because I loved reading magazines." In her twenties, Moore especially enjoyed *Sports Illustrated,* the Time, Inc. publication where she worked for ten years. "If you're a sports fan, how much fun is it to work at *Sports Illustrated?* There are real psychic rewards." These days Moore is proud of her company's newest publication, *Real Simple,* because "It helps women organize their lives and relieve their stress. It has become the hottest magazine in America. Women de-stress these days by reading, and chances are they are reading a Time, Inc. magazine. I am in awe of the importance of what we do."

Cesar Conde is vice president of Univision, the largest Spanish-language television network in the United States. After the Castro revolution, his grandparents helped his mother flee Cuba for the United States because they wanted her to have better chances. At Univision, which employs many first- and second-generation Hispanic Americans, Conde seeks to create similar opportunities for his coworkers.

One day his boss took him to look at the company parking lot and told him, "Fifteen years ago the parking lot was full of rickety old cars owned by our employees. With the company's success, the cars are new and employees can afford to send their kids to good schools." Conde said, "I can identify with his pride. It is motivating to realize I have the opportunity to do something great for other people."

Donna Dubinsky, CEO of Palm and cofounder of Handspring, sees technology as a way to change the world in fundamental ways. She recalls the day when she was introduced to VisiCalc, the first personal computer spreadsheet program. "That moment changed my life," she said. "I had been a banker doing spreadsheets by hand and realized this was going to be huge. Throughout my career I have been motivated to make computing tools more accessible to people." Dubinsky's passion for using technology earned her a spot in *Fortune*'s Innovators Hall of Fame.

Discovering your intrinsic motivations may come from surprising sources. In his mid-twenties, Bob Fisher, now chairman of Gap, Inc., was feeling increasingly stressed at work and needed a new focus. "I got immediate pleasure out of growing the men's knit top business, but it's here today, gone tomorrow. Just selling another shirt was not turning me on." His roommate and friends convinced him to join them for a fly-fishing weekend. Fisher immediately fell in love with the sport. "I got consumed by fly fishing," he said. "After spending numerous weekends on Northern California's rivers, I discovered my passion for the outdoors."

One day, as he fished in the North Fork of the Feather River, Fisher came across the remains of rusted gold mining equipment, a discovery that ultimately changed his life. In harsh contrast to the tranquil river settings to which he was accustomed, mining equipment was everywhere. "The equipment had been there since the early twentieth century and had created a huge mess. That introduced me to environmental problems." Shortly thereafter, Fisher joined the board of the NRDC. He educated himself about environmental issues for the next eight years. At Gap, Fisher organized other employees to look at what the company could do to recycle. Spearheaded by Fisher's leadership, the grassroots effort grew into Gap's highly admired corporate social responsibility initiative.

Avoiding Traps

Many people never tap into their most powerful motivations. With society's unprecedented attention on material gain, temptations and social pressures cause many leaders to seek the world's acclaim rather than doing what motivates them internally. The pressure starts early, when college graduates compare salaries. It evolves as they compare apartments or new home purchases. Alan Horn, president of Warner Brothers, describes how he consciously avoids these traps:

> *Early in your career the incremental dollar can change the incremental quality of life because it enables you to buy a better car, a better house, etc. At some point, however, the incremental dollar does not change the quality of life at all. In fact, incremental purchases just increase the complexity of life, not the enjoyment of life. I don't want more things because they simply wouldn't make me happier.*

Many leaders advised emerging leaders to beware of getting caught up in social, peer, or parental expectations. Debra Dunn, who has lived in Silicon Valley for decades as a Hewlett-Packard executive, acknowledged the constant pressures from external sources: "The path of accumulating material possessions is clearly laid out. You know how to measure it. If you don't pursue that path, people wonder what is wrong with you. The only way to avoid getting caught up in materialism is to understand where you find happiness and fulfillment."

Moving away from the external validation of personal achievement is not easy. Achievement-oriented leaders grow so accustomed to successive accomplishments throughout their early years that it takes courage to pursue their intrinsic motivations. But at some point, most leaders recognize that they need to address more difficult questions in order to pursue their true motivations. McKinsey's Alice Woodwark, who at twenty-nine had achieved success at each stage in her life, noted:

> My version of achievement was pretty naive, born of things I learned early in life about praise and being valued. But if you're just chasing the rabbit around the course, you're not running toward anything meaningful.

Many leaders turned down higher-paying jobs in early career decisions in order to pursue roles they would enjoy. They came out ahead in the end—in both satisfaction and compensation—because they were successful in doing what they loved. Ann Moore had a dozen job offers after business school and took the lowest-paying one—with Time, Inc. "I had student loans hanging over my head, but I took the job because I loved magazines. At the time nobody in my class understood why I made that choice, but at our twenty-fifth reunion they understood completely."

Donna Dubinsky took a job at Apple Computer for half of what she could have earned in a professional services firm. Ann Fudge, CEO of Young & Rubicam, also took the lowest-paying offer she received out of business school. She explained, "You can't make career decisions just based on money. I hoped that the money would come, and it did, but if I had made my career decision based on the money, I would have been on a totally different career path."

In his twenties, Howard Schultz was afraid to tell his mother he was leaving a high-paying sales job at Xerox to pursue the venture that eventually became Starbucks. "I was paying college loans until I was God knows how old. If I stayed at Xerox two more years, though, I knew I would be locked in. It was like a relationship that is safe, but you're not in love."

Citing a recent visit with business school students, Dave Cox, former CEO of Cowles Media, quoted one as saying, "Maybe I have to get my satisfaction someplace else and I'll just do the business part to make money." Amazed by the comment, Cox raised his eyebrows quizzically, "Why would you want to spend your time doing work you don't enjoy? These should be the best years of your life. There is so much energy that results from feeling valued and connecting with what you're enthusiastic about. That is when you add the greatest value."

Many young leaders are tempted to take high-salaried jobs to pay off loans or build their savings, even if they have no interest in the work and do not intend to stay. They believe that after ten years they can move on to do the work they love. Yet many become so dependent on maintaining a certain lifestyle that they get trapped in jobs where they are demotivated and unhappy. Locked into the high-income/high-expense life, they cannot afford to do work they love. *Ironically, not one of the leaders interviewed wound up taking a position predicated upon establishing wealth early so that they could later pursue roles they would enjoy.*

Jean-Pierre Rosso, former CEO of Case-New Holland and currently chair of the World Economic Forum USA, recalled, "I always focused on being happy in what I was doing. If I was motivated and did my job well, I knew the money would follow." Per Lofberg, former CEO of Medco, challenged young business leaders to think carefully about the lifestyle they choose for themselves: "It is dangerous to get overcommitted to a high-flying lifestyle at a young age."

Many people would like to give up a cushy corporate job for a high-risk entrepreneurial opportunity, but they are afraid because it seems too risky and they have committed themselves to a large mortgage or too many cars. That holds a lot of people back from pursuing what motivates them and brings them satisfaction.

Balancing Your Motivations

For leaders with a high-achievement orientation, external motivations and positive validation by the outside world are a natural consequence. They appreciate the recognition that comes with their accomplishments. *The key to developing as an authentic leader is not eschewing your extrinsic motivations but balancing them with intrinsic motivations.*

Many leaders want to ascend to senior roles in order to be central to the action. Marianne Toldalagi, former general manager of American Express Consumer Travel, acknowledged: "I don't like hiding in the shadows. I like visibility and power and thrive on recognition." Ecolab CEO Doug Baker recognized from a young age that he wanted to be in charge. "In a new situation, it doesn't take long before I want to run the show. I don't know where this comes from, but I've always had it."

It is natural to seek recognition from peers, promotions in title, and positive media accolades. These are all positive outcomes of achieving success in the eyes of the world. The danger comes when leaders become so enamored of these external symbols that they can never get enough. At this point they are at the greatest risk of losing touch with their intrinsic motivations and abandoning things that give them a deeper sense of fulfillment.

Many leaders have learned the hard way that external recognition can be a fickle lover. When things do not go their way, their external sources of gratification disappear very quickly. So do superficial friends and acquaintances who are more interested in associating with them as a success than they are in being there for them when things go poorly. The key to avoiding these traps is finding a balance between your desires for external validation and intrinsic motivations that provide fulfillment in your work.

Finding Your Motivated Capabilities

The term *motivated capabilities* is used to describe the alignment of your motivations with your strongest capabilities in order to find the *sweet spot* for your leadership. (See Figure 6.1.) When we talked with Claremont professor Mihaly Csikszentmihalyi, a pioneer in the field of positive psychology, he provided the following advice about motivation: "Find out what you are good at and what you like

Figure 6.1 The Sweet Spot of Your Motivated Capabilities

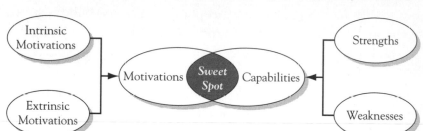

to do." In these two simple dimensions, Csikszentmihalyi cut through the jargon and summed up what our interviewees learned through hundreds of years of experience.

In reflecting on what she had learned through her work experience as a star consultant at McKinsey, Alice Woodwark noted that she tended to focus on negative feedback. The cycle continued until she realized she was spending so much time responding to negatives that she did not celebrate or take advantage of her strengths. "No one achieves anything brilliant by mitigating their weaknesses," she explained.

Brilliance comes only from exploiting your strengths. Many of the most extraordinary people in history were tremendously flawed individuals. Margaret Thatcher, Gandhi, and Napoleon all had striking weaknesses. Yet there was a part of them that was ridiculously gifted and enabled them to achieve amazing things through their leadership.

Through intense reflection, Donna Dubinsky came to a similar realization in her mid-thirties. After ten years of eighty-hour weeks at Apple Computer and Claris Software, she was burned out and decided to take a yearlong sabbatical to live in Paris. There she found an apartment, learned to paint, studied French, and thought about what she would do next. "I reflected on what I am good at, what I'm not good at, and what value I could bring. I realized I am not an innovative thinker and will never have the product savvy of Steve Jobs. I had been in the technology industry for ten years and had never thought of one big new idea."

As she thought further about her capabilities, she acknowledged her ability to recognize other people's good ideas, build a strong team, and design key business processes. "I had everything except the ability to envision the next great product," she concluded.

When I returned to Silicon Valley, I had a clear focus. I knew I needed to find a great product person to team with me. It wasn't so much about the product as it was finding a partner who is skilled where I am not.

Donna eventually found Jeff Hawkins, the talented product developer who created the Palm Pilot, and she became Palm's CEO in 1992. The two have such complementary skills that they are considered inseparable business partners around Silicon Valley and are currently working on their third venture, Numenta.

Warren Bennis gained an understanding of his motivated capabilities in the 1970s when he served as president of the University of Cincinnati. "Some people know their talents earlier than I did. I learned the hard way that being a university president is not for me." A year into his tenure, Bennis was mired in paperwork one evening when he saw that the clock read 4 A.M. "I had a moment of truth. Either I couldn't manage the place or it was unmanageable."

From that experience, Bennis recognized that he derived his greatest motivation from interacting with people, especially students. He did not enjoy the transactional aspects of being president, such as writing 150 letters a day to alumni. "I realized my personal truth: I was never going to be able to be happy with positional power. What I really wanted was personal power: having influence based on my voice," Bennis said.

Returning to teaching and writing at the University of Southern California, Bennis found his *sweet spot*. He has profoundly influenced a generation of students and has written twenty books on leadership. He noted, "My real gift is what I can do in the classroom or as a mentor."

When leaders step out of their comfort zones to take on new challenges, they often discover capabilities they did not know they had. When the late John Gardner joined the U.S. Marine Corps during World War II, he discovered he enjoyed action as much as reflection. That led him to become president of the Carnegie Corporation and secretary of Health, Education and Welfare in the Johnson administration. Gardner went on to found the White House Fellows Program, Common Cause, the Independent Sector, Urban Coalition, and the American Leadership Forum, as he encouraged the next generation of leaders to engage in public service. Gardner once said, "There were some qualities that life was waiting to pull out of me." When you also challenge yourself by taking risks, you may be surprised to find leadership abilities you did not know you had.

You will be most effective as a leader when you find opportunities that highly motivate you and utilize your greatest capabilities. One without the other is insufficient. To find them, you must understand your deepest motivations and be honest with yourself about your capabilities. Being motivated by something you are not good at will not enable you to succeed as a leader, nor will pursuing leadership roles that do not motivate you. But when you find a role that meshes your motivations with your capabilities, you will discover the sweet spot that maximizes your effectiveness as a leader.

Note to the reader: Before going on to Chapter Seven, you may want to complete the Chapter Six Exercise found in Appendix C.

7

BUILDING YOUR
SUPPORT TEAM

Have some group that will tell you the truth and
whom you can tell the truth. If you have people
like that around you, what else matters?

—*Warren Bennis*

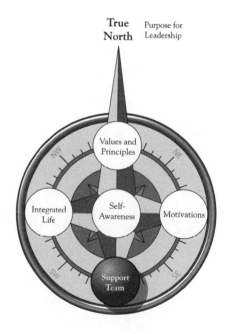

Your support team, which sits at the base of your compass, is the
fourth element of your development plan. Members of your team
help you stay focused on your True North, keep you grounded in
reality, and provide the support you need as you venture on your
leadership journey.

Leaders do not succeed on their own. The loneliness of leadership has been well documented, but the remedies have not. Everyone has insecurities; some are just more open about them than others. Even the most outwardly assured executives need support and appreciation. Authentic leaders build support teams that will counsel them in times of uncertainty, be there in times of difficulty, and celebrate with them in times of success.

Strong support teams provide affirmation, advice, perspective, calls for course corrections when needed, and, above all, love. After their hardest days, leaders find comfort in being with people on whom they can rely so they can be open and vulnerable. During the low points, they cherish the friends who appreciate them for *who* they are, not *what* they are.

It is easy to be tempted or seduced by the interests and expectations of others. The people with whom authentic leaders surround themselves ground their values and help them stay on track, especially when outside forces pressure them to take another course. Without strong relationships to provide perspective, it is very easy to lose your way.

How do you go about building your support team? Most authentic leaders have a multifaceted support structure that includes their spouse or significant other, family members, mentors, close friends, and personal and professional support groups. Many experienced leaders have built their support networks over time, as the experiences, shared histories, and willingness to be vulnerable with people close to them create the trust and confidence they need in times of trial and uncertainty. *Leaders must give as much to their relationships as they get from them so that mutually beneficial relationships can develop.*

The Most Important Person to Your Leadership

Your support team starts with having at least one person in your life with whom you can be completely vulnerable and open, warts and all, and still be loved unconditionally. Often that person is the only one who can tell you the honest truth.

Most leaders have their closest relationships with their spouses, although some develop these bonds with other family members, a close friend, or a trusted mentor. When leaders feel unconditionally loved by another person, they are more likely to accept themselves for who they really are. This enables them to become less dependent on external reinforcement.

Paula Rosput Reynolds, CEO of Safeco, found such a person in her second husband.

> *When you go home at the end of the day and your employees think you're a jerk, or something has gone so wrong it seems hopeless, you've got to have somebody who says, "I love you unconditionally." I always had that with my parents and my son. I'm fortunate now to have it with my husband. I know I can always go home and he will love me.*

Reynolds did not have that relationship in her first marriage. She was focused on her own shortcomings and the lack of feeling acknowledged for her accomplishments. As she matured and became less dependent on the need for acknowledgment, she found that she could make her marriage flourish as well.

Your partner is someone with whom you share mutual commitment, dedication, and love, someone who can hold up a mirror to tell you the truth in a compassionate way when you have strayed from your True North. In your partner's eyes, positions and accomplishments mean little, but the essence of who you are means everything. Because most leaders are so well defended against criticism, only those with whom they have a genuinely loving relationship can penetrate the armor protecting their core.

Big Brothers Big Sisters' Judy Vredenburgh and her husband each have a deep appreciation for the values, character, and humanity of the other. She said, "I married someone who is not threatened by my power or position."

> *He made it clear that my position would not give me negotiating strength in our relationship. He doesn't care about the things that impress the*

*external world. He deeply values my humanity as well as my achievement
orientation, my sense of responsibility, and my values.*

Leaders also described ways in which they have nurtured their
relationships over time. Stanford MBA Ryan Frederick and his
wife, Abi, put a lot of time and effort into developing their relationship. They took a personality test together to understand their
respective interests and how to communicate better. They also
sought out older couples from whom they could learn. "When we
find an older married couple we respect, we find it very helpful to
learn from them because it helps us grow intellectually, spiritually,
and in our relationship," Frederick said.

Many relationships grow over time through an expression of
shared values that lead to a common purpose. Randy Komisar said his
marriage to Debra Dunn has been successful and lasting because it is
rooted in similar values. "When couples have very different experiences, their values, principles, and needs may diverge over time."

*Debra and I are very independent, but extremely harmonious in terms of
our personal aspirations, values, and principles. We have a strong resonance around questions like, "what is your legacy in this world?" We
didn't start with that resonance, but it has grown over time. It is important to be in synch about what we do with our lives.*

Although Komisar's career path as an entrepreneur was very different from Dunn's role as a senior executive of HP, both have
always been determined to make a positive social impact through
business. She said, "We each have a clear sense of our own identity,
but also this positive overlap."

Families

Most leaders find comfort in being with their families. Younger
leaders maintain close connections with their families of origin,
seeking out opportunities to share high-quality time with siblings,

parents, and grandparents. In knowing their parents at a deeper level and learning more about their past, they wind up understanding themselves better.

At twenty-nine, Julian Flannery has worked in the White House as assistant to the president's chief of staff and is currently working for John Mack, CEO of Morgan Stanley. An only child, he has been close to his mother since he was three, when his father left the family. While in college, Flannery supported his mother throughout his stepfather's extended illness. These days he consults with his mother like a best friend.

With increasingly long working hours, some leaders have sharply limited their social lives. eBay president John Donahoe and his wife imposed a moratorium on social events so that they could spend quality time with their four children. When George Shultz was U.S. secretary of state, he and his wife skipped all Washington social events unless the president or vice president insisted they attend.

Marianne Toldalagi, formerly of American Express, emphasized the importance of developing trusting relationships with her twin children. "As a parent, I want my children to feel comfortable in their skin. I am building a trusting relationship with them, so we can talk about everything when they get into the teenage years."

Whether with employees or with your kids, you can never take trust for granted. It requires time to build and has to be earned. The key is making sure other people feel respected without being judged. I try to help my children know who they are and help them feel good about themselves. What could be better than an environment of trust where people feel strong, know who they are, and know how they can contribute?

Mentors

Many authentic leaders have had a mentor who has changed their lives by helping them develop the skills to become better leaders and the confidence to lead authentically. But what some people fail to recognize, especially aspiring leaders, is the importance of the two-way relationship with their mentors. *Lasting relationships must flow both ways.* The best mentoring interactions spark mutual learning, exploration of similar values, and shared enjoyment. But if people are only looking for help from their mentors, instead of being interested in their mentors' lives as well, the relationship will not last for long. It is the two-way nature of the connection that sustains it.

Coach Campbell: Mentorship in Action

Currently chairman and formerly CEO of Intuit, Bill Campbell is the dean of mentoring in Silicon Valley. Many venture capitalists and board members in northern California will not hire a new CEO without first checking with Campbell. Although he keeps a low public profile, "Coach Campbell" is one of Silicon Valley's most respected executives.

Campbell has mentored dozens of entrepreneurs and business leaders, including three of the leaders we interviewed: Randy Komisar, Donna Dubinsky, and Bruce Chizen. People are drawn to him because they consider him a great mentor and leader who has helped them unleash their own leadership potential. His selfless spirit, cultivated on the football fields of his youth, has enabled him to develop a loyal network of mentees, supporters, and friends.

Campbell played offensive guard at Columbia University and supported the point scorers with a sheer intensity that still emanates from his eyes. On first impression, his broad shoulders, tight jaw, and tough talk make it seem like he is going to tackle you. Beneath the façade, he genuinely cares about people. "When you're with Bill," said Komisar, "you never have the sense he's worrying about himself."

While an executive at Apple Computer, Campbell led the spin-off of Claris Software in 1987 and recruited a talented young team to join him, including Komisar, Dubinsky, and Chizen. Each of the three speaks with great nostalgia about the Claris years and their strong affection for Campbell. They still call him regularly for wisdom, advice on difficult decisions, friendship, and laughter. They are like a tight-knit family, and a very powerful one at that.

The relationships between Campbell and his mentees have been highly interdependent. Dubinsky, Komisar, and Chizen recognized that Campbell could help them enhance their skills while they helped him to build Claris. Dubinsky said, "Bill taught us how to communicate with employees, how to build a team, and how to operate the company." Chizen recalled watching Campbell during quarterly operating reviews: "He taught me how to understand a profit-and-loss statement, how manufacturing worked, and how to package products. He gave me my MBA." In building a diverse team, Campbell relied upon Komisar, a trained lawyer, to master contractual details while Dubinsky spearheaded the supply chain and Chizen motivated the sales force.

Campbell also helped them discover their authentic leadership by modeling it for them and pushing them to get outside themselves. Dubinsky recalled the respect he showed for others. "Bill would walk in and spend a few minutes every day talking to the receptionist. He knew what the receptionist's problems in life were and could relate to what her kids were doing." Campbell also knew how to give tough love. He challenged his team to think beyond their own narrow interests in order to focus on the entire company. Dubinsky noted, "He pushed me a lot. He saw me as a champion for my people, but insisted that I look out for the company's best interests as well."

Most important, Campbell empowered all three by regularly asking them for advice and by revealing his own vulnerabilities. Komisar recalled, "One of the things that Bill did was expose himself as a human being."

> He would give a speech to the whole company, imploring us, "We're going to do this!" Then we would go in his office, shut the door, and he would say to me, "I'm worried. Do you think the team can do this?" I got to see a vulnerable human being and to support him when he was down. He was not a caricature.

By being vulnerable and making subordinates his advisers, Campbell gave Komisar, Dubinsky, and Chizen the confidence

and license to be authentic in their own right. Komisar said he learned to be comfortable with himself from being mentored by Campbell:

Bill brings tremendous knowledge and experience to the table. He does not give you a fish but teaches you how to fish. You sense from Bill an overwhelming belief in you and a deep caring for what happens to you. That is the highest expression of love.

The best mentors put the interests of those they are mentoring above their own. These relationships can grow into strong personal friendships, especially when the participants are no longer in the same professional context. The cycle then continues when those who benefited from strong mentoring offer to mentor others.

Recruiting Mentors

Mentoring relationships provide both the mentor and person mentored with opportunities to learn and grow while working toward common goals. Many people are afraid to approach potential mentors because they do not want to ask for something. They fail to realize how much they can contribute to the mentor. To have great mentors, Warren Bennis tells young leaders, they have to recruit them. He likens this to a dance where the two engage in mutual learning. Reflecting on how he developed close relationships with his mentors, he recalled, "They appreciated my openness, energy, follow-up, and discipline."

As a young entrepreneur building a fledgling company, Howard Schultz realized he needed someone with whom he could share his fears and vulnerabilities. When Starbucks was just an eleven-store chain, Schultz heard Bennis lecture on leadership and said to himself, "This is someone I can learn from."

Who do you talk to when you're afraid to demonstrate vulnerability and insecurity to others? You can talk to your wife or close friends, but you also

need advice from someone who has been there before. I asked Warren for
his help, calling him once or twice a month. He taught me that vulnera-
bility is a strength and a characteristic that people value. Demonstrating
your values, emotions, and sensitivities empowers others, as no one is
impervious to having doubts.

Contrasting Mentors

Mentors are not necessarily people who make you feel good about
yourself or tell you that you can do anything you want to do.
Sometimes the best mentors provide tough love by being critical
as a means of teaching. Kroger's Dave Dillon told the story of two
contrasting mentors he had early in his career. At age twenty-
nine, he was named merchandising vice president for the Fry's
supermarket division of the Dillon Company (prior to its acquisi-
tion by Kroger), where he served under its president and his mentor, Ray Rose. In spite of Dillon's lack of merchandising experience,
Rose believed that anyone who could manage people could do
any job well.

One day Dillon got a call from Chuck Fry, the entrepreneur who
had sold his family business to the Dillon Company, inviting him to
walk through a Fry's store with him. As they stopped in front of a soft
drink display, Fry spent a long time questioning Dillon about what
he saw. "He made sure I realized I was not observing what was happening in the store and that I had missed the whole point. He
explained that the display had not been built with the customer in
mind, but was based on maximizing the vendor's profits."

Years later, Dillon learned that the real purpose of Fry's visit was
to decide whether or not young Dave would be willing to learn from
him as a teacher and mentor. If he wasn't, Fry planned to have him
pulled out of his job. Every day for the next year, Dillon and Fry
spent an hour a day together, in person or on the phone.

Looking back, I realize I was failing terribly as merchandising VP, but
didn't even recognize it. I also learned that Ray Rose was wrong about

this point. You can't take people who know how to manage people, put them into a totally foreign job, and expect them to perform. You have to teach them the leverage points of that job, not just the things you read in a book. It was a very valuable lesson. Without Chuck, I would not be successful in the grocery business.

Dillon's story illustrates the importance of having mentors who challenge rather than just support you. Too many leaders prefer mentors who are always there for them but don't push them to change or improve. As a mentor, it is relatively easy to be a good listener and support other people's ideas but harder and riskier to point out their weaknesses and blind spots.

Close Friends: Growing Redwood Trees

Having a close network of friends on whom they can call when in doubt or in need of help has proven to be extremely important for many authentic leaders. Close friendships are built over years of shared experiences, with each person having a genuine appreciation for the other. Most have no more than a handful of close friends, but they stay in regular contact with them. DaVita CEO Kent Thiry uses redwood trees as a metaphor for the way to develop close relationships. "Redwood trees are the tallest, strongest, longest-living tree in the forest. How do you get a tall, strong, long-lived redwood tree? It takes time."

After college, Thiry worked hard to maintain close contact with a handful of friends, traveling to see them and organizing reunions throughout the year. He is systematic in maintaining his friendships, using a spreadsheet to keep track of how many high-quality interactions he has had with each friend throughout the year. He also lets them know how much their friendship means to him. "You can start to grow another tree, but it's going to take ten years or more. Wouldn't it be a crime to cut a tree down just because you were tired of it?"

Close friends provide reinforcement when leaders feel discouraged and need a boost. They shake them from blind overconfidence when they are arrogant. It is often by sharing vulnerabilities that their friendships deepen, because openness is the sine qua non for cultivating relationships. Like mentoring, friendship is a two-way street where both parties benefit from the relationship. If it devolves into a situation where one person is doing all the giving and the other all the receiving, the friendship will not last for long.

When people grow together through various phases of life, they develop a deeper understanding of each other. Having been through it all together, close friends notice the little things, like when you need a kick, even when no one else can see that. They can sense when you are getting off track and are not afraid to tell you.

Traditions help create lasting friendships. Chris O'Connell, president of Medtronic Emergency Response Systems, has a group of seven classmates from business school who are among his closest friends. "Once a year, we get together for four days on a retreat. In the twelve years since we've been out of school, not one person has missed a single year. We probably spend more time planning and getting excited about the next trip than being on the trip itself. We will go to our graves doing this every year."

Many leaders prefer to build their close relationships outside their organizations and business circles. Jack Brennan, Vanguard's CEO, is close friends with doctors and lawyers who have no interest in his business. "It is nourishing to have close friends outside my professional circle."

It is during the most turbulent moments of their lives that leaders find out who their real friends are. Donna Dubinsky noted, "I was a 'paper billionaire' before the bubble burst in 2001, and people started running after me like crazy to be my friend. When much of this paper fortune disappeared, those people all left, but my real friends remained."

When Richard Tait reached his lowest point, he desperately needed a close friend. Before founding the board-game company Cranium, Tait had been one of Microsoft's stars, selected as "Employee of the Year" in 1994. After ten years of eighty-hour weeks, he was burned out and decided to quit in his early thirties. He recalled, "I got to the point where I was lost. I knew that it was better for me to leave."

For several months, Tait shuffled around his house, trying to think of entrepreneurial ideas. "That was a very dark period. I was so depressed that I spent my days in the basement in my jammies. The only reason I got dressed was to greet my wife coming home from work."

During that period Tait's friend Bruno, whom he had known when they worked together at Microsoft, came to his house for long conversations. "He's one of my most trusted friends. He has been my gladiator three times in my life," said Tait. "I can be completely vulnerable with him. Bruno gave me confidence and enabled me to be true to myself. He always said, 'You'll have another idea.' After six months, the idea for the board game Cranium finally came to me."

Your Personal Support Group

Personal support groups are one of the most powerful ways of gaining wisdom and advice that will help you grow as a leader. The most effective groups are made up of peers who meet on a regular basis and talk about what is important in their lives. Some structure can help immeasurably to ensure that the conversation does not degenerate into casual talk about current events. Instead, a carefully conceived structure causes members of the group to probe their beliefs and relationships and to describe the challenges they face.

In preparing for the unexpected in life, Warren Bennis tells leaders, "Have some group that will tell you the truth and to whom you can tell the truth."

If you have people like that around you, what else matters? You're never going to be prepared for 9/11, nor can you figure out what's going to hap-

pen. All you can do is make sure there's some way of understanding reality beyond what you know yourself.

In 1974 I joined a men's group that formed after a weekend retreat in which we all participated. More than thirty years later, we are still meeting every Wednesday morning for seventy-five minutes before the workday begins. After an opening period of catching up on each other's lives and dealing with any particular difficulty someone may be facing, one of the group's eight members leads a discussion based on a topic he has selected, such as the legacies we want to leave behind. These discussions are open, probing, and often profound. The key to their success is what we call "honest conversations," saying what you really believe without fear of judgment, criticism, or reprisal.

Over the years, we have developed shared life histories as members of the group have gone through the birth of children and grandchildren, divorce, promotion and job loss, life-threatening illness, and even death. Occasionally, the group goes on a retreat or gets together socially with our spouses, but the essence of the group is the Wednesday morning meeting. We all consider that the group has been one of the most important aspects of our lives, enabling us to clarify our beliefs, values, and understanding of vital issues, as well as providing a source of honest feedback when we need it most.

Piper Jaffray's Tad Piper is a member of three groups that have been essential during the difficult times of his life. He noted,

If you had told me twenty years ago that I would be part of three groups that meet regularly and talk about things like feelings and God, I would have said, "Thank you, but I don't do groups." Now they are incredibly important parts of my life. I look forward to being there, because they help fill me up as a person.

Fifteen years ago, Piper went through treatment for chemical dependency and afterward joined an Alcoholics Anonymous group. He noted, "These are not CEOs."

They are just a group of nice, hard-working people who are trying to stay sober, lead good lives, and work with each other about being open, honest, and vulnerable. We reinforce each other's behavior by talking about our chemical dependency in a disciplined way as we go through the twelve steps. I feel blessed to be surrounded by people who are thinking about those kinds of issues and actually doing something, not just talking about them.

Not many of us will be as fortunate as Piper to have three regular groups in our lives, but wouldn't it be great if we could all have one? Having a small group of people that you share with confidentially on a regular basis is an invaluable way to stay grounded and to get advice and support when you need it most.

Creating a Professional Support Network

Many leaders develop professional peer networks both within and outside their organizations to consult with them about important issues and to provide counsel and guidance. eBay's Donahoe noted, "You can learn a little bit from a lot of people." Rob Chess, chairman of Nektar Therapeutics, commented, "If someone does something very well, I try to understand how I can apply it to my work."

Some leaders mentioned the value of their involvement with executive roundtable groups and professional organizations like the Young Presidents' Organization (YPO). YPO provides a forum where members can talk openly about their challenges and a network to exchange ideas and learn from each other.

Having a peer support structure within your organization can be invaluable, because colleagues may be facing comparable experiences, have insights about things you do not see, or be in a position to offer you real-time feedback on your leadership. Because being on top of an organization can be lonely and isolating, some leaders use their subordinates as an advisory network, even in the most difficult business circumstances.

Your Personal Board of Directors

CEOs look to members of their board of directors for advice at crucial points, so why not have *your own personal* board of directors? Your board might include several highly trusted personal and professional advisers, people you respect for their professional expertise, insights, and wisdom, and for their commitment to your personal well-being. Your team can also include close friends, mentors, your lawyer, financial planner, or personal coach. You can meet with them for counsel and advice on a regular basis or when you are facing especially difficult decisions.

Your journey to leadership is likely to take many unexpected turns. Life is full of challenging situations, including ethical dilemmas, midcourse career changes or burnout, seemingly intractable interpersonal challenges with colleagues, marriage and family issues, failures, and loneliness. At times you may feel you are losing your way or have gotten off the course of your True North.

Getting back on track alone is very difficult. That is when you most need your support team. It is important to build your team long before there is a crisis in your life, because that assures you that people will be available to help when you need them most.

Note to the reader: Before going on to Chapter Eight, you may want to complete the Chapter Seven Exercise found in Appendix C.

8

STAYING GROUNDED:
INTEGRATING YOUR LIFE

The world will shape you if you let it.
To have a sense of yourself as you live,
you must make conscious choices.
—John Donahoe, president, eBay

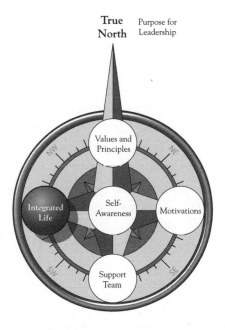

On a tranquil Boston evening in the fall of 1983, eBay's John Donahoe, then an energetic twenty-three-year-old, enjoyed a relaxing dinner with his fiancée, Eileen. Just a year out of college, Donahoe had already earned an excellent reputation as a consulting analyst at Bain. His eyes lit up as he talked about his career prospects.

As dinner wore on, Eileen became more concerned about the toll John's career could take on his life. She expressed concern about how the long hours, constant travel, and stress might limit his ability to have close relationships. Then she asked him pointedly, "Is that really what you want in life?" John answered adamantly, "No!" He reached into his wallet to find a piece of paper and wrote on the back of a Shawmut Bank receipt, "I will not live the life of a management consultant," and signed his name. John recalled, "Her challenge to me was, 'Be who you are.'"

As Donahoe rose through the ranks to become worldwide managing director at Bain, he worked hard at leading an authentic life. "My ultimate goal is to have an impact and be an authentic businessperson, as well as the kind of father, husband, friend, and human being I want to be. The human-being side is the highest goal and the ultimate challenge."

For authentic leaders, being true to themselves by being the same person at work that they are at home is a constant test, yet personal fulfillment is their ultimate reward. According to Donahoe, "Leading a satisfying life is a quest worth taking." Donahoe feels strongly that integrating his life has enabled him to become a more effective leader. "There is no nirvana," he said.

> The struggle is constant, as the trade-offs and choices don't get any easier as you get older. My personal and professional lives are not a zero-sum trade-off. I have no doubt today that my children have made me a far more effective leader in the workplace. Having a strong personal life has made the difference.

Integrating their lives is one of the greatest challenges leaders face. To lead an *integrated life*, you need to bring together the major elements of your personal life and professional life, including work, family, community, and friends, so that you can be the same person in each environment. Donahoe stressed that being authentic takes continuous effort. "The challenge of maintaining authenticity, a sense of self, of learning and growing, is the same no matter where you are."

Authentic leaders are constantly aware of the importance of staying grounded. In doing so, they avoid getting too cocky during the high points and forgetting who they are during the low points. Spending time with their families and close friends, getting physical exercise, having spiritual practices, doing community service, and returning to places where they grew up are all ways they stay grounded. This grounding is essential to their effectiveness as leaders, because it enables them to preserve their authenticity.

"The world can shape you if you let it. To have a sense of yourself as you live, you must make conscious choices," said Donahoe. "Sometimes the choices are really hard, and you make a lot of mistakes." One of his first big decisions came during his first year at business school. The first term was the most intense academic experience of his life. On the eve of finals, Eileen went into labor with their first child. When Donahoe asked himself what was more important, the birth of his child or his grades, the answer became obvious.

Having achieved in every academic environment he had been in, he had to let go of his desire to get top grades. "In a strange way, I had an excuse for not doing well. I had to accept the fact that I was not going to get straight A's." As finals approached, Donahoe spent more and more time with Eileen. As his colleagues became increasingly stressed, he felt oddly relaxed.

Much to his surprise, Donahoe earned the highest grades possible that quarter. "It was only because I had a bit of perspective. I certainly was not the smartest person in the room," he said. "I remember watching the inefficiency that kicked in when people stressed out." That experience showed him that life could be his friend.

A few years later, Donahoe faced another difficult set of choices that confirmed his belief that he could integrate his life in an authentic way. After graduating from law school, Eileen received an offer to clerk for a federal judge, but the job required her to be at work by 7:30 A.M., and John's job required him to travel extensively. John had no alternative but to take their two kids to school every day.

Donahoe went to Tom Tierney, managing director of Bain's San Francisco office, and told him that he had no choice except to quit. Tierney just laughed and said, "John, we can find a way to work around this." He reassigned Donahoe to a local client, enabling him to take his kids to school before arriving at the client site.

Donahoe was amazed that his clients appreciated the choices he was making. He told his client honestly, "It is important to me to be doing this. It's not that I'm not committed to working hard, but I can't be there before 10 A.M."

The client responded positively as he appreciated my commitment and my contribution even more. I'm not sure I had the courage to think about it that way before. There's an inclination in business to put on a tough exterior to give the impression that you have everything under control. This was a defining year for me.

Donahoe also learned that the more he integrated his life and embraced his humanity, the more effective he became as a leader. "That was my best year of client work. Our client understood, and I became more relaxed," he recalled. By showing his team and clients his vulnerabilities, he discovered that the teams performed better and his client relationships strengthened.

The following year he was named head of Bain's San Francisco office. After six years in that role, he felt burned out by the fast-paced life and wanted to spend more time with his two oldest sons before they became teenagers. So he handed off his work to his colleagues and took a three-month sabbatical. "It was the right time for repotting, and an opportunity to bring our family closer together." First, the family went to Europe, and then Donahoe took separate weeklong trips with his wife and each of his four children.

He returned to Bain reenergized and a year later was named worldwide managing director, succeeding Tierney. The announcement came just as the economy was plummeting. At the same time, a family health issue with one of his children arose that tested him as never before. "The health issue emerged soon after I became managing director, and just as the consulting industry faced its biggest downturn in thirty years."

> *It was the hardest thing I've ever had to work through in my life. My family, friends, coaches, and colleagues were unbelievably helpful. Real life forced me to bring a sense of authenticity and vulnerability to the workplace, because life humbles you.*

Sharing his personal situation openly helped him connect with his partners so they could rally during the downturn. By accepting his vulnerabilities, Donahoe was able to maintain an even keel. "I had faith in our people. We could talk about where we were going and how we were going to make it happen." He believes he was effective precisely because he was able to integrate his personal and professional lives during the stressful circumstances. "Because much of my emotional energy was going to my family, I didn't take the downturn personally. As a result, I was more effective as a leader. My legacy to Bain partners will probably be the way I led us through the downturn."

Although twenty years have passed since their conversation that night in Boston, Eileen Donahoe has not forgotten the signed Shawmut Bank slip. "I still keep it inside my purse," she says. "I've brought it out many times over the years." The Donahoes have successfully weathered challenging stages of their lives and continue to strive for an authentic life together. Their partnership serves as an excellent example of not only how to be intentional in building meaningful lives but how rewarding it can be.

Making Choices and Trade-Offs

Warren Bennis does not like the word *balance*. "*Balance* is an engineering term that means you put the little weights on each side, and if you're really a good person, you'll come out equal. We have to be aware that we swing back and forth. It is choices all the time, not balance."

Without realizing it, we make hundreds of choices every day, many of them subconscious or intuitive, and try to learn from those that turn out to be mistakes. *Ultimately, our life stories become an expression of the choices we make.* Young & Rubicam's Ann Fudge emphasized the importance of people making choices based on what you value and according to what is important to you.

> *The most important thing is to put aside the immediate impact of our choices and ask, "What am I going to contribute? What can I learn?" I don't know how much time I have. I hope to go to my grave having no regrets.*

When leaders talked about their crucibles, they said those experiences forced them to ask themselves, "What is important to me in life?" Asking that question allows leaders to make conscious choices. Xerox's Anne Mulcahy said, "I like to work hard and have a serious career, but the most important thing to me in my life is my family. I love Xerox and I'd kill for it, but it is not even on the same scale as my family. As a family, we made a lot of choices. It is all about trade-offs."

She and her husband, a thirty-six-year Xerox veteran who traveled a great deal himself, decided that one of them would be at home with their kids every night. They also decided they would not move. So they commuted, even when their jobs required them to travel great distances. "To be CEO of Xerox, and never having moved, is quite extraordinary, but it's doable. At Xerox we expect people to put their families first. Unacceptable trade-offs should not be part of the work environment."

Twenty-three-year-old David Darst, one of the youngest leaders interviewed, has worked incredibly hard in founding both a for-profit company and a nonprofit start-up. He makes a conscious effort to bring fun into his work, taking time for exercise, listening to music to alleviate stress, and seeking interactions with close friends. It is not easy. "I would sacrifice these things only for an opportunity I am truly passionate about," he explained.

Dermot Dunphy, retired CEO of Sealed Air, has worried about the impact of personal and family problems on the ability to lead at work. Although most people try to separate these areas, it is inevitable that problems in one area will impact performance in the other. Dunphy noted, "There's no doubt in my mind that a happy personal life is a valuable facilitator for balanced leadership."

The Buckets of Your Life

Many leaders think about integration in terms of bringing the major parts of their lives together: family, work, friends and community, and personal time. Phil McCrea, founder and former CEO of Vitesse Learning, said, "I have four buckets representing the important areas of my life."

> *One is my career. The second is my family. The third is my community and personal friendships, and fourth is the personal activities I enjoy. The third and the fourth are very removed for me right now. This is not frustrating for me because I'm tremendously fulfilled by the first two today. By age forty, I'd like to be in a position where I have a better ability to fill buckets three and four—community, friendships, and personal activities. Long term, I will not continue to pursue the career I'm in if it leaves a void.*

McCrea and his wife, Annika, who has a promising career herself as a consultant, made the difficult decision to plunge ahead with starting a company just as they were starting their family. Living in San Francisco, McCrea soon found that he was traveling coast-to-coast virtually every week because his software programmers were based in California and his customers—primarily large pharmaceutical companies—were on the East Coast. Eventually, he was faced with a stark choice: give up his family life or move his family to New Jersey to be close to his customers. They chose the latter route, as Annika was able to convince her company to transfer her to its Connecticut headquarters. Thus far, the

Figure 8.1 Integrating Your Life

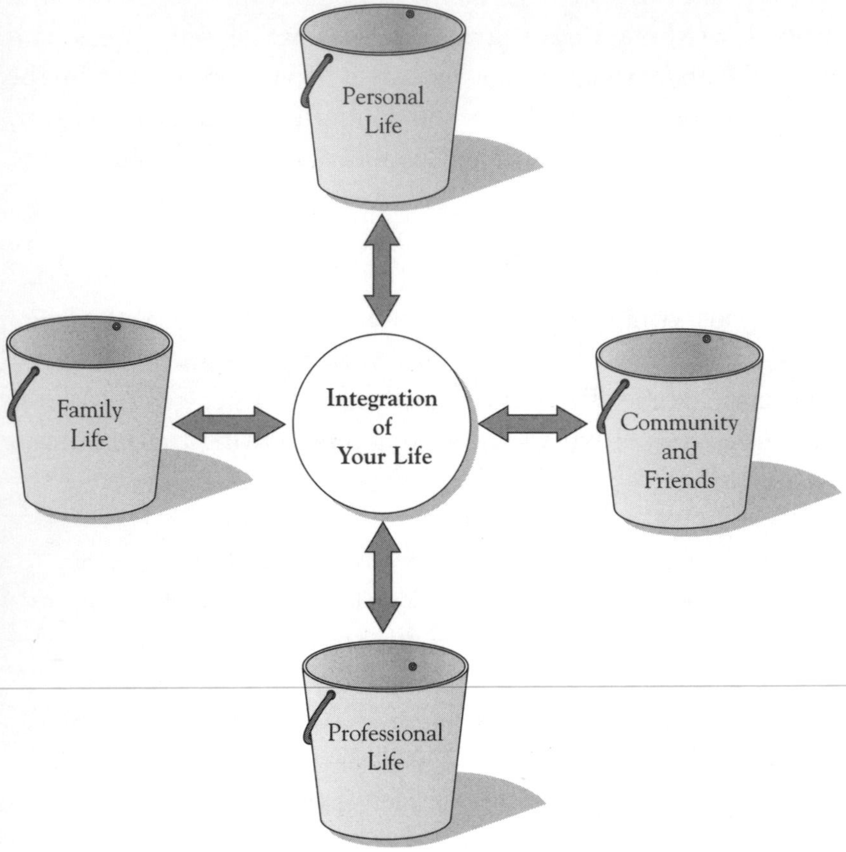

relocation has worked well; the travel demands have not gone away but have shrunk in duration.

Leadership can require significant sacrifices, especially during intense periods, when certain buckets get less time. Former AT&T executive Gail McGovern framed it concisely. "A lot of people ask if it is possible to have a rich personal life and a great work life. I say unequivocally, it is entirely possible. You just have to recognize you can't give 110 percent to everything. There are many mundane things in your life you have to let go of and not feel guilty about."

To ease the pressures, McGovern hires people to help with child care and does not worry if her house isn't perfectly clean or if video rentals are overdue. "If you realize you can't be super housewife, super career person, super mom, and super wife, there is absolutely no reason why you cannot have it all," she concludes.

Staying Grounded by Integrating Your Life

To integrate your life, you must remain grounded in your authentic self, especially when the outside world is chaotic. Well-grounded leaders have a steady and confident presence. They do not show up as one person one day and another person the next. Integration takes discipline, particularly during stressful times when it is easy to become reactive and slip into bad habits.

Leading is high-stress work. There is no way to avoid stress when you are responsible for people, organizations, outcomes, and the constant uncertainties of the environment. The higher you go, the greater your freedom to control your destiny but also the higher the level of stress. The question is not whether you can avoid stress but how you can control it to maintain your own sense of equilibrium. As a former colleague used to say, "The state of zero stress is death."

When Medtronic's Chris O'Connell gets stressed, he says, "I can feel myself slipping into a negative frame of mind. When I'm at my best, I'm very positive and feel I can accomplish anything, both at work and home." When O'Connell's frame of mind becomes negative, "I lose effectiveness as a leader and become even less effective at home. Both positive and negative emotions carry over between work and home."

Amid the turmoil, it is important to maintain your perspective. To keep his perspective, Belkin Corporation's Mark Reynoso imagines a simple analogy: "If I have a hundred balls coming at me and can grab only two, I can stress out about missing ninety-eight balls or accept the reality I can grab only two—and make sure they are the most important ones."

Your Family

Avon Products CEO Andrea Jung recalled the morning she was anxious to get to work because she was being named Boss of the Year. When she told her son to hurry up, he looked at her and said, "You are not the boss of me." She explained, "Here I was going to speak in front of three thousand people who thought I was boss, but I was forced to acknowledge I had zero control over my own child."

Family grounds you, no matter who you are. Warner Brothers' Alan Horn makes the final decision about which of twenty-five movies the company will produce every year, a job that puts him on *Entertainment Weekly*'s Executive Power List. Every holiday he gets cards and gifts from the megastars. Unlike most Hollywood producers, who routinely display pictures of themselves with Tom Cruise, Julia Roberts, or Brad Pitt, Horn has few traces of Hollywood in his office. Instead, pictures of his family members are everywhere.

Horn pointed to his desk chair and said, "The moment someone else takes that chair, all that glamour is gone. These people move on to the next person, but my kids won't move on." Horn then paused and with obvious emotion said, "My father was just a bartender, but he's still the most important person to me."

Fadi Ghandour, founder and CEO of Aramex International, is a well-respected Middle East businessman who takes his sons on annual scuba diving trips. Ghandour started the tradition because he did not see his own father often enough when he was growing up. "It was a conscious effort on my part," he said. "It's a great way for me to connect with my kids and is the most relaxing and enjoyable time for me."

Kris Johnson: You Cannot Do It All. With the rise in two-career marriages, younger leaders wrestle with questions of life choices and integration more than previous generations did. There is never enough time for two full-time careers and raising a family with young children as well as for personal time and community involvement.

Kris Johnson was a rising star at Medtronic who took the company's external relations and business strategy to new levels of sophistication in the 1980s. Then in the 1990s she built the company's implantable defibrillators into a $3 billion business. She and her husband, Rob, one of Cargill's top executives, shared the parenting of the couple's two daughters, with Kris carrying more of the emotional load. Kris loyally attended her daughters' sporting events and frequently took them along on trips to out-of-town company meetings.

Kris and Rob were not afraid to get outside help to ease their busy schedules. She recalled the advice of a mentor who told her, "You ought to pay somebody to do whatever you don't want to do. You've got enough money. Use it to buy time." Johnson was embarrassed to tell her mother she needed help but soon found that the change was necessary. Eventually, she became comfortable with not being able to do it all.

After being promoted to run Medtronic's global vascular business, Johnson found she was spending too much time away from her family on grueling international trips. At first, she tried returning to the more stable life of the Medtronic corporate staff but eventually realized a major change was required to give her greater control over her schedule and more time with her teenage daughters.

At this point she left Medtronic to become a partner in a mid-sized venture capital company focused on health care. Her new job gave her the freedom to find the proper balance between her work and her family. Just a few years later, an unexpected health crisis brought home to her that she had made the right decision. "Opportunities to be with your daughters at the most important events or to visit them at college don't come around again if you pass them up," she said.

Kris Johnson's story illustrates that you can have it all but not all at once. As two active executives, Kris and Rob made conscious decisions about their family and their careers to ensure that they were there for their daughters during the vital growing-up years while continuing to pursue active and successful leadership roles in business and in nonprofit organizations.

Staying True to Your Roots

Returning to where you came from is another important way to stay grounded. Just as Howard Schultz goes back to Brooklyn from time to time, Bill Campbell stays in regular contact with his old friends in Homestead, Pennsylvania, which helps keep perspective on life in Silicon Valley. Akshata Murthy, who grew up in Bangalore as the daughter of Infosys CEO Narayana Murthy, returns to India regularly to see her old friends and extended family. She is committed to making an impact there someday.

To restore themselves and their sense of perspective, many have a special place they can go with their families on weekends and vacations. For decades, former Secretary of State George Shultz and his wife went to an old family farm they own in Massachusetts. "I once told the president, 'This is my Camp David.' When I go there, I put on an old pair of pants and shoes I have worn for a long time. I am so relaxed I don't worry about anything."

Finding Time for Yourself

To manage the stress created by our leadership roles, we need personal time to relieve the tension. Some people practice meditation or yoga to center themselves and relieve anxiety. Others find solace in prayer. Some people find they can release tension by jogging at the end of a long workday. Still others find relief through laughing with friends, listening to music, watching television, attending sporting events, reading, or going to movies.

It does not matter *what* you do, as long as you establish a routine that enables you to manage the stress in your life and gives you time to think clearly about life, work, and your personal issues. It is critical to avoid abandoning these routines when you are going through an especially busy or difficult period, because that is precisely when you need your stress reduction techniques to kick in.

Buzz McCoy, who led Morgan Stanley's real estate division, coped with the stress of his job by running nearly every day. "My relief came through physical activity to burn off the edge. I knew I had to be in shape physically because I'd fly at night."

Warner Brothers' Alan Horn wakes up each morning at six o'clock to exercise; if he misses one day, he goes for two hours the next. When John Morgridge was CEO of Cisco, he also went jogging at 6 A.M. because, as he said, "In the technology industry, you have to get going early. I could just throw my running shoes into my bag wherever I was traveling."

Spiritual and Religious Practices

Understanding our role in the world by asking questions like "What is the meaning and purpose of my life?" or "Why am I here?" is the most personal and profound area of our leadership development. Many leaders have an active religious or spiritual practice to engage these issues, either privately or with like-minded people. Some seek the answers through a process of introspection. Others explore them through discussions with the people closest to them.

Authentic leaders who are religious talked about the power of prayer, being a part of church groups, and finding solace at church. Commenting on his faith, Vitesse Learning's Phil McCrea said, "I take the kids to church every Sunday, which is rewarding and fulfilling. In addition to the religious aspect, there is also a meditative aspect. While sitting in the church pew, I have a solid hour of reflective time."

Venture capitalist Denise O'Leary, who sits on several prestigious corporate boards, listens to Gregorian chants at a local church, while her husband, DaVita CEO Kent Thiry, reads Buddhist texts to center himself. She explained, "This is the place where I find real solace. I remember loving this style of music as a child. It is my meditation as it allows me to be introspective." Debra Dunn, who used to do yoga in her office on executive row at Hewlett-Packard, finds renewal in nature. "I realized that I needed to get out of Silicon Valley in order to get centered."

Taking Sabbaticals

Taking sabbaticals is another way in which authentic leaders ground themselves. John Donahoe's sabbatical lasted three months. Brenda Barnes was away from the workplace for several years to focus on her family before she returned to the corporate world as president of Sara Lee. Many other leaders, such as Joe Rogers Jr., also took sabbaticals.

Rogers did not take long to become CEO. At twenty-six he was put in charge of Waffle House, a chain of breakfast restaurants owned by his family. After early success in his new role, relationships with his people grew strained as he tried to change the firm's direction. He explained, "By the end of the 1970s, I was fed up. A lot of people were opposing what I was trying to get done. Finally, I just threw up my hands and asked myself, 'Do I want to keep beating my head against this wall?'"

Rogers took a six-month sabbatical and went to Solana Beach outside San Diego. He lived on the beach for six months, ran every day, and learned to surf while he thought about his options. "Finally, I said to myself, 'Is this really my people's fault? Maybe I'm the problem. I may have the right ideas, but I'm not providing the right leadership.'"

He returned to the business and unveiled a new corporate strategy. He told his team, "We're stopping the growth and committing to quality first. It's no longer bigger and better. It's better before bigger. If we don't get better, we haven't earned the right to get bigger." Rogers's organization quickly solidified around the new strategy as Waffle House was transformed into a success story that has been sustained for thirty years.

Friends and Community

Genuine friends—those we can count on in good times and bad—are an invaluable resource in helping us stay grounded. They are always willing to provide candid feedback, constructive criticism when appropriate, and encouragement when most needed. Some of Howard Schultz's closest friendships are those he made during college and in his twenties. He says, "There is a core group of people you meet in life who are your friends because your relationships really matter, not because of who you are or what you have done. It is important to stay close to those people because your relationships with them ground you and keep you humble."

Being in direct contact with those who are less fortunate also provides leaders with an invaluable perspective about who they are and what is happening in the world around them. Lisa Dawe, a regional operations director with DaVita, emphasized that human interactions in an AIDS hospice helped her stay in touch with reality. "In the rush of day-to-day leadership responsibilities, I risk losing perspective on my core motivation."

> *It is crucial to connect with people one-on-one, not just to create a fundraising plan. Being in touch with AIDS victims enabled me to feel human. I sat by the bedsides and watched, one by one, as people died. That helped me understand what I'm going to do when I get to that point and provided perspective on how fortunate I am. It helped me get to the core of what it means to be human.*

Measuring Success

Have you defined what success means for you and for your life? Unless you have thought through the answer to that question, you are at risk of letting others define success for you or trying to keep up with their definitions of success. Only when you can define what is most important in your life can you set the right priorities for your life and become an integrated leader.

The specific choices will differ for each of us. John Donahoe developed his own scorecard to measure his success. His criteria are the number of lives he can influence while being the type of husband, father, friend, and person he would like to be. Dermot Dunphy of Sealed Air encourages entrepreneurs to start off by defining their personal standards of success. "I use three points to define success," he says.

> *The most important is to love and be loved. The second is to be respected. The third is to possess a sense of honor. It's how you feel about yourself early in the morning when you get up and look at yourself in the mirror.*

Living with Integrity

What does it mean to live your life with integrity? Real integrity results from integrating all aspects of your life so that you are true to yourself in all settings. Think of your life like a house, with a bedroom for your personal life, a study for your professional life, a family room for your family, and a living room to share with your friends. Can you knock down the walls between these rooms and be the same person in each of them?

When you can act the same in each setting, you are well on your way to living your life with genuine integrity. Living that way, you will be an authentic leader who leads a fulfilling life.

Note to the reader: Before going on to Part Three and Chapter Nine, you may want to complete the Chapter Eight Exercise found in Appendix C.

Part Three

Empowering People to Lead

Having focused on how leaders discover their True North, let's explore the ways authentic leaders empower people through their leadership. The crucial first step is to find the purpose of their leadership by reframing their life stories and following their passions. Then they are prepared to inspire others to step up and lead around a common purpose and shared values.

To optimize their effectiveness, leaders build their influence by honing their style and making authentic use of their power to generate superior performance from their teammates. Superior results build the reputations of authentic leaders and their teammates and earn them added responsibility and resources. Through the reinforcement of the effectiveness of authentic leadership, the virtuous circle is completed and others are encouraged to become authentic leaders and join in the shared purpose.

The Effectiveness of Authentic Leaders

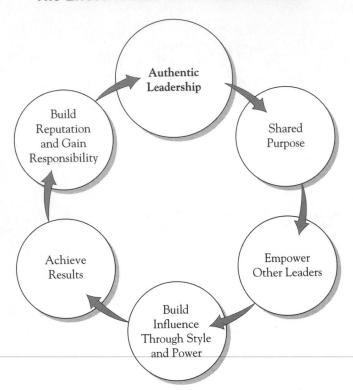

9

LEADERSHIP WITH PURPOSE AND PASSION

Tell me, what is it you plan to do
with your one wild and precious life?
—*"The Summer Day," by Mary Oliver*

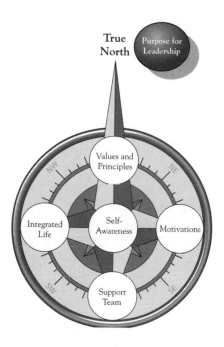

In 1998 Andrea Jung was facing the most difficult decision of her long and successful career. Four years after joining Avon Products, she had just been passed over for promotion to CEO in favor of one of the company's outside board members. "I had an offer to become CEO at another company, but Ann Moore, CEO of Time, Inc. and an Avon board member, advised me to stay," she recalled. "She told me, 'Follow your compass and not your clock.'"

> I had fallen in love with what Avon does. I realized I would prefer to be number two in a company with this impact on society than to be number one in another company without it. If you don't love your work, it is too great a sacrifice.

Jung decided to stay, becoming president of Avon and a board member. The decision changed her life. Just twenty months later, the new CEO retired, and Jung was named his successor in November 1999, becoming Avon's first female CEO. Reflecting on her decision, she notes, "If people can't tell that I love this company, it's hard to be a lasting leader."

> Passion is such an important quality. The infectiousness of your leadership must be apparent to the people, or you can't charge forward. If you don't love it, you can't fake it.

Jung is a leader who has found her passion and fulfilled it through the company she leads. From the time she joined the firm, she saw Avon as not just a cosmetics company but an organization that improved women's lives, both in the company and around the world. Soon after Jung became CEO, Avon adopted a new vision statement, "*The* Company for Women." This mission, which was aligned with Avon's business model, provided clarity of direction throughout the company. Jung explained:

> We wanted a catalyst for a fast, clear, and universal understanding of this mission. What we do is to elevate women in the community. It is purposeful work. We create commerce that can better their families' lives, particularly in emerging markets.

What is the purpose of *your* leadership? Are you following the True North of your compass or the timetable of your clock? Do you understand your passion for leading, as Andrea Jung does? These questions are not easy to answer. For some of us, it takes many years to find the purpose of our leadership—and the right place to devote our passions.

If you examine your True North again, you will find that it points the way to the purpose of your leadership—the difference you make in the world and the legacy you leave behind. When you understand your purpose, you are ready to find an organization—or to create one—where you can fulfill your purpose.

Even for a gifted and passionate leader like Andrea Jung, finding her purpose wasn't easy. She was born in Toronto to a family of Chinese immigrants who valued education, perseverance, hard work, and humility above all else. Her father was an architect, and her mother was the first female chemical engineering graduate of the University of Toronto. Her parents instilled in her the sense she could accomplish anything.

Jung is proud of the influence of her parents' work ethic. "The principles were to try and give back, improve, teach, and make things better," she explained.

You just don't give up on anything. I can remember being at the piano for fifty-two minutes when my parents would say, "It is sixty minutes. You do not get up yet." The last eight minutes are important. Achievement was less about getting all A's and more about trying.

Graduating from Princeton in three years, Jung joined Bloomingdale's management training program, where she quickly became frustrated doing menial tasks. "I felt my education was being wasted in a back stockroom, changing clothes from vendors' hangers to the store's hangers," she recalled. After a few months on the job she decided to resign, as did three-quarters of her fellow trainees, but her parents told her, "You will not quit."

If you were being mistreated, it would be different, but you're quitting because you don't have the perseverance. You don't want to get your hands dirty. We don't quit in this family. We persevere.

Jung stayed with the program and became one of Bloomingdale's youngest vice presidents, heading a department of people that averaged twenty years older than herself. "I was only twenty-three," Jung said, "and it was my first tough experience." She did not fit the mold of the aggressive retail executive because she had been taught to be deferential and mindful of elders and others in authority. "I had to become more assertive," she recalled.

> *No longer was I just an individual contributor. I had to be a leader now. What I did was irrelevant. It was all about people underneath me. There were personnel changes to be made, and a new strategy to be designed. I followed the principles of having compassion and respect for people and to understand and value the human spirit along with the work.*

After six years with Bloomingdale's, Jung followed her mentor to San Francisco as senior vice president of I. Magnin and later moved to Dallas to become executive vice president of Neiman Marcus. As an Asian woman and single mother of a two-year-old daughter, Jung found life in Dallas very challenging. "It was brutal," she recalled. "I loved the work, but there was a lot of travel and that was tough with a young child. It was also difficult being a minority in Dallas."

> *My British nanny always took my daughter, who is half-Asian, to school. The first time I went to the school, they said to me, "We have been waiting for a long time to meet Lauren's nanny." I said, "No, I'm her mother."*

While in Dallas, Jung began to feel that focusing her career on upscale department stores selling to the high-end luxury market was not in the real world. Although she had risen rapidly, she could not find her passion, nor did her work relate to the family values with which she had been raised. She resigned from Neiman Marcus without having another job.

Shortly thereafter, she was approached by Avon to evaluate its entry into retail. After six weeks of study, she recommended against retail distribution. When she presented her marketing ideas to

Avon CEO James Preston, he was so impressed he offered her a job immediately. Jung learned that Preston was committed to the advancement of women at Avon. "I noticed a picture behind his desk," she recalled.

> *It had four footprints to depict the evolution of leadership: first, the footprint of an ape, followed by the bare foot of a man, then a man's wing-tipped shoe. The fourth footprint was a woman's high-heeled pump. This was the early 1990s, when no women were leading companies in the Fortune 500. I asked him, "Do you believe in that?" He said, "I imagine Avon will be one of the first companies to have women at the top."*

Once at Avon, Jung discovered her real purpose for leading: to empower women. Throughout its history, Avon had been a leader in providing women with earnings opportunities as independent sales representatives; by 1994 its ranks had grown to 1.5 million people, 95 percent of whom were women. Jung was excited about having a global platform so that she could help women in developing countries as well.

During her twelve years with Avon, Jung has increased the number of sales representatives to five million. By 2006 women accounted for three of Avon's nine outside directors, seven of its seventeen senior managers, and three-quarters of its 1,400 U.S. district sales managers. "Our business is built on the belief that your dreams can come true, that women can do anything, and that they can be self-sufficient and empowered," said Jung. "To be a female CEO of this company reflects that belief at the highest level."

In spite of her passion for Avon, staying focused on her mission has not been easy in the face of pressures to meet Wall Street's near-term expectations. After five years of rapid increase, the company's revenue growth in 2005 slowed to 5 percent and earnings were flat; Avon stock tumbled 30 percent. Jung responded quickly by cutting management levels from fifteen to eight, eliminating 25 percent of the management positions, and reducing the sales force by 6 percent.

She chose to reinvest a significant portion of the $300 million of annual savings in reigniting the company's growth and suspended earnings forecasts to get shareholders to focus on the company's long-term prospects. By staying true to her principles, Jung garnered full support for the changes from her employees.

"Being able to reinvent yourself personally as a leader is just as important as reinventing the company and its strategy," Jung reflected.

> You have to keep both fresh and relevant. Compassion, understanding of people, and fairness are important. I feel responsible not to let the people in the company down. There is a lot of pressure that comes with that. When you take it to heart, it becomes your life, not just a job.

Andrea Jung is representative of the new breed of authentic leaders who have taken over major companies since 2000. She is passionate about the purpose of her organization and works tirelessly to align her employees with the company's mission. Like all leaders, she has to make difficult trade-offs between meeting short-term objectives and fulfilling the mission. Jung's leadership shone through when she faced a bump in the road. She took decisive action without sacrificing the company's values or its long-term goals, demonstrating her adaptability in guiding her organization through challenging times.

Discerning Your Passions

How do you discern your passions? For most leaders passion comes from their life stories, as it does for Andrea Jung. By understanding the meaning of key events in your life story and reframing them, you can discern what your passions are. That in turn will lead you to the purpose of your leadership.

Understanding your passions is not as easy as it sounds. For some leaders, a transformative event in their lives awakens them to seeing what their passions are. For others, finding their passion

Figure 9.1 Understanding Your Passions and Purpose

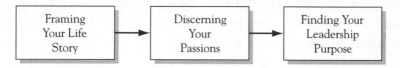

requires letting go of their security blankets and stepping back from the expectations others have of them.

Steve Rothschild described the process he went through at General Mills:

> *When you're focused on something professionally for so long, you're afraid to let go. It's like standing inside a giant hoop. When you let go a little bit, you do so with one arm. You're afraid to let go with two arms and fall out of the hoop altogether, because you could fall flat on your face. In my case I had to let go of the hoop altogether.*

A year after leaving General Mills, Rothschild was one of the two finalists for an important CEO position. "I got a call, saying they had chosen the other guy. Instead of feeling disappointed, I was relieved. I realized I wasn't interested in the job because I wasn't excited about returning to the business world.

> *My decision to start Twin Cities RISE! evolved out of the recognition that I like solving important and meaningful problems. And here was one that wasn't being adequately addressed. The nature of the problem shifted from building a business to building lives.*

Having made the decision to get out of the frying pan at General Mills, Rothschild decided not to jump back into the fire. Instead, he gave himself the time and the freedom to understand his real passions and to recognize he wanted to work on issues that meant something to him.

Former LucasArts CEO Randy Komisar did just the opposite. Frustrated by the involvement of founder George Lucas, he abandoned his job at LucasArts to join its smaller competitor, Crystal Dynamics. Komisar confesses: "My purpose for going to Crystal was very thin. It was to re-create Lucas. Once there, I couldn't find my muse, my reason for being there. Coming out of Crystal, I never wanted to live without a purpose again. I realized that without a purpose, nothing mattered."

When you meet Komisar, you are struck by his openness, his willingness to be vulnerable, and his insight into himself and other people. It is unlikely he could have come so far without facing what is important in his life.

It is difficult to determine your passions in the abstract. Discerning them takes a combination of introspection and real-world experiences before you can determine where you want to devote your energies. Without that understanding, you are vulnerable to jumping from one high-status role to another without ever finding fulfillment.

Trammell Crow's former CEO, Joel Peterson, believes that many people are cause-driven and don't start out thinking about being leaders. "They have so much passion for the cause that they naturally become the leader. When they are pulled to something that matters a great deal, leadership follows their passion." Penny George represents the kind of person Peterson is describing.

Penny George: It's Never Too Late to Become a Leader. My wife, Penny, never thought of herself as a leader, nor was she encouraged to become one by her parents. Quite the contrary; they discouraged her from taking the risks that come with leading. She became a skilled organizational psychologist, valued by her clients for helping talented individuals realize their potential, but she avoided organizational leadership roles, even on nonprofit boards. In 1995 she reached the pinnacle of her academic achievements when she received her doctorate in psychology.

Disaster struck just six months later, as she and a partner were launching their new consulting psychology firm. She recalled, "A day after a routine mammogram I returned home from work to a message on my answering machine: 'Penny, it appears you have breast cancer. Please schedule an appointment with a surgeon.'"

Although her oncologist told her, "The goal is cure," she went on an emotional roller-coaster, convinced that she was going to die. She opted for a modified radical mastectomy, followed by seven months of chemotherapy and five years of hormonal therapy, yet she had a constant fear that the cancer would return. Unwilling to be passive, she experimented with many complementary therapies. She embraced rigorous lifestyle changes with new dietary, exercise, stress reduction, and herbal medication regimes and did psychotherapy to reframe the difficulties of her teenage years. She found that taking responsibility for her return to wellness was profoundly healing and restored her sense of control.

As part of her recovery, she went on an eleven-day Vision Quest in the barren Four Corners region of Colorado, including a four-day solo fast. After her return, she decided to abandon her practice of psychology to concentrate her energies on advancing integrative medicine. Her vision of the new medicine combined the best of traditional Western medicine with complementary therapies to treat the whole person, just as she was doing for herself.

One day as we were driving to Colorado, she told me with determination, "We are going to change the way medicine is taught and practiced." From my work at Medtronic, I knew how intractable the medical establishment was to fundamental change. I asked her, "Do you realize the magnitude of what you're taking on?" With tears in her eyes, she looked at me and said, "Don't you believe in me?" I felt ashamed and sheepishly replied, "Of course I believe in you. I'll do everything I can to support you."

Penny proposed that she run the family foundation we had created in 1994. With the help of an exceptional foundation director, she directed over half our giving to integrative medicine. Together they conceived an innovative idea to bring together medical leaders of integrative medicine with philanthropists who were funding in the area. This led to the formation of the Bravewell Collaborative, a group of thirty foundations that agreed to pool their funding to support the transformation of medicine.

Although her leadership of the collaborative was acclaimed by its members, she kept insisting, "I am not a leader." Why this dichotomy? Rather than be the powerful out-front leader, she was quietly leading from behind by encouraging individual members of this peer network to step up and lead. It was her passion and vision, coupled with the values of collaboration, that inspired the group's members. Her story illustrates how discovering your passion can empower you to step up to lead, even if you do not see yourself as a leader.

What's the Purpose of Your Leadership?

Following your passions will enable you to discover the purpose of your leadership. When you do, you are ready to make a difference in the world.

When Baxter Healthcare's Michelle Hooper was a child, she had a close friend who lived on her street. One day when she was in sixth grade, she went to her friend's house but was met at the door by her father. "He told me my friend was no longer allowed to play with black children. That had a huge effect on me. It was horrible." The shock of that blatant discrimination stuck with Hooper and provided the impetus for her leadership.

After that painful experience, she was driven to excel academically and to be somebody. "I planned to use my intellectual capacity as a stepping stone to get ahead," she said. Although she had no role models in the corporate world, she decided to become a corporate leader because she excelled at economics and business courses.

At Baxter Healthcare, Hooper earned her first general management opportunity: to lead the turnaround of its Canadian operations. She found the work so stressful that she broke out in hives and acne. Yet, she said, "I could not quit because I was the first black female to run an organization like that and first in my family to move into these lofty executive ranks. I could not fail."

As she advanced to other leadership roles at Baxter, she found her purpose: to be a role model for people coming up and to provide them with opportunities such as she had. Hooper believes that many talented people never get the opportunities they deserve because no one recognizes their potential.

> *It goes back to my days when I was rejected by my friend's father. You have to accept people for who they are.*
>
> *There are so many good people out there. All they need is an opportunity and a platform. People gave me that in my career and allowed me to take stretch assignments to grow in ways that I would have never dreamed.*

Cranium founder Richard Tait launched his board game company to introduce games that were not win-lose but enabled everyone to shine. "What drives me is not financial gain, recognition, or power; it's the letters from customers thanking us for creating these games and the moments and memories in their lives." Tait worries about the entertainment choices available today, especially those aimed at young people.

> *Recently I watched an eight-year-old boy play Grand Theft Auto. That kid is being taught by the most powerful medium in the world—the television—to shoot at cars, to steal, and to trade prostitutes to make money. His face was so tortured and angered. When I was eight, I was outside kicking a ball in the street and laughing with my friends as we created fantasy worlds.*

Tait's calling is to create something more worthwhile—something able to keep that eight-year-old boy from getting drawn into violent games. "It takes courage and a sense of advocacy to stand up for something that's pure and simple," he said.

These stories reflect both the struggle that leaders go through in discerning their purpose and the fulfillment they feel when they find it and can share it with others. Ann Fudge sees leadership as serving, not self-serving. She asks, "How can I use my talents to give back in some positive way?"

> *Any of us can figure out ways to drive a business for two years and make a boatload of money and move on. That's not leadership. That's playing a game. Leadership is leaving something lasting, whether it is how you treat people or how you deal with a problem.*

Aligning Your Purpose

In the introduction, we defined a leader as someone who brings people together to pursue a shared purpose. Gaining alignment around purpose is the greatest challenge leaders face. To sustain the motivation of teammates and a successful track record, authentic leaders like Andrea Jung convey such a sense of passion for their purpose that people share it and feel inspired by the mission.

When he was chairman and CEO of Merck, Roy Vagelos had great passion for discovering lifesaving drugs. He had been a medical researcher for nineteen years when he was asked to become dean of two prestigious medical schools, the Universities of Chicago and Pennsylvania. Vagelos turned down the opportunities because he believed being a dean was a dead end. "I was horrified about becoming a dean, because you don't teach or do research; you just shuffle papers and push people around," he explained. Then he got an offer to become head of research for Merck.

> *I thought if I could use my knowledge of biochemistry to discover new drugs, I could impact human health far beyond what I could do as a practicing doctor, and I could possibly change the technology of drug discovery. I never thought of myself as being a leader, but asked myself instead if I was contributing something to what's going on in the world.*

I first met Vagelos when he was selected for the U.S. Business Hall of Fame by Junior Achievement for his leadership in eliminating the African disease known as river blindness. Merck discovered a cure, the drug Mezican, but market projections indicated Africans could not afford it. Instead of shutting down the discovery process, Vagelos decided to complete development of the drug and distribute it for free in Africa.

You may be asking, "Where's the shareholder benefit in that?" Vagelos used the decision as tangible evidence of Merck's purpose and as a way of conveying a sense of meaning to his organization. He explained, "Here's a drug that can prevent blindness in eighteen million people. That single decision put Merck in a position where we could recruit anybody we wanted for the next decade."

During that decade, Merck had the most productive record in producing lifesaving new drugs of any pharmaceutical company, in large part because of the inspiration that Merck's researchers drew from Vagelos's passion and sense of purpose. Not surprisingly, Merck's shareholder value increased ten times during that decade. "Given a choice of working just to make a living, or benefiting the people of the world, the majority of people will choose the latter," Vagelos concluded.

The cynics would say it is easy to create a sense of purpose when your team or company is saving lives like Merck, but what about the grocery business? CEO Dave Dillon is a strong believer in creating shared purpose throughout the Kroger organization. Kroger may not save lives, but it is a company where employees feel they are part of something important. Dillon has gained alignment around the proposition that serving the public in a service-oriented grocery operation is a dignified, proud profession. "All human beings want to find meaning in their lives. Our objective is to help give them that meaning," he said.

We have the opportunity to make customers' lives better by making them feel good about the world around them because someone was friendly to them. Little touches of human kindness can literally change their day. If I am the deliverer of human kindness, I wind up feeling better about myself as well. At the end of our careers, we can look back and say, "I was part of something special."

Former Tropicana CEO Ellen Marram is critical of leaders who pay lip service to saying their mission is to serve customers but do not fully engage their employees with customers. "Many leaders don't understand that unless the customer is ultimately satisfied they are not going to have a business," she explains.

They smoke their own exhaust and see the world from the inside out. To switch someone's perspective, you have to get your employees to interact with customers. When you send R&D and manufacturing people to customer focus groups, all of a sudden they understand how consumers use their products. Customers don't care about the technology used to make a product; they care only about how a product benefits them in the end. As a leader, you always have to keep people's eyes on the endpoint. We may not be selling defibrillators that save lives, but people feel good when they provide a product or service that people really want.

The reason for Medtronic's success is the alignment its employees feel with the company's mission of restoring people to full life. The highlight of Medtronic's year is not the annual shareholder meeting but the annual holiday party. At this event, all Minneapolis-based employees gather in the company's large atrium auditorium, with thousands more watching via webcast, to hear from six patients who have received the company's products. These six patients are representative of the seven million people whose health has been restored in the past year by company products.

As the patients tell personal stories of how their lives have been changed by Medtronic products, the room fills with emotion. Through those feelings, Medtronic employees rediscover what their work is all about—not just making money for themselves or the company but making a difference in the lives of others. By seeing their impact on these patients, they understand the meaning of their work.

What Is the Purpose of Business?

With all the frenzy in the 1990s around maximizing short-term shareholder value, we lost sight of the purpose of business. It is not simply to reward its shareholders in the near term but to create an entity that has lasting value for all its constituencies.

Harvard University professor Michael Porter, an economist famed for his breakthroughs in strategic planning, has challenged those who claim the only measure of a company's worth is its shareholder value at a given instant. "Shareholder value," he says, "does not equal economic value."

Given the vicissitudes and volatility of the stock market, shareholder value may fluctuate a great deal, but the only sustainable value for the company is building its economic value, and ultimately, the company's shareholder value will reflect that sustainable economic value. Companies that attempt to increase shareholder value by hyping their stocks without building economic value are likely to go the way of Enron and WorldCom.

Infosys founder Narayana Murthy believes that the purpose of business must go beyond maximizing shareholder value. He says, "You cannot sustain long-term shareholder value unless you create sustainable value for your customers, while assuring fairness to all stakeholders: customers, employees, investors, vendor partners, governments, and society."

> *The best index of success is longevity. If you have existed for a long time, that means you have gone through thick and thin, learned to strengthen your character, focused on clients, and tightened your belt. That is what makes you stronger.*

Leaders can sustain their effectiveness only if they empower employees around a shared purpose. As a leader, you must convey passion for the business every day while maintaining clarity about the mission of your organization. Andrea Jung is as clear about her passion and purpose as any leader we know: "I love Avon because it changes women's lives."

> *There is purpose in my work: enabling women to be self-empowered, learn to run their own businesses and achieve economic means to provide education. At the end of the day, that trumps all things.*

> *Note to the reader: Before going on to Chapter Ten, you may want to complete the Chapter Nine Exercise found in Appendix C.*

10

EMPOWERING PEOPLE TO LEAD

> I get things done by identifying with the people in
> the company and by trusting them. I care most
> about building a good team to lead the company.
> —*Anne Mulcahy, Chair and CEO, Xerox*

Watching the brilliant young Norwegian conductor Arild Remmereit lead the Dallas Symphony Orchestra, I realized that an entirely new version of the "conductor as metaphor for leadership" has emerged, one that is consistent with our vision of how the new breed of authentic leaders empowers others to step up and lead.

Remmereit's style was in sharp contrast to the great showmen who led major orchestras in years past, when the conductor was out front taking all the credit. As he prepared to conduct Mendelssohn's Scottish Symphony, Remmereit spoke to the audience in his Norwegian accent. "The musicians know within five minutes whether a new conductor is any good or not," he said, "and soon you will learn what they think of me as their leader."

For the next forty-seven minutes he demonstrated that his quiet confidence was well placed. Without using a single sheet of music to conduct the complex work, he knew every bar of the symphony as well the parts for each instrument and how he wanted them played. His demeanor on the podium was engaged and inspiring.

When the orchestra finished the finale, the audience rose in unison for a standing ovation. Unwilling to take credit, Remmereit insisted that the entire orchestra rise to take their bows and hurried from the stage. Returning to the audience's rhythmic applause, he wandered through the rear of the orchestra, asking the musicians to stand and take the credit, instead of mounting the podium as other conductors do. Eventually making his way to the podium, he again refused the solo bow and would only be recognized with the entire orchestra.

Remmereit's leadership is a metaphor for the best of today's business leaders:

- He knew his True North: being true to the music as originally intended.
- He knew his purpose: producing beautiful and inspiring music.
- He knew his subject in amazing detail.
- He was highly authentic and humble in a confident way.
- He knew how to get the best out of his musicians by empowering them.
- Finally, he was challenging, inspiring, respectful, and willing to share the credit.

Anne Mulcahy: Empowering People Through a Crisis. Xerox CEO Anne Mulcahy is an exceptional leader who has demonstrated a remarkable ability to empower a large, diverse organization around a common mission. Back in 2000, becoming CEO of Xerox was the furthest thing from her mind. One day, as she was preparing for a business trip to Japan, chairman Paul Allaire came to her office and told her he planned to recommend that the Xerox board terminate its current CEO and promote her to COO and eventually CEO. She was so shocked that she asked for the evening to discuss it with her family. The next day she accepted the job.

The board's decision surprised Mulcahy as well as everyone else. Since joining Xerox twenty-five years before, she had worked in field sales and on the corporate staff but not in finance, R&D, or manufacturing. At the time she was enjoying her first general management assignment, running a relatively small business outside the Xerox mainstream. "It was like going to war," she recalled, "knowing it was the right thing for the company and there was so much at stake."

> *This was a job that would dramatically change my life, requiring every ounce of energy that I had. I never expected to be CEO, nor was I groomed for it.*

What no one understood was that Xerox was facing a massive liquidity crisis and was on the verge of bankruptcy. Its revenues were declining, its sales force was unraveling, and its new-product pipelines were depleted. The company had $18 billion in debt, and all lines of credit were exhausted. With the share price in free fall, morale inside the company was in disarray. Xerox had just one week of cash on hand as key advisers recommended that the company consider bankruptcy. To make matters worse, Xerox's chief financial officer was preoccupied with an SEC investigation into the company's revenue recognition practices.

As the situation went from bad to worse, Mulcahy recognized just how great the risks of bankruptcy were.

> *My greatest fear was that I was sitting on the deck of the* Titanic *and I'd get to drive it to the bottom of the ocean—not exactly a moment to be proud of.*
>
> *Nothing spooked me so much as waking up in the middle of the night and thinking about 96,000 employees and retirees and what would happen if things went south.*

How could Mulcahy cope with this crisis when she had had no financial experience? She brought to the CEO's role relationships built over twenty-five years and an impeccable understanding of the organization. She bled for Xerox and everyone knew it. To ameliorate the gaps in her experience, she was tutored on finance by the treasurer's office and surrounded herself with a diverse set of leaders.

As Mulcahy recognized the depth of the company's problems, her purpose became crystal clear: to save the company from bankruptcy and restore Xerox to its former greatness. Her challenge was to unite the disheartened organization and to get leaders throughout the company to step up to the challenge.

"I get things done by identifying with the people in the company and by trusting them," she said. "I care most about building a good team to lead the company." She met personally with the top one hundred executives to ask them if they would stay with the company despite the challenges ahead. "I knew there were people who weren't supportive of me," she said.

> So I confronted a couple of them and said, "Hey, no games. Let's just talk. You can't be thrilled. If you choose to stay, either we're totally in synch or when you go, it won't be pleasant, because I have no appetite for managing right now. This is about the company."

The first two people she talked to, both of whom ran big operating units, decided to leave, but the remaining ninety-eight committed to stay. They did so because Mulcahy appealed to their character and to the purpose of saving the company they loved. One of them, Ursula Burns, noted, "I have a wonderful life and great friends because of my partnership with this company. What do you say when times are tough? 'Thank you very much, I'll see you later?' That's not what my mother taught me."

In spite of the pressures and endless rounds of meetings at headquarters, Mulcahy decided to get into customers' offices and ride with field salespeople to see if she could help stem the tide of customer defections and field-sales resignations. She told her sales force, "I will go anywhere, anytime, to save a Xerox customer." Her customer-engagement contrasted sharply with her predecessor, who had rarely been seen outside the headquarters building. It sent an important signal that solidified the Xerox field organization and restored customer confidence.

Yet Mulcahy was both challenging and demanding, as she held people publicly accountable for their results. Despite the tremendous pressures the company was under, she set realistic expectations, "You can't wish your way to good performance," she said. "If you set the bar someplace that buys you ninety days of stock-market esteem, you will eventually get killed. Boy, is it ugly."

She encouraged senior managers to engage each other directly. "We talk about everything," said Burns. "Anne is really clear: 'Make sure you get it.'" Mulcahy did not take the lead in every discussion, playing instead what Burns described as an orchestrating role. "She's very good at reading people," Burns explained, "and getting us to work together."

The bankruptcy question came to a head in the third week of October 2001. Earlier in the month, Mulcahy candidly told the company's shareholders that Xerox's business model was unsustainable. The next day the stock dropped 26 percent. Mulcahy noted, "This was my baptism by fire."

Mulcahy had traditionally drawn support by interacting with her peers, but in her new role she had to provide her team with confidence that the company could survive—in spite of any personal doubts she had. "As a touchy-feely people person, the hardest thing was that my new role required some distance I wasn't prepared for."

Yet Mulcahy was not immune from uncertainty and stress. "One day I came back to the office from Japan and found it had been a dismal day," she explained.

> Around 8:30 P.M. on my way home, I pulled over to the side of the Merritt Parkway and said to myself, "I don't know where to go. I don't want to go home. There's just no place to go."

Have you ever felt like that? In my experience, feelings of despair among leaders are quite common, but most do not have the courage to admit it. In times like these, you need the support of your colleagues. Mulcahy explained, "I picked up my voice mail and listened to a message from chief strategist Jim Firestone: 'This may seem like the worst day, but we believe in you. This company will have a great future.'" That was all Mulcahy needed to drive home and get up the next day. "The team gave me incredible supportive strength. We fight, we debate, but at the end of the day, they've been extremely loyal and supportive."

When the company's external advisers argued that Xerox should prepare for a bankruptcy filing to relieve the $18 billion debt burden, Mulcahy exploded:

> I told them, "You don't understand what it's like to be an employee in this company—to fight and win. Bankruptcy's never a win. I'm not going there until there's no other decision to be made. There are a lot more cards to play." I was so angry because they could not comprehend the passion and drive that's required to succeed and the impact of bankruptcy on the company's employees. Our people believed we were in a war we could win.

Anne Mulcahy did win in the end. She staved off bankruptcy by cutting billions in operating expenses without touching R&D or field sales and by reducing debt by 60 percent. In launching sixty new products with new color and digital technology, she restored revenue and profit growth. What distinguished her leadership throughout this crisis was her ability to empower people to rise to the challenge and to keep them focused on the shared mission of saving and restoring Xerox.

Mutual Respect: The Basis for Empowerment

To bring out the best from teammates, authentic leaders must develop trusting relationships based on mutual respect. There is no substitute. Like loyalty, respect provides a basis for empowerment, but it must be earned. Here are some of the things leaders do to gain the respect of their colleagues:

- Treating others as equals.
- Being a good listener.
- Learning from people.
- Sharing life stories.

Treating Others as Equals

We respect people who treat us like equals, especially when they are successful investors like Warren Buffett. Buffett has the same sandwich and Cherry Coke combination with a group of wide-eyed students as he does with his close friend Bill Gates. He does not rely upon his image to make people feel he is important or powerful. He genuinely respects others, and they respect him as much for those qualities as for his investment prowess. Although Anne Mulcahy had never met Buffett, she felt able to fly to Omaha to get his advice over his traditional steak dinner. By being authentic in his interactions, Buffett empowers people to lead in their own authentic ways.

Being a Good Listener

We are grateful when people genuinely *listen* to us. Active listening is one of the most important abilities of empowering leaders, because people sense such individuals are genuinely interested in them and not just trying to get something from them.

Learning from People

We feel respected when others believe they can learn from us or ask for our advice. When Warren Bennis, now in his eighties, meets with his incoming class of USC undergraduate students each year, he tells them, "I know I have a lot to learn from you." The students find that hard to believe at first, but they soon see how their feedback helps him understand how younger generations think.

Sharing Life Stories

When leaders are willing to be open and share their personal stories and vulnerabilities, people feel empowered to share their own stories and uncertainties in return. On Thanksgiving eve in 1996, I sent an e-mail to all Medtronic employees expressing my gratitude for the support Penny and I received following her ordeal with breast cancer and chemotherapy. We were overwhelmed by the number of people who spontaneously shared their stories with us.

Sharing our life stories can free us from our defenses and open us to authentic relationships. Safeco CEO Paula Rosput Reynolds described a prior experience in leading a team that had very low trust. One person in particular was viewed as too opinionated and unable to work well with colleagues until she asked him to share his story with the team. He explained that his older brother and father died during his preteen years, and he felt obligated to carry on for them, including working for the same company his father had worked for. "All of a sudden, everyone understood and was willing to work with him," Reynolds explained. "That is why leadership must be personal."

Empowering People to Lead

If mutual respect provides the foundation for bringing out the best from people, what are the steps needed to empower them? The skills of empowerment take many forms, from simply showing up to engaging people, helping them, challenging them, stretching them, and aligning them with the mission. Effective leaders use all of these approaches at different times, depending on the capabilities of the people involved and the situation they are facing.

- Showing up.
- Engaging people.
- Helping teammates.

- Challenging leaders.
- Stretching people.
- Aligning everyone around a mission.

Showing Up

Woody Allen once remarked, "Eighty percent of success is showing up." Surprisingly, many leaders get so busy they don't take the time to be there for people. They don't bother to attend award ceremonies, company picnics, sales meetings, and even business and project reviews. Nor do they show up around the offices, factories, labs, and field sales and service locations. Often they are too busy to come to important customer meetings or trade shows. As a result, their teammates never get to know them on a personal basis. Their only contact with their leaders is through impersonal media like speeches, voice mail, videotapes, and web-streaming of company events.

Howard Schultz told of visiting a Starbucks store one Saturday morning:

> I walked in, dressed so that nobody would recognize me. As soon as I sat down, the manager came up and said, "Howard, is that you?" I said, "Yes, it is." She was telling me about receiving Starbucks stock, and what it did for her and her family. Then she started crying and said, "I'm so moved that you're in my store." Later I got voice mail from her, saying what that moment was like for her. I immediately called her back and thanked her for sharing with me.

Stories of basic human interactions like this one are very powerful. All Schultz had to do was show up. Showing up at important events or at unexpected times means a great deal to people and enables them to take their leaders off their proverbial pedestals and see them as real people.

Engaging People

The most empowering leaders are those who engage a wide range of people. That means being with them face-to-face; inquiring about their work, their families, their personal lives, and their careers; and being open and vulnerable with them. This degree of intimacy with people they don't know well makes some leaders uncomfortable, but it is a powerful means of establishing deeper connections.

One of my MBA students shared a story about working for Procter & Gamble in Chile:

> We had the first visit ever from CEO A.G. Lafley. Lafley asked in advance to visit the homes of poor people the day before our meeting. This surprised all of us, since we generally do not go into the homes of poor people. The next morning I was at my desk at 7:30 A.M. when Mr. Lafley came walking down the hall. He stopped at my desk, put out his hand, and said, "My name's A.G. Please tell me about your work." When I nervously concluded explaining how we were expanding the market for P&G products in Chile, again he shook my hand and said, "Thank you. Your work is vital to the future of P&G and our ability to grow in countries like Chile. I came here to see firsthand how we can expand our business in developing markets and reach a broader range of consumers."

That is empowerment. Your first reaction may be that Lafley reached only one of the hundred thousand P&G employees, but the reality is that my student and his colleagues told that story to hundreds of people inside and outside the company to illustrate the personal qualities of their leader.

Helping Teammates

Authentic leaders help their teammates, whether it is with a personal problem or a career problem, by counseling with them, offering suggestions, or assisting them in making vital contacts. That in turn is highly empowering.

Merck CEO Roy Vagelos ate regularly in the company cafeteria, where he asked people about their work and the challenges they were facing. He took notes about the conversations and then thought about the specific problems for a few days before calling the employees back with his ideas.

Imagine how Merck researchers must have felt when they picked up the phone to hear Vagelos getting back to them. "I'd call them up and say, 'That's a tough problem, but here are a couple things you might try,'" Vagelos said. "People love to have involvement of the leader. They feel you want to help them and are part of the solution." These interactions reinforced the importance of the researchers' work and had a multiplier effect upon employees.

Challenging Leaders

Empowering people is much more than a series of positive interactions. Often, the most empowering response is to challenge people's ideas, to ask why they are doing something a particular way, and to help them sharpen their ideas through dialogue. Although people may feel uncomfortable in being challenged at first, they are usually engaged with their leaders and anxious to respond.

Jack Welch was a master at asking challenging questions that caused GE leaders to set higher standards for themselves and their teams and to think more deeply about important issues of their business. He wouldn't hesitate to get on the phone and challenge managers who were several levels below him.

Stretching People

Most people want to be stretched in assignments that enable them to develop. The leader's key is to sense when people are ready for such challenging experiences, of the sort Jeff Immelt had in GE's plastics division.

Yet it is also important for your team to know that you will be there to support them if necessary. Medtronic's Martha Goldberg

Aronson tells the story of a boss who was willing to bet on her in stretch roles while supporting her. On taking a new position, Aronson said, her new boss advised her,

> *On certain days you will feel that you're way out on this limb. The wind is going to start to blow, and you're going to feel like the limb is going up and down. You're going to hear it crack, and you're going to come crashing down. That's when I'll be there to catch you.*

It wasn't long before Aronson encountered a quality problem with her new line of catheters. She noted, "The branch cracked a few times, and my boss was really there." Just knowing you have support from your leaders if things go wrong is very empowering. It enables you to recognize that you will not be hung out to dry, so you can take on stretch goals and significant challenges without fear of someone sawing off the limb behind you.

Aligning Around a Mission

The most empowering condition of all is when the entire organization is aligned with its mission, and people's passions and purpose are in synch with each other. It is not easy to get to this position, especially if the organization has a significant number of cynics or disgruntled people. Nonetheless, it is worth whatever effort it takes to create an aligned environment.

Individuals usually have their own passions that drive them. If the organization's leaders can demonstrate how they can fulfill their purpose while achieving the organization's mission, then alignment can occur.

Several years ago I visited Medtronic's heart-valve factory in southern California, where employees reconfigure valves from pig hearts to replace human heart valves. Because the process is more art than science, it requires extremely skilled workers. On the factory floor I met the top producer, a Laotian immigrant who made a thousand valves a year. When I asked her the key to her process, she looked at me with passion in her eyes and said, "Mr. George, my job is to make heart valves that save lives."

> *Before I sign my name to a completed valve, I decide whether it is good enough to put in my mother or my son. Unless it meets that standard, it does not pass. If just one of the valves I make is defective, someone may die. To the company 99.9 percent quality may be acceptable, but I could not live with myself if I caused someone's death. But when I go home at night, I fall asleep thinking about the five thousand people who are alive today because of heart valves I made.*

Can there be any question that she is a leader among her peers? She has a passion for her work that is tied directly to the company's mission; she sets high standards for herself, and she sets the example for everyone else to emulate.

Marilyn Carlson Nelson: Building an Empowered Culture. Marilyn Carlson Nelson, CEO of travel-and-leisure conglomerate Carlson Companies, has dramatically transformed the company founded by her father, Curtis Carlson. Carlson was a consummate salesman and a tough, demanding boss. Seeing an employee leaving the office at 7:30 P.M. one night, Carlson asked if he had lost his enthusiasm for the business. "Monday through Friday are about staying even with the competition," he often said. "Saturday is when you get ahead."

The elder Carlson taught his daughter about business but never encouraged her to join his company, believing that women were not meant for the workplace. After giving birth to her first child, Nelson worked from her home as publisher of Carlson's employee newspaper. After she produced a catalog of the company's products, she was promoted to department head. When she reported this news to her father, his response was blunt: "You're getting too involved in the business. You should be at home with your children." Added Nelson, "My father fired me on the spot. I left the building with tears running down my face."

While raising her family, Nelson got deeply involved in the Minneapolis community, chairing the Minnesota Orchestral Association, creating "Scandinavia Today," and bringing the 1992 Super Bowl to Minnesota on the coldest weekend of the year. She also became the first woman to serve on the boards of major local corporations and was co-owner of a rural bank. As her business profile continued to rise, her father repeatedly rebuffed her interest in his company.

When her last child went off to college, Nelson finally rejoined Carlson—at age forty-eight. In her first month she accompanied her father to a presentation by MBA students at Minnesota's Carlson School about their research into Carlson Companies' corporate culture. Nelson recalled asking, "How do the students see Carlson?" No one dared to answer. Finally, one student said, "Carlson is perceived as a sweatshop that does not care about people. Our professors don't recommend that we work for Carlson." Nelson was stunned. "That meeting lit a fire under me," she said. She realized then she needed to change the corporate culture away from her father's top-down, autocratic style.

When her brother-in-law abruptly departed as CEO two years later, her eighty-year-old father returned to active management, and Nelson took on more prominent operational roles but still was not designated as successor. Meanwhile, the management turmoil continued as key executives left the company, frustrated by Carlson's command-and-control management style. Eventually, Nelson assumed responsibility for key Carlson divisions and began to reshape the company's leadership and strategy. At the celebration for her father on the company's sixtieth anniversary, she was named CEO.

Undaunted, Carlson cautioned his daughter against relying on others. "Be very careful," he told her. "You can't trust anyone besides yourself." Nelson had just the opposite point of view, feeling that trust would work in a caring environment. "If you create a supportive environment, you can attract people who are trustworthy, so long as you trust them and you are trustworthy yourself," she explained.

In place of the company's founder-driven culture, Nelson focused on employees and customers. "In the command-and-control environment," she explained, "my dad robbed himself of the opportunity to hear contrarian views."

> *The contrarian view forces you to either understand or change your position. I moved to a collaborative mode of management. Now we rely on everybody to bring their wisdom and experience to bear on decisions. I believe that collective wisdom has great value when it comes from solid thinking. Ultimately, the leader still has to make the final decision.*

Nelson decided to reinvent Carlson as a company that cared for customers by creating the most caring environment for its employees. She shifted emphasis away from stewardship of financial capital toward acquiring and cultivating human capital with experience, wisdom, and collective-thinking skills. She looked for three characteristics in employees: character, competence, and caring. "The need for character as absolute trustworthiness, and competence in the form of global experience, expertise, and judgment, are not surprising," Nelson explained, "but the characteristic of caring was not self-evident."

> *I looked for people who had "a servant's heart." Servant leadership is an important driver of the culture we want to create. A satisfied employee delivers a satisfied customer. In the service business, customers understand very quickly whether you legitimately care about serving them.*

Recognizing that these values had to be embraced by Carlson locations worldwide if they were to become key behaviors for every Carlson employee, Nelson traveled tirelessly to meet with company employees and customers around the world. "We can build relationships only if an employee is affirmed and empowered, enjoys clarity of direction, and understands the vision and mission of the company," she said.

We cannot just teach restaurant employees to put a meal on the table. In a restaurant you can customize the experience if you know when customers want privacy or when they want fun.

Reflecting on the changes she had wrought over the course of nine years, Nelson said that these days no follow-up study by MBAs could conclude that Carlson does not care about people. "You cannot change a culture in six months," she explained. "If you change the business model and build transparency and collaborative discussion into the culture, it will eventually take hold, but it takes time."

Having suffered from her own daughter's death twenty years before, Nelson never lost sight of her personal mission "to use every tool at hand as an opportunity to give back or make life better for people." Her transformation of Carlson to a collaborative culture is a remarkable example of how a leader can inspire employees around a common vision and empower them to lead.

Leaders like Mulcahy and Nelson have discovered that the results achieved by empowering people throughout their organizations with passion and purpose are far superior to what can be accomplished by getting them to be loyal followers. By giving others the latitude to lead within the organization's broad purpose, they are able to delegate more of their leadership responsibilities and still expand the scope and reach of their leadership through more people.

Note to the reader: Before going on to Chapter Eleven, you may want to complete the Chapter Ten Exercise found in Appendix C.

11

HONING YOUR LEADERSHIP EFFECTIVENESS

> My height was a very clear reminder to me that
> I couldn't simply emulate this man. In a symbolic
> way it reminded me that I had to find my own
> style of being effective, rather than
> trying to imitate someone else.
> —*Ellen Marram, Tropicana*

In the Introduction, we noted that the leaders interviewed believed they were more effective and got better results when they were authentic. In this final chapter, we explore how you can optimize your leadership effectiveness. Once you empower people to lead around a shared purpose, you are well positioned to achieve superior results through your organization. The final step in maximizing your effectiveness as an authentic leader is to hone your leadership style and make authentic use of your power.

Producing superior results through your leadership will generate greater influence for you and your teammates and provide you with opportunities to take on added responsibility. The process produces a virtuous circle that will encourage others to join you and sustain your effectiveness on an ongoing basis. This reinforcing cycle is precisely what leaders like Dick Kovacevich, Dan Vasella, Andrea Jung, Howard Schultz, and Marilyn Carlson Nelson have used throughout their careers to produce superior results.

Optimizing Your Leadership Effectiveness

The topic of style has been saved for last because the style of an effective leader must come from an authentic place. That will only happen when you have a high level of self-awareness, are clear about your values, and understand your leadership purpose.

Without this clarity, your style will be shaped by the expectations of your organization or the outside world and will not be seen as authentic. Nor will it be empowering to people. Using your power is directly linked to your style, as you convey power through style.

Yet your use of style and power must fit the situation you are facing, and you have to be versatile to maximize your effectiveness *in that situation*. In the aftermath of the attacks of September 11, 2001, New York Mayor Rudy Giuliani acted decisively to get urgently needed resources in place. He had no time to build consensus. In situations like these, people need decisive leaders to guide them efficiently and calmly to solutions. On the other hand, when trying to create a future vision for their organizations, leaders need to use a more participative style that involves a wide range of people and gets them engaged and committed to that vision.

You also need to adapt your leadership style to the capabilities of your teammates and their readiness to accept greater power and responsibility. For example, if your teammates need clear direction, they may not be ready to respond to a consensus style. Conversely, creative or independent thinkers will not respond positively to a directive style. As you think about your leadership style and power, ask yourself these questions:

- Is your leadership style consistent with your leadership principles and values? Is it ever inconsistent?
- How do you adapt your style to the circumstances facing you and to the capabilities of your teammates?
- How do you optimize the use of your power in leading others?

- In situations in which you used your power over others inappropriately, how did they respond?
- How do you respond to powerful people who use their power over you? What is the most appropriate way to deal with very powerful people?

John Whitehead's Consensus Leadership. John Whitehead of Goldman Sachs has led just about every possible organization, from one of the world's great investment banks to the U.S. State Department, the New York Federal Reserve, major educational institutions, and other nonprofit organizations. But on the morning of June 6, 1944, as a twenty-one-year-old ensign in the U.S. Navy, Whitehead faced one of the greatest leadership challenges of his life. He was leading six boats in the first wave of the massive invasion fleet nine miles off the shore of Normandy. The rain was coming down in sheets, and the ocean surged and chopped with fury. Just before the sun came up, Whitehead gave the signal to proceed to land.

Amid an increasing artillery barrage, his boat encountered a long string of metal bars embedded in the ocean floor that blocked the designated route. Disobeying orders, Whitehead directed his boats to turn parallel to shore to look for an opening in the barricade before turning toward the beach. "Because of the delicate coordination of the invasion," he said, "I was under strict orders to proceed directly to the beach and not deviate for any reason. Had I followed those orders, we would have been hung up on the barricade and blocked all the boats coming in behind us."

> Sometimes you have lots of time to make a decision. I had maybe ten seconds to think about this one. There was no time for consensus or to consult with anybody. There are very few decisions in life where you don't have some time to think about what your decision should be as a leader. This was the fastest decision that I made. I used my instinctive reactions to decide what should be done.

The small flotilla soon found a break and headed for the beach again. As the boats came under heavy fire, the pins that held the bow doors malfunctioned, preventing the launch ramp from going into the water. Whitehead climbed forward in the boat to hammer them out so the infantry troops could advance to the shore. "Half the people in my boat were killed or wounded in the first hundred yards up the beach," said Whitehead. "It was very, very heavy fire, and I was lucky to escape it."

On D-Day, Whitehead relied on his intuition and used a very direct leadership style to make the decision to countermand the orders he had been given. It was a far cry from the consensus-driven approach that he had developed as president of the student council at Haverford College. Haverford, founded by Quakers, required weekly attendance at Quaker meetings and perpetuated traditions of rectitude, modesty, and consensus-based decision making that made a lasting impact on him.

I never was a convert to Quakerism or pacifism, but I was influenced by Quaker principles like reaching consensus and respecting other people's viewpoints. Quakers never vote, but continue to talk until reaching consensus.

After the war, Whitehead went to business school and then joined Goldman Sachs in 1947. He started as a statistician, sitting in an unheated former squash court, doing unglamorous, highly quantitative work. At this time, the firm was controlled by five partners, but its fortunes depended on the country's best-known investment banker, managing partner Sidney Weinberg. Noticing Whitehead's work ethic and character, Weinberg made him his assistant and became his mentor and role model.

In one instance, Whitehead drafted a confidential report for Weinberg detailing the company's overdependence on Weinberg's relationships and outlining a plan to build new business relationships for the firm. After being elected partner the following year, Whitehead circulated the report to the other fifteen partners. Hearing no opposition, he started the new business department, hiring four people to solicit business from the largest companies in the country.

Because he worried that the ethos of the firm could be lost to rapid growth, Whitehead decided Goldman Sachs needed a clear set of business principles that all employees would adhere to in their business dealings. Working at home one Sunday afternoon, he drafted the ten essential points that made Goldman Sachs distinctive. Known as "Our Business Principles," the document reflected Whitehead's leadership philosophy. "With the exception of two principles added by the lawyers," he said, "Goldman Sachs today operates with the same business principles I wrote on that yellow pad."

When Weinberg's successor, Gus Levy, experienced a fatal stroke in 1976, Whitehead was an obvious choice to become co-chairman. In contrast to the rough-and-tumble style of his competitors, Whitehead continued to use the consensus style he had learned years before at Haverford to build equality among his partners. He retired from Goldman in 1984 after a remarkable thirty-seven-year career, but his legacy continues to this day. Principles like "Our clients' interests always come first" and "Teamwork in everything we do" are still part of the modus operandi of the firm.

For Whitehead, the word *retirement* proved to be a misnomer. Again and again, he stepped up to important leadership roles, including deputy secretary of state, chairman of the New York Federal Reserve, and chair of the board of trustees of more than a dozen nonprofits, including his alma maters. It is especially noteworthy that in all these situations, he continued to use his consensus style and to use his power modestly.

Yet Whitehead never hesitated to exert his influence over decisions, employing his persuasive powers and tenacity to win people over to his point of view. When Goldman's partners were deciding whether to take the firm public in 1999, Whitehead got involved to make sure the firm maintained its unique partnership culture and its business principles. As a former client and now a board member of Goldman, I have had the opportunity to witness firsthand just how widely those principles are practiced.

Whitehead's consensus style faced its greatest challenge after September 11, when New York Governor George Pataki recruited him to chair the Lower Manhattan Development Corporation (LMDC) to rebuild the World Trade Center. The politicized atmosphere in which the LMDC operated was a new environment for Whitehead. When he stepped down from his formal role as chairman four years later in May 2006, he acknowledged, "The job is still not done."

> *Reaching decisions in the intense political atmosphere is the toughest assignment I've ever had. Both the governor and the mayor were running for office and worrying about their public impression. There is a very high level of public interest over what gets rebuilt in Lower Manhattan. There are eight million people in New York and eight million ideas as to what should be rebuilt at Ground Zero.*

Across this wide range of for-profit, government, and nonprofit leadership situations, John Whitehead has demonstrated his ability to master the context and make optimal use of his consensus style of leadership, without deviating from his principles. His story illustrates that you can be an effective leader in very different situations if you listen to the people around you, work hard at understanding the challenges you face, and employ an empowering leadership style that optimizes the use of your power.

Defining—and Refining—Your Leadership Style

How do you know what leadership style fits you best? Are you concerned about whether your authentic style will be acceptable and effective in the organizations you join? Do you worry that you may have to modify your style to get ahead before you have organizational power?

Many organizations work hard to get young leaders to embrace the company's normative leadership style, sending them to training programs to bring their styles into line. Therein lies the risk: Will you have to compromise who you are in order to succeed in the organization? If you do, you will feel like an imposter, trying to be something you are not.

Many of the best leaders wrestled with those exact questions early in their careers. Iconic CEOs like Jim Burke of Johnson & Johnson and Jack Welch of GE quit their jobs within the first year because they refused to conform to company norms, yet powerful mentors attracted them back.

If you simply adopt an organization's normative style or try to emulate someone else's style, your lack of authenticity will show through. Under pressure and stress, leaders tend to revert to their least attractive styles—from being highly directive or passive aggressive to completely withdrawn. That is why you should find a leadership style that is authentic to you and continue to refine it.

Ellen Marram of Tropicana learned that early in her career. One of the first division heads she worked for would stand up when he wanted to make a point convincingly. He was a full foot taller than Marram, who recalled, "It sounds silly, but my height was a very clear reminder to me that I couldn't simply emulate this man. In a symbolic way it reminded me that I had to find my own style of being effective, rather than trying to imitate someone else."

In thinking about your leadership, consider where you fit among the six leadership style categories shown in Exhibit 11.1.

The directive style of leadership was common in the past, especially in military and manufacturing operations. It is still needed during crises like September 11, when time is of the essence. As more companies are built around knowledge workers, the directive

Exhibit 11.1 Leadership Styles

• Directive Leaders	Demand compliance and obedience with rules
• Engaged Leaders	Mobilize people around shared purpose and values
• Coaching Leaders	Develop people for leadership roles
• Consensus Leaders	Build agreement through participation
• Affiliative Leaders	Create emotional bonds and harmony
• Expert Leaders	Expect competence and self-direction

style has proven ineffective in motivating people to take initiative or be creative.

The most common style to emerge in recent years is the engaged style. Engaged leaders like Anne Mulcahy are actively involved with people at all levels of the organization—questioning them, listening to them, motivating them, and encouraging them to perform at a higher level—but always within the shared purpose and values of the organization.

Coaching leaders like John Donahoe bring out the best in people and develop them for future leadership roles. Usually such leaders are more concerned with people's development in order to achieve long-term results than they are in immediate outcomes.

Consensus leaders like John Whitehead treat everyone on the team as an equal and work toward consensus by encouraging everyone to participate in decision making. They are quite willing to take the time to reach conclusions, even to the point of postponing decisions, until a consensus emerges. Most nonprofit organizations need consensus leaders to motivate the various constituent groups.

Affiliative leaders build bonds of trust among people. Keeping harmony among team members and their leaders often takes precedence over getting near-term results. These leaders are often most effective at bringing out the best in their teammates by giving the impression that they are not leading at all. Their leadership is subtle and restrained.

Expert leaders such as Craig Venter, sequencer of the human genome, rely heavily on their own knowledge and expertise. They are often found in scientific organizations, consulting, and financial services, where the individual stars rise to leadership positions. They tend to listen primarily to other experts while demanding that their teammates exhibit equally high levels of knowledge and individual performance.

Authentic leaders use directive or expert styles when needed to get things done, but their primary leadership styles are engaged, coaching, consensus, and affiliative.

Using Power Wisely

The effective use of power in relationships is essential to achieving one's goals. After negotiating nuclear arms reduction treaties with the Soviet Union and presiding over the Bechtel Corporation, George Shultz understands power as well as anyone. His advice: "Don't be afraid of power, but be responsible with it."

Many leaders feel powerless without the benefit of title, rank, and large organizations to support them. When they do not use their power, leaders find themselves at risk of being dominated by powerful people. Yet they have more power than they realize, if only they assert themselves. Earlier in my career, I found myself backing off to a powerful executive. A colleague challenged me: "Why are you giving away so much power to him?" Recognizing that he was right, I started challenging the executive more and found he was willing to let me take the lead.

Traditionally, power has meant dominance over others. Indeed, many leaders in high-level organizational roles use their positional power to dominate others. Often, however, they underestimate their impact on other people and do not realize that their intimidating style and excessive use of power shuts down the contributions of others. They never understand why they do not get the best out of their people and why their organizations are not performing.

Many of the most effective leaders gain influence by using power more subtly. Engaged leaders influence people by getting them involved in decisions and persuading them. Coaching leaders gain influence by their ability to counsel with people and help them think through issues and improve the way they perform.

Although some would view consensus and affiliative leaders as relatively less powerful, just the opposite is the case. Their ability to gain agreement around their point of view gives consensus leaders great influence over others. Affiliative leaders use empathy and concern for others to generate support and emotional bonding. When they ask for help, people are more than willing to respond.

Expert leaders' power is entirely different from the other leadership types. It derives from their intellect and the depth of their knowledge, which generates respect from and influence over others.

These more subtle forms of power and influence—persuading, counseling, gaining agreement, empathy, and knowledge—are generally much more effective than the use of positional power and dominance in increasing your impact as a leader.

The irony is that the more power one accumulates, the less it should be used. Viewed another way, by exerting your power, you are taking away the power of others. Authentic leaders understand they need power to get things done, but they learn to use it in subtle ways. They prefer to persuade others to adopt their point of view or to build a consensus rather than forcing subordinates to go along with them. In so doing, they win the trust, loyalty, and support of their teammates. That in turn leads to better decisions and a higher level of commitment to shared goals.

Linking Style and Power

Your style and your use of power are inextricably linked. Your style conveys your sense of power, just as the way your use of power is reflected in your leadership style. Table 11.1 illustrates this linkage and indicates the kind of teammates who flourish with each style of leadership.

Directive leaders create dependent relationships with their subordinates, who obediently carry out their orders and respond to their demands. On the other hand, engaged leaders establish interdependent relationships by empowering and influencing members of the team. Anne Mulcahy gains power with her teammates by asking probing questions and listening carefully. Her team thus becomes more open to new ideas and more effective in working out creative solutions to difficult problems. As a result, she has no need to use her positional power to force people to support her.

Table 11.1 Leadership Style and Power Grid

Leader's Style	Use of Power	Teammates' Style	Relationship Established
Directive	Dominating, Positional	Obedient	Dependent
Engaged	Persuading	Empowered	Interdependent
Coaching	Counseling	Receptive	Interdependent
Consensus	Gaining Agreement	Equality	Interdependent
Affiliative	Empathy	Team-Oriented	Interdependent
Expert	Knowledge	Autonomous	Independent

Coaching leaders create interdependent relationships the way Bill Campbell did with Randy Komisar, Donna Dubinsky, and Bruce Chizen. Those three needed Campbell's help to develop as leaders, just as he needed them to build a great company. Coaching leaders believe people must learn from their own experiences, especially when failing. They do not jump in and correct employees too soon in order to avoid negative outcomes. They are most effective with teammates who are receptive to coaching and genuinely want to grow.

Consensus leaders use power in subtle ways to reach agreement without hurting feelings or isolating people with different points of view. They are masters at working behind the scenes to develop long-term, interdependent relationships to bring people together around common goals. Consensus building works less well when time is short.

Affiliative leaders are embraced by others for their highly empathic relationships. Their power comes through the strength of the relationships they build, which create loyalty and mutual trust. Such leaders are most effective with people who are committed to being team players and treasure interdependent relationships.

Expert leaders believe knowledge is power and that being right and efficient is more important than the relationship. Offering little empathy or emotional support, they are most effective in settings where teammates are autonomous and results depend on knowledge and expert judgment.

Adapting to the Situation . . .

As leaders mature through multiple experiences, they develop an authentic primary leadership style that works well for them and makes effective use of their power. That style is effective as long as their situation or context stays the same. But what happens when the context changes? Will consensus or affiliative leaders be able to shift to a more urgent style to address the immediate situation?

In leading, you must always understand the situation in which you are operating, as well as the performance imperative. As Narayana Murthy said, "Leadership must always be put in a context. If you take the best corporate leaders and make them senators or president, they may not succeed because that is a different context." Once you understand the context, however, you can adjust your communication and leadership style to get results.

Amgen CEO Kevin Sharer's experience at MCI taught him the value of a flexible leadership style, one that could vary with the needs of the business and the readiness of his team to operate autonomously. Sharer described flexibility as a matter of the appropriate "altitude" for the level of abstraction or specificity of the task at hand.

> At the highest altitude, you're asking the big questions: What are the company's mission and strategy? Do people understand and believe in these aims? At the lowest altitude, you're looking at on-the-ground operations: Did we make that sale? What was the yield on the last lot in the factory? In between, you ask questions like: Should we invest in a small biotechnology company that has a promising new drug? How many chemists should we hire this quarter?

As a CEO you've got to be working at all of these levels simultaneously, and that's not easy. I learned from Jack Welch the skill of rapidly shifting between levels, or even engaging several levels at once. Most CEOs tend to gravitate toward the altitude where they're most comfortable. Unfortunately, they get in trouble because they get stuck at a particular altitude.

Sharer acknowledged his own tendency to be preoccupied by the nitty-gritty details of a problem: "When I go into my submarine mode—when I go very, very deep into a problem—I tend to think I can solve it myself and am at risk of ignoring the advice of experts and closing down debate."

I've paid a price for this—for example, in forging ahead with a product that others were saying didn't have sufficient commercial promise. Mainly, I prefer to work at a middle-to-high altitude. I'm fascinated with strategic alternatives. This can also be destabilizing to the organization. People begin wondering, "What idea is Kevin going to have next?" I've learned to be careful about ruminating on these things with the wrong audience. But moving nimbly in and out of a variety of areas and at different altitudes is crucial to leadership success, particularly in times of rapid growth and uncertainty.

Sharer has worked hard to improve the effectiveness of his leadership style and his use of power. He has developed a more effective style and learned to use his power in more subtle ways. He credited the 360-degree review process with helping him improve. "My model as CEO is the prime-ministerial one," he said, "where if you don't have the support of independent, strong, and knowledgeable cabinet members, you don't have a job."

... and to Your Teammates

In determining the style and power you want to use in a given situation, you should consider the readiness of your teammates to accept greater power and authority. For example, teammates who are used to taking clear direction may not be ready to adapt to a leader with a consensus style; conversely, followers who are highly creative and independent will not respond positively to a directive style. You should also think carefully about the kind of relationship you want to have with your teammates and what type of relationship will enable your team or organization to achieve its business imperatives. These relationships generally fit one of three types: dependent, independent, and interdependent.

In creating dependent relationships, leaders must recognize that their teammates will rely entirely on their direction and their decisions. Dependent subordinates tend to be lost without clear, specific guidance from the leader.

At the opposite end of the spectrum, independent relationships give teammates the autonomy and freedom to act on their own, but there is little bonding or group support. Academics and scientists generally work well in this environment.

In creating interdependent relationships, engaged, coaching, consensus, and affiliative leaders share power with teammates and bring out their best qualities. They believe interdependence creates better decisions and greater commitment to ensuring success.

Optimizing Effectiveness
to Achieve Superior Results

The bottom line for *all* leaders is to optimize their effectiveness to achieve superior long-term results. Authentic leaders are more effective at doing this because they have a clear sense of their moral compass and are explicitly committed to building their organizations over time. By developing an authentic leadership style, they get the best from their teammates and their organizations.

Through multiple experiences, authentic leaders learn how to use their power and style in a nuanced and flexible manner to adapt to the situation they are facing and to rally people to the cause. In so doing, they improve both their effectiveness and the results their organizations generate.

Leaders who produce superior results—whether they are leading a team for the first time or at the top of their organizations—build credibility and influence within their organizations and in the world around them. Without results, credibility suffers and influence is lost. Those who build credibility and influence also gain responsibility within the organization and the resources that go with it. Added responsibility and resources position them to take on even greater challenges and give them the ability to sustain superior results. This is just as true for a young engineering project leader in a computer company as it is for IBM CEO Sam Palmisano.

Every leader has to meet the bottom-line test. When you do so authentically, you find yourself in a virtuous circle in which your results reinforce the effectiveness of your leadership. Your success attracts talented people, both inside the company and outside, who join your team and commit themselves to the common purpose, thus sustaining the cycle of success.

Superior results over a sustained period of time are the ultimate mark of authentic leaders. At the end of the day, you can honestly say that you followed your True North and made a difference in the world through your leadership.

Figure 11.1 illustrates the linkage between your life story, your development of the five dimensions of an authentic leader, and the transformation that enables you to empower other leaders. In the end, this approach to discovering your authentic leadership enables you to make an impact and get results.

Note to the reader: Before going on to the Epilogue, you may want to complete the Chapter Eleven Exercise found in Appendix C. Once you've read the Epilogue, you'll be ready to prepare your Personal Leadership Development Plan, also in Appendix C. You can update it regularly to incorporate your experiences.

Figure 11.1 Getting to Results and Making an Impact

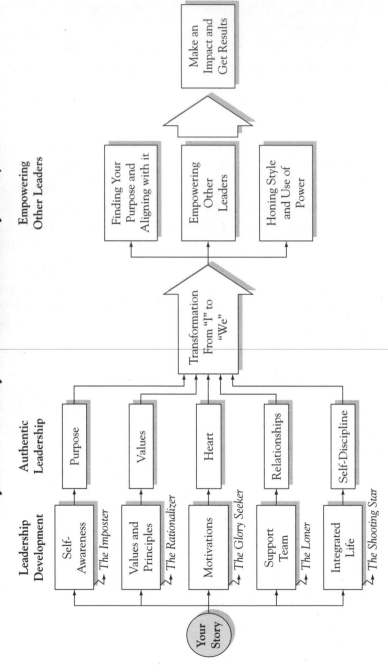

Epilogue

The Fulfillment of Leadership

Just for a moment, envision yourself at the end of your life. You are at home in your bedroom. All the children, grandchildren, and great-grandchildren have gathered around you to say good-bye. Your adorable great-granddaughter looks up at you with her bright brown eyes and says, "Please—tell us what did you do in your life to make a difference in the world?"

Tears well up in your eyes and a lump forms in your throat as the important people and events of your life flash before your eyes. You think back to all the moving speeches given at your ninetieth birthday party and recall that you never had the opportunity to say what your life and leadership were all about. Now you have that opportunity. In the presence of your entire family, what are you going to say? What will your legacy be?

Why not take the opportunity to think about that question right now, while you are still writing your life story? Just as it is never too late to lead, it is never too late to make a difference in the world and to leave a legacy for those who come along after you. But *only you* can answer that question. When you know your answer, you will also recognize why leadership is so fulfilling.

A close friend of mine devotes his time to working with businesspeople in their fifties and sixties who have achieved great financial success but find their lives are hollow because there is no fulfillment in them. *It is never too late . . . or too soon to step up to leadership*.

After studying numerous cases of failed executives in my MBA class, a student asked, "Is leading an organization worth the risks of failing, of being criticized, of being sued, or even of being dis-graced?" She was correct in assuming that being an authentic leader means taking all those risks.

In my closing talk for that class, I quoted Theodore Roosevelt's famous 1910 speech at the Sorbonne, "The Man in the Arena."

> *It is not the critic who counts; not the man who points out how the strong man stumbles, or where the doer of deeds could have done them better. The credit belongs to the man who is actually in the arena, whose face is marred by dust and sweat and blood; who strives valiantly . . . who knows great enthusiasms, the great devotions; who spends himself in a worthy cause; who at the best knows in the end the triumph of high achievement, and who at the worst, if he fails, at least fails while daring greatly, so that his place shall never be with those cold and timid souls who neither know victory nor defeat.*

Are you prepared to enter that arena, to dare greatly, to know the great enthusiasms and the great devotions, and to spend your-self in a worthy cause? If you are, in the end you will also know the triumph of high achievement.

That is the fulfillment of leadership.

You cannot find that fulfillment by observing leaders from the sidelines or by being a brilliant observer from the press box, high above the arena. You have no choice but to get in there and get your face marred by dust and sweat and blood.

That is what life and leadership are all about. Your fulfillment comes not from the money, the titles, the awards, or the recogni-tion. These fleeting symbols of external gratification will vanish like the wind.

What will remain are the memories:

- Working together toward shared goals with a group of people you care about.
- Being passionate about helping other people or righting soci-etal wrongs.

- Toiling long hours to get it right.
- Debating and arguing to understand each other's points of view.
- Failing and then regrouping to learn from your mistakes.
- Growing together as leaders.
- Making a difference in the world through your combined efforts.

After reaching your goal together, pause long enough to celebrate your success before going on to the next challenge. Then pass it on to those who carry on after you.

That is the fulfillment of leadership.

It is knowing who you are and staying on the course of your True North. And of knowing that when you found you were off course, you were able to correct your direction and get back on track.

There is no satisfaction in your professional life that can compare to this sense of fulfillment. No individual achievement can equal the pleasure of leading a group of people to achieve a worthy goal. When you cross the finish line together, all the pain and suffering you may have experienced quickly vanishes. It is replaced by a deep inner satisfaction that *you made a difference in the world*.

Countless numbers of people, many as yet unborn, will benefit from your efforts. They will pass on your legacy to those who come along behind, because at the end of the day, the only thing you take with you is what you leave behind.

Is that what you will tell your great-granddaughter? If it is, she will stand on your shoulders and see an even greater vista ahead to explore on her journey to authentic leadership. Your legacy will be complete.

You followed your True North.

You discovered your authentic leadership.

The world is a better place because of you.

That is the fulfillment of leadership.

The discovery of your authentic leadership is well on its way as you become a True North leader. Good luck and Godspeed on your journey.

Appendix A

RESEARCH STUDY ON DEVELOPMENT OF AUTHENTIC LEADERS

Our research question: *"How does one become and remain an authentic leader?"*

Research Team

Bill George, Professor of Management Practice, Harvard Business School.

Diana Mayer, MBA, Harvard Business School.

Andrew McLean, Ph.D., Research Associate, Harvard Business School.

Peter Sims, MBA, Stanford Graduate School of Business.

Definition of "Authentic Leader"

The five dimensions of authentic leadership:

- Pursuing purpose with passion
- Practicing solid values
- Leading with heart
- Establishing connected relationships
- Demonstrating self-discipline

Authentic leaders are genuine people who are true to themselves and to what they believe. Rather than letting the expectations of others guide them, they are prepared to be their own person and go their own way. As they develop as authentic leaders, they are more concerned about serving others than they are about their own success or recognition. And they are constantly looking for ways to grow personally. Authentic leaders develop genuine connections with others and engender trust. Because people trust them, they are able to motivate people to high levels of performance by empowering them to lead.

Field Interviews

The research was based on field interviews with leaders deemed to be both authentic and successful. The interviews were conducted in person, except in a few cases when it was not possible to coordinate logistics for a personal meeting. The interviews lasted on average seventy-five minutes. All interviews were audio recorded with the permission of the interviewee in order to preserve the accuracy of the statements and quotations. Interviews were then professionally transcribed to provide a written record.

All interviews were conducted by Bill George, Diana Mayer, or Peter Sims between April and November 2005, with the exception of one preliminary interview conducted in October 2004. In some cases two of these interviewers participated in the interviews, and in others Andrew McLean also participated.

The interviewers used a common set of questions, but interviewees were permitted to guide the interview to subjects of greatest importance to them in responding to the questions. In several cases, time did not permit the entire list of questions to be asked. No statistical records on the interviewees were established as this was not the intent of the research project.

A typical interview followed this basic structure:

1. Early Influences and Development (fifteen minutes)
   - Impact of key people and experiences
2. Discovering Authentic Leadership (thirty minutes)
   - Motivations

- Strongest growth experiences
- Key turning points
- Lessons from failures
- Relevant personal life experiences

3. Approaches to Leadership Development (twenty minutes)

- Most important practices or resources
- Maintaining authenticity under pressure
- Greatest personal challenges

4. Leadership Purpose and Legacy (ten minutes)

- Purpose of leadership
- Aspired legacy

Interview Subjects

In total, 125 leaders were selected for the study, based on their reputation for being authentic and successful. An attempt was made to include a diverse set of people in the interviews. As a result, 28 percent of the interviewees were women, 8 percent were racial minorities, and 12 percent were born outside the United States. No explicit attempt was made to determine religious affiliation or sexual preference, although informal comments suggest diversity along these dimensions as well.

We looked for a minimum of fifteen interviewees for each age bracket, with the exception of those over seventy. As it turned out, the age distribution at the time of interview was

70–93	14 (11.2 percent)
60–69	18 (14.4 percent)
50–59	38 (30.4 percent)
40–49	22 (17.6 percent)
30–39	18 (14.4 percent)
23–29	15 (12.0 percent)

Selection Criteria

Interviewees were selected based on their perceived authenticity and established success in leadership roles. In a number of cases interviewees were recommended by other participants, by academics engaged in leadership, and by colleagues of the interviewees.

After the interviews were complete, the authenticity of the interviewees was assessed by the interviewers, using the definition of an authentic leader stated here and contained in *Authentic Leadership*. Success in leadership roles was determined by the qualitative judgment of the research team and not by quantitative measures.

Assessment of Transcripts

Transcripts of the interviews were read multiple times by members of the research team, with individual summaries prepared for each. Then the interviewees' responses were categorized by major topics addressed in each interview. After discussion at frequent team meetings between May 2005 and March 2006, generalized conclusions were drawn. These conclusions are presented throughout this book.

Appendix B

AUTHENTIC LEADERS INTERVIEWED FOR *TRUE NORTH*

Here are the 125 individuals interviewed for this book, by age bracket.

Leaders over Seventy

Warren Bennis	University Professor and Distinguished Professor of Business Administration, University of Southern California
Sir Adrian Cadbury	Chairman, Cadbury Schweppes (1965–1989)
T. J. Dermot Dunphy	Chairman, Kildare Enterprises LLC; Chairman and CEO, Sealed Air Corporation (1971–1999)
Fisher Howe	Former Associate Dean, School of Advanced International Studies, Johns Hopkins University
Sidney Knafel	Managing Partner, SRK Management Company; Chairman, Insight Communications Company, Inc.; Chairman, Vision Cable Communications, Inc. (1971–1981)
John Mackowski	Chairman and CEO, The Atlantic Mutual Companies (1985–1988)
John Morgridge	Chairman, Cisco Systems (1996–2006); CEO, Cisco Systems (1988–1995)

Zygmunt Nagorski	Founder, Center for International Leadership
George Shultz	U.S. Secretary of State (1982–1989); President, Bechtel (1975–1979)
Helmut Sihler	Chairman, Porsche AG; Chairman of the Central Board Management, Henkel KGaA (1980–1992)
John Smale	Chairman, General Motors (1992–1996); Chairman and CEO, Proctor & Gamble (1981–1990)
Dr. Roy Vagelos	Chairman and CEO, Merck & Co. (1985–1994)
John Whitehead	Co-chairman, Goldman Sachs (1976–1984); U.S. Deputy Secretary of State (1985–1989)
James "Jimmy" Williams	Chairman and CEO, SunTrust Banks (1985–1998)

Leaders in Their Sixties

Ned Barnholt	Chairman and CEO, Agilent (1999–2005)
Richard Braddock	Partner, MidOcean Partners, LLP; President and COO, Citicorp (1990–1992)
Bill Campbell	Chairman and CEO, Intuit (1994–1998)
Marilyn Carlson Nelson	Chairman and CEO, Carlson Companies
Reatha Clark King	Chairman, General Mills Foundation (1998–2002)
David Cox	President and CEO, Cowles Media (1981–1998)

Ian Cumming	Chairman, Leucadia National Corporation
Robert Day	Chairman and CEO, The TCW Group, Inc.
Brad Freeman	Founder and Partner, Freeman Spogli & Co.
David Gergen	Director, Center for Public Leadership, Kennedy School of Government; Harvard University; White House adviser to U.S. Presidents Nixon, Ford, Reagan, and Clinton
Alan Horn	President and COO, Warner Bros.
Jon Huntsman	Chairman, Huntsman Corporation
Dick Kovacevich	Chairman and CEO, Wells Fargo
Bowen "Buzz" McCoy	Adjunct professor, USC; past Partner, Morgan Stanley
Jean-Pierre Rosso	Chairman, World Economic Forum USA; Chairman and CEO, Case-New Holland (1996–2004)
Robert Ryan	Senior Vice President and CFO, Medtronic (1993–2005)
Charles Schwab	Chairman and CEO, The Charles Schwab Corporation
Manny Villafana	Founder, Cardiac Pacemakers Inc. (now Guidant Corporation), St. Jude Medical, and ATS Medical
Sam A. Williams	President, Metro Atlanta Chamber of Commerce

Leaders in Their Fifties

Brenda Barnes	Chairman and CEO, Sara Lee Corporation

Nancy Barry	President, Women's World Banking
John Brennan	Chairman and CEO, The Vanguard Group
Ellen Breyer	CEO, Hazelden Foundation
Mike Buhrmann	Partner, 1024 Partners, LLC; Founder and CEO, @mobile
Donald Carty	Chairman, Virgin America; Chairman and CEO, American Airlines (1998–2003)
Lady Lynn Forester de Rothschild	Founder and CEO, EL Rothschild, Ltd; Founder, FirstMark Communications, U.S. (1995–1997), Europe (1998–2000)
David Dillon	Chairman and CEO, Kroger
Robert Fisher	Chairman, Gap, Inc.
Ann Fudge	Chairman and CEO, Young & Rubicam
Paul Garcia	Chairman and CEO, Global Payments
Judy Haberkorn	President, Consumer Sales & Services, Verizon Communications, Inc. (1998–2000)
Michelle Hooper	Managing Partner, The Directors' Council; past CEO, Voyager Expanded Learning; Vice President, Baxter Healthcare
Kris Johnson	Managing Partner, Affinity Capital; past Senior Vice President, Medtronic
Lois Juliber	Chief Operating Officer, Colgate-Palmolive (2000–2004)
David Kelley	Cofounder and Chairman, IDEO; Professor of Design Division, Department of Mechanical Engineering, Stanford University
Randy Komisar	Partner, Kleiner Perkins Caufield & Byers; CEO, LucasArts (1994–1995)

Per Lofberg	CEO, Merck Capital Ventures, LLC; Chairman, Medco Health (1993–2000)
Ellen Marram	Operating Advisor, North Castle Partners; President and CEO, Tropicana (1993–1998)
Gail McGovern	Professor, Harvard Business School; President, Fidelity Personal Investments (1998–2002); EVP, Consumer Markets Division, AT&T (1996–1998)
Ann Moore	Chairman and CEO, Time, Inc.
Anne Mulcahy	Chairman and CEO, Xerox
N. R. Narayana Murthy	Cofounder and Chief Mentor, Infosys; Chairman and CEO, Infosys (1981–2002)
Stephanie Odegard	President, Odegard, Inc.
Joel Peterson	Lecturer, Stanford Business School; Managing Partner, Trammell Crow Company (1988–1991)
Addison "Tad" Piper	Vice Chairman, Piper Jaffray Companies; CEO, Piper Jaffray (1983–2000)
David Pottruck	Chairman and CEO, Eos Airlines; Co-CEO and then CEO, Charles Schwab Corporation (1998–2004)
Joe Rogers Jr.	Chairman and CEO, Waffle House
Steve Rothschild	Founder and Chairman, Twin Cities RISE!; past EVP, General Mills
Jon Rounds	Chief Operating Officer, Risc Ventures, LLC
Lewis Sanders	Chairman and CEO, AllianceBernstein, L.P.
Howard Schultz	Chairman, Starbucks; CEO, Starbucks (1987–2000)

Kevin Sharer	Chairman and CEO, Amgen
John Thain	CEO, New York Stock Exchange
Jim Thompson	Founder and Executive Director, Positive Coaching Alliance
Marianne Toldalagi	President, MCT Associates; SVP and General Manager, Consumer Travel Division, American Express (1995–2000)
Dr. Daniel Vasella	Chairman and CEO, Novartis AG
Judy Vredenburgh	CEO, Big Brothers Big Sisters of America

Leaders in Their Forties

Doug Baker Jr.	Chairman and CEO, Ecolab
Mike Baker	CEO, Arthrocare
Robert Chess	Chairman and CEO, Nektar Therapeutics
Bruce Chizen	CEO, Adobe Systems
Chip Conley	Founder and CEO, Joie de Vivre Hotels
John Donahoe	President, eBay Marketplace; Worldwide Managing Director, Bain & Company (1999–2005)
Donna Dubinsky	Cofounder and CEO, Numenta; Cofounder and CEO, Handspring (1998–2003); CEO, Palm, Inc. (1992–1998)
Mark Ernst	Chairman and CEO, H&R Block
Mark Feidler	President and COO, BellSouth Corporation
Fadi Ghandour	Founder and CEO, Aramex
Andrea Jung	Chairman and CEO, Avon Products

Keith Krach	Founder and former CEO, Ariba, Inc.
Vanda Marlow	Zen Hospice Project
Denise O'Leary	Director, Medtronic; former Partner, Menlo Ventures
Karl-Henrik Robert	Founder, The Natural Step
Paula Rosput Reynolds	President and CEO, Safeco Corporation
Louise Sams	President, Turner Broadcasting System International
Dan Schulman	CEO, Virgin Mobile USA
Michael Sweeney	Managing Director, Goldner-Hawn Johnson & Morrison
Richard Tait	Founder and Grand Poo Bah, Cranium
Kent Thiry	Chairman and CEO, DaVita
Carol Tomé	CFO, The Home Depot

Leaders in Their Thirties

Ian Chan	Founder and former CEO, U.S. Genomics
Cesar Conde	Vice President, Univision
Lisa Dawe	Regional Operations Director, DaVita
Stephen DeBerry	Investment Director, Omidyar Network
Charles Dimmler	General Manager, Geron Corporation
Martha Goldberg Aronson	Vice President, Investor Relations, Medtronic
Jamie Irick	Vice President, General Electric
Wendy Kopp	President and Founder, Teach For America
Chris Landon	Director, Medtronic Cardiac Rhythm Management
Bernard Looney	Vice President, BP, Plc.

Philip McCrea	Founder and former President, Vitesse Learning
Chris O'Connell	President, Medtronic Emergency Response Systems
Michal Petrzela	Associate, Lightyear Capital
Mark Reynoso	Senior Vice President, Sales & Marketing, Belkin Corp.
Shailendra Singh	Vice President, Sequoia Capital India
Ronald Sonntag	Founder and Chairman, Utah Vacation Homes
Kristopher Woolley	Vice President, Greystar Real Estate Partners
Sam Yagan	Cofounder and CEO, OkCupid

Leaders in Their Twenties

David Darst	Cofounder, Potentia Pharmaceuticals and Cofounder, Medicine in Need
Jonathan Doochin	McKinsey & Company; Founder, Harvard Leadership Institute
Julian Flannery	Staff Assistant to CEO, Morgan Stanley; Assistant to Chief of Staff, The White House
Ryan Frederick	Associate, CoastWood Capital Group
Jared Hutchings	Cofounder and Managing Director, University Venture Fund
Sarah Molloy	Vice President, Acadian Asset Management
Akshata Murthy	Student, Stanford Business School
Kristin Ostby	Director of Central American Operations, Boys & Girls Hope
James "Than" Powell	Marketing, Eli Lilly

Margaret Booth Powell	Marketing Manager, Eli Lilly
Daniel Salvadori	Associate, New Leaf Ventures
Scott Starr	Management Training Program, General Electric
Sara Strammiello	Founder and Executive Director, Year Up Providence Office
Nichole Taylor	Assistant Product Manager, Frito Lay
Alice Woodwark	McKinsey & Company

Leaders Profiled from Public Sources and Personal Discussions

Earl Bakken	Founder and former CEO, Medtronic
Lord Browne of Madingley	Group Chief Executive, BP, Plc.
Warren Buffett	Chairman and CEO, Berkshire Hathaway
James Burke	Chairman and CEO, Johnson & Johnson (1976–1989)
Jeffrey Immelt	Chairman and CEO, General Electric
Alan "A.G." Lafley	Chairman and CEO, Procter & Gamble
Samuel Palmisano	Chairman and CEO, IBM
Henry Paulson	U.S. Secretary of the Treasury; Chairman & CEO, Goldman Sachs (1999–2006)
Oprah Winfrey	Chairman, Harpo

Appendix C

LEADERSHIP EXERCISES FOR EACH CHAPTER

For all of these exercises, you should use a notebook or a journal that you can keep as a record of them and update them whenever appropriate.

Introduction Exercise: Your Development as an Authentic Leader

After reading the Introduction, think about the basis for your leadership and the process you need to go through to become an authentic leader. The following exercise will get you started.

1. What leaders, past or present, do you admire most?
   - What is it about them that you admire?
   - Which of these leaders do you consider to be authentic leaders?
   - What can you learn from their leadership?
2. Thinking back over all your leadership experiences in your lifetime, which ones are you proudest of?
3. Think about the basis for your leadership and the kind of leader you would like to be as you answer these questions:
   - What qualities do you bring to leadership?
   - What leadership qualities would you like to develop further?
4. Assess yourself against the five dimensions of an authentic leader:
   - Do you understand your purpose?
   - Do you practice your values?
   - Do you lead with your heart?
   - Do you establish connected relationships?
   - Do you demonstrate self-discipline?
5. Do you feel that you are more effective as a leader when you are authentic, or does being authentic constrain your leadership effectiveness?
6. Are you consciously developing your leadership abilities at this time?

Chapter One Exercise: Your Story and Journey to Authentic Leadership

After reading Chapter One, it's important to examine your life story and leadership opportunities to this point, with an emphasis on the influences of your early years and instances of your leadership.

Discover Your Leadership in Your Life Story

1. During your early years, which people had the greatest impact on you?
2. Starting with your earliest memories, which experiences marked key turning points in your life?
3. In which experiences did you find the greatest inspiration and passion for your leadership?
4. Looking at patterns from your early life story, what people, events, and experiences have had the greatest impact on you and your life?
5. Can you identify instances where you were dissatisfied with your leadership or received constructive feedback from others about it?
6. Has there been an instance in your life where you have felt like a victim?
7. Do the failures or disappointments you experienced earlier in your life constrain you, even today, or have you been able to reframe them as learning experiences?

The Journey to Authentic Leadership

1. Do you currently view your life and leadership as a destination to a certain point or as a journey in which you seek to maximize your learning and experiences?
2. What are the most significant leadership experiences you have had to date and what did you learn from them?
3. What experiences do you need to develop your leadership to take it to the next level?
4. If you are just entering a new phase, have you assessed the goals and experiences you would like to have during the phase?
5. Do you think you need to make any adjustments to your personal and leadership development as a result? If so, what are they?
6. How can you take your previous experiences and apply them more optimally to your leadership now?

Chapter Two Exercise:
The Risk of Losing Your Way

After reading Chapter Two, think carefully about whether you see any of yourself in each of the five archetypes of leaders who lose their way and get derailed. In completing the exercise, be honest with yourself and attempt to see yourself as others see you.

Why Leaders Lose Their Way

Think through the underlying reasons why so many leaders in the recent past have lost their way and wound up failing as leaders.

1. Have you seen leaders lose their way or worked with someone who fits any of the archetypes particularly well?
2. What are the behaviors and warning signals you have seen in others at risk of losing their way?

Derailment

Referring back to the five archetypes that lead to derailment:

1. Can you see any of the qualities of the Imposter in yourself?
2. Can you see any of the qualities of the Rationalizer in yourself?
3. Can you see any of the qualities of the Glory Seeker in yourself?
4. Can you see any of the qualities of the Loner in yourself?
5. Can you see any of the qualities of the Shooting Star in yourself?

Losing Your Way

1. Can you envision a situation in which you could lose your way in the future?
2. To what extent are you prepared to go your own way and be your own person, despite external pressure?
3. Do you have a fear of failing? In what ways? Is it because you are afraid of what other people would think about you? Is it personal pride?
4. How is your fear of failing impacting your decisions about leadership and your career? Are you consciously or unconsciously avoiding situations in which there is a risk of failing?

5. How could the experience of failing help you achieve your ultimate goals?

6. In what ways do you crave success?

7. How is your craving for success impacting your decisions about leadership and your career? Are you consciously or unconsciously choosing situations that give you a high probability of success?

Prevention

1. What steps can you take to prevent being derailed during your career?

Chapter Three Exercise:
Your Greatest Crucible

After reading Chapter Three, think back over your life and recall the experience that involved the greatest pressure, stress, or adversity.

1. Write freely about your greatest crucible and describe it in the following ways:

   - How did you feel at the time?
   - What resources did you call upon?
   - How did you resolve the issues, if you have?
   - How did it shape you and your views about the world?

2. Describe any relationships, such as those with mentors, that had a transformative effect on you and your leadership. What did you learn from that relationship and how did it shape who you are?

3. Describe any other experiences that triggered significant leadership development.

   - In looking back on these experiences, what did you learn from them?
   - In what ways have they helped you to grow?

4. How can you use these experiences to reframe your life story and to understand yourself and your life more fully? Are there ways in which these experiences are holding you back today?

5. Transformation from "I" to "We."

   - Are you on "the hero's journey"? Do you ever see yourself as the hero of your own journey?
   - Have you made the transformation from "I" to "We"? If so, what triggered this transformation for you?
   - If you have not yet made this transformation, what would have to happen in your life and leadership for a transformation like this to occur?

Chapter Four Exercise:
Knowing Your Authentic Self

After reading Chapter Four, this exercise will help develop your self-awareness by assessing your leadership strengths, your shortcomings, and your development needs.

Basic Self-Awareness Assessment:

The following questions will allow you to compare your evaluation of yourself with how others view you. Rate yourself from 1 to 10 (with 10 being "Very," 5 being "Moderately," and 1 being "Barely") then support your assessment by answering each question. Then choose two people who know you well to rate you using the same scale and provide their assessments.

Question	Self-Rating (1–10)	Feedback 1 Rating (1–10)	Feedback 2 Rating (1–10)
How self-confident are you?			
How aware are you of your moods and emotions?			
How effective are you in regulating your moods to minimize their impact on other people?			
When confronted with situations that are displeasing to you, how well do you take the time to think clearly about them before responding or reacting?			
When you receive critical feedback from others, how well are you able to take in the feedback and respond in a constructive manner without acting defensively?			
How well do you understand the emotional makeup of others and their needs?			
How sensitive are you in relating to others' needs and helping them?			
How skillful are you in building lasting relationships?			

How well do you network with others and create networks of people with common interests?

How effective are you in leading teams?

Do others follow your lead voluntarily?

How persuasive are you in convincing others of your mutual interests?

After reviewing the feedback, to what extent do you see yourself as others see you? How strong is your basic self-awareness right now?

Strengths and Development Areas

1. What are your strongest capabilities or talents?
2. What are your strongest attributes as a leader?
3. What are your greatest needs for development as a leader?

Needs

1. Do you need structure in your job? To what extent are you comfortable with ambiguity and change?
2. What level of financial security will allow you to feel comfortable?
3. To what extent do you need to be leading a team?
4. How much time do you need with your family or loved ones each week?
5. How much personal time do you need each week to recharge?

Your Authentic Self

1. What are your vulnerabilities, blind spots, and shadow sides?
2. To what extent do you use defensive armor as a shield to protect yourself from exposing your vulnerabilities with others?
3. How can you become more comfortable in sharing your vulnerabilities with others?
4. How comfortable are you with who you are right now?

Chapter Five Exercise:
Practicing Your Values and Principles

In this exercise, you have the opportunity to set forth the values, leadership principles, and ethical boundaries that will guide your leadership as an authentic leader. The intent of this exercise is to be explicit about the values that are important to you, the principles you will use in leading, and the ethical boundaries that you will adhere to, even under great pressure.

Values

1. List the values that are important to your life and your leadership. After you have done so, go back and rank them in order of their importance to you.

   - Which of your values are inviolate?
   - Which ones are desirable but not mandatory?
   - Do some of your values depend upon the situation that you are facing?

2. Recall a personal situation in which your values conflicted with each other.

   - How did you resolve this conflict?
   - How pleased were you with the outcome?

3. Recall a situation in which your values were tested under pressure.

   - To what extent did you deviate from your values under that pressure?
   - What resources did you call upon under this pressure?
   - What would you do differently if you had it do all over again?

Principles and Boundaries

1. List the leadership principles you use (or want to use) in leading others. Then go back and rank-order them depending on which are most important to you.

2. List the ethical boundaries that you will not cross. Then rank-order them in terms of their importance to you.

3. Recall a situation in which you deviated from your True North and your values in order to achieve your goals.

   - How will you handle this situation if you face it in the future?
   - How can you sense "the slippery slope" of minor deviations leading to major ones later on?
   - When you find yourself being pulled away from your True North, how do you get back on track?

Chapter Six Exercise: Your Motivations and Motivated Capabilities

The following exercise provides you with the opportunity to understand your motivations. After completing the sections on your motivations, you can explore ways in which you can mesh your motivations with your capabilities to find your *sweet spot*—that zone where you are able to use your abilities to the fullest and where you are highly motivated. This sweet spot may reveal valuable insights about your career and life choices.

1. What is motivating you to be a leader?
2. What are your sources of motivation?
3. What are your extrinsic motivations? Note them on the following chart with a check mark. After you have completed the list, rank-order your greatest extrinsic motivations (from 1 to 5, with 1 being the greatest).

Observed   *Rank Order*

1. Monetary compensation
2. Having power
3. Having a title
4. Public recognition
5. Social status
6. Winning over others
7. Being associated with prestigious institutions
8. Other:

4. What are the traps set by your extrinsic motivations that you could foresee yourself falling into? What are you doing to avoid these traps?
5. What are your intrinsic motivations? Please note them below with a check mark. After you have completed the list, rank-order your greatest intrinsic motivations.

Observed   *Rank Order*

1. Personal growth and development
2. Satisfaction of doing a good job
3. Helping others
4. Leading and organizing others

Observed   *Rank Order*

   5. Being associated with people you care about

   6. Finding meaning from your efforts

   7. Being true to your beliefs

   8. Making a difference in the world

   9. Having influence on others

  10. Other:

6. Conflicts between extrinsic and intrinsic motivations:

   - Recall and then list one or more instances in which your extrinsic motivations conflicted with your intrinsic motivations. What did you do?

   - How did you go about resolving these conflicts?

   - What steps can you take to balance your extrinsic and intrinsic motivations?

7. Your motivations (in rank order):

   Combine your lists of extrinsic and intrinsic motivations and rank-order those that most highly motivate you today from 1 to 5, with 1 being the greatest motivation. Put an asterisk next to those that are intrinsic motivations.

8. Your capabilities:

   List your capabilities or your strengths. Then rank-order your five strongest capabilities today from 1 to 5, with 1 being your greatest capability.

9. Your developmental areas:

   Compile a list of your developmental needs, as you see them today. Then rank-order them from 1 to 5, with 1 being your greatest developmental need.

10. Your motivated capabilities: Make a list of your motivated capabilities—the areas where you are both highly motivated and very capable.

11. Using your motivated capabilities: Make a list of future situations that you can envision that would enable you to apply your motivated capabilities and then rank-order them from 1 to 5, with 1 being the best use of your motivated capabilities.

Chapter Seven Exercise:
Building Your Support Team

After reading Chapter Seven, this exercise will allow you to prioritize the important relationships in your life today and the kind of support team you would like to build.

1. Current and past relationships: Make a list of the most important relationships in your life, right now and in the past.
   - What is your most important relationship?
   - Why is this person important to you? In what ways do you look to this person for support?

2. Your family of origin:
   - What role has your family of origin played in your life and specifically in your development as a leader?

3. Relationships with teachers, coaches, or advisers: Have you had a particular teacher, coach, or adviser who has been influential in your interest in leadership and your development as a leader?

4. Mentors:
   - Who are the people who have mentored you in your leadership development?
   - Which mentors have been most important in your development as a leader?
   - In what ways have they helped you develop?
   - How have you helped your mentor and built a two-way relationship?
   - What more can you bring to your mentoring relationships?

5. Friends:
   - In what ways have your friends helped you become a better leader?
   - Which of your friends could you count on if things did not go well for you?
   - Do you have friends with whom you can share the challenges you face openly? Can you give each other honest feedback?
   - Describe a relationship that has been mutually beneficial to you over an extended period of time. What qualities did you bring to the relationship that made it meaningful and enduring?
   - Describe a relationship that did not work out for you for which you feel some degree of responsibility. What would you do differently if you had the opportunity to do it over again?

6. Personal support group:
   - Do you have a personal support group? If so, what is its value and meaning to you and your leadership?
   - If you have never had such a group, would you like to form one? If so, what kind of people would you like to have in your group?

7. Professional support network:
   - Do you have a professional support network or would you like to build one?
   - What would such a network look like for you?
   - Who are some of the people you would like to have in your network?

8. Personal board of directors:
   - Would you like to create a personal board of directors? If so, what types of people you would like to have on your board?
   - Who specifically would you like to be part of your board?
   - How would you use your board? What would you contribute to your board members?

Chapter Eight Exercise:
The Integrated Leader

In this exercise you will examine how you can bring together all aspects of your life into an integrated whole so that you can live your life with integrity. The underlying belief here is by bringing together all aspects of your life into an integrated whole, you will be a more effective leader and have a more satisfying and fulfilling life.

Personal Life

1. What is most important to you in your personal life?

2. In what ways do you set time aside for yourself and your personal development?

3. In what ways do you nurture your inner life?

4. Optional: Do you have a regular religious or spiritual practice? In what ways does it contribute to your having an integrated life?

Family Life

1. What are the most important aspects of your family life?

2. In what ways will your life and time commitments change as you take on additional family commitments?

3. How do you manage the time requirements and conflicts?

Friendships and Community

1. In what ways do friendships enable you to lead a more integrated life? How much time do you devote to developing and nurturing your friendships?

2. Is your community an integral part of your life?

3. In what ways do you serve your community?

4. How can community service help you become a better leader?

5. In what ways would you like to serve your community in the future?

Professional Life

1. What do you do to ensure that you stay grounded professionally?
2. In what ways do your family life, personal life, friendships, and community life add to or detract from your professional life?
3. How do you cope with the seductions and pressures of professional life and still stay focused on your True North?

Making Choices and Trade-Offs

1. What is the most difficult choice or trade-off between various aspects of your life that you have made in the past? What would you do differently in the future?
2. What is the most difficult trade-off or choice that you are facing right now?
3. How will you balance the time requirements of each part of your life?

Measuring Your Success

1. How do you measure success in your life right now? What is your personal scorecard?
2. What are the long-term achievements you would like to realize in your life?
3. What will bring you the greatest amount of happiness in your life?
4. What is the positive impact on others that you would like to have?

Integrating Your Life

Think of your life as a house with a bedroom for your personal life, a study for your professional life, a family room for your family, and a living room to share with your friends.

1. Can you knock down the walls between these rooms and be the same person in each of them?
2. Are you able to be the same authentic person in each environment, or do you behave differently at work than you do at home, with your friends, or in the community?

Chapter Nine Exercise: The Purpose of My Leadership

In this exercise, you will focus on the purpose of your leadership and how your purpose is derived from your life story, your passions, and your motivated capabilities.

Discerning Your Passions Through Your Life Story

Recall your early life story (addressed in the exercises for Chapter One and Chapter Three) and use it to identify sources of your passions that are close to your heart.

1. By reframing your life story, can you discern your passions more clearly?
2. In what ways do your passions lead you to the purpose of your leadership?

The Purpose of Your Leadership

Write an essay to yourself describing the long-term purpose of your leadership.

1. For the near term, what is your purpose in leading?
2. In what ways does the purpose of your leadership relate to the rest of your life? Is it integral to it or separate from it?

Chapter Ten Exercise:
Empowering Other Leaders

After you read Chapter Ten, this exercise will help you empower other leaders.

Leadership Relationships

Leadership relationships can take many forms. The following is a list of the roles leaders play in developing relationships with others in their organization. *Please assess your effectiveness in each type of leadership relationship (from 1–10, with 10 being "Very Well," 5 being "Satisfactory," and 1 being "Poorly")*. Put a check mark next to those items you would like to focus on for improvement and an asterisk next to those items that are your strengths.

Rating (1–10)	Strength	Needs Improvement
	Directing	Giving people directions about work to be done
	Organizing	Organizing people to get things done
	Delegating	Giving others authority and responsibility
	Persuading	Convincing others of your point of view
	Listening	Hearing clearly what others are saying
	Motivating	Inspiring people to achieve the task
	Empowering	Encouraging others to reach their potential
	Discussing	Talking through different points of view
	Learning	Gaining understanding through others
	Teaching	Transmitting understanding to others
	Advising	Counseling others on their challenges
	Coaching	Guiding others accomplishing their tasks
	Mentoring	Helping others grow as leaders
	Following	Following the leadership of others

1. What are your greatest strengths in establishing relationships?

2. What areas do you intend to improve upon?

Leadership Relationships in the Workplace

Describe the kinds of leadership relationships you have in the workplace with your superiors, peers, subordinates, and external constituencies.

1. Bosses: What kind of relationship do you have with your boss? How could you make it better?
2. Peers: What kind of relationship do you have with your peers at work?
3. Subordinates: What kind of relationships would you like to have with your subordinates? How could they be improved?
4. Organizational networking: How effective are you in building a network of relationships in your organization? What can you do to improve your networking?

Empowering Other Leaders

1. Describe an example from your past where you have been effective in inspiring other leaders around a common purpose and shared values.
2. How effective are you today at empowering other people to step up and lead? How do you go about doing this? What are you doing to improve your effectiveness?
3. Recall a situation in which you faced a conflict between empowering other people and reaching your performance goals.
   - How did you resolve the conflict?
   - Did you give preference to reaching your goals or to your relationships?
   - Would you act differently in the future when facing a conflict between relationships and performance?

Chapter Eleven Exercise: Honing Your Leadership Effectiveness

The following exercise will allow you to examine ways to improve your effectiveness as a leader, including your use of flexible leadership styles and power in your relationships. Refer back to the definitions of leadership style in Chapter Eleven and Table 11.1, "Leadership Style and Power Grid."

1. Preferred leadership style:
   - What is your preferred leadership style?
   - Why is it your preferred style?
   - Which of your skills does it use?
   - In what situations do you use your preferred style?
   - Is your style consistent with your leadership principles and values? Is it ever inconsistent?
   - What are you doing to improve your preferred style?

2. Backup style:

   Your backup style is one you often revert to when you are under pressure or when you find your preferred style is not working.
   - What is your backup leadership style?
   - In what situations do you revert to your backup style?
   - Which of your leadership skills does your backup style use?
   - As compared to your primary style, what are the negative consequences of your backup style? What are the positives?

3. Flexible leadership styles:
   - What are your flexible leadership styles?
   - In what situations do you use each of them?
   - What leadership skills does each of your flexible styles require?
   - How do you adapt your leadership style to the circumstances facing you?
   - How do you adapt your leadership style to the readiness of your team to take on greater leadership?
   - How can you use flexible styles and still be authentic?

4. Using power:
   - What is the role of power in your leadership?
   - How do you gain power or influence within your group?
   - How do you use power effectively in leading others?

- Think of an example in which you used your power over others with negative consequences. How did people respond?
- What went wrong? What would you do differently if you had it to do over again?
- How do you respond to powerful people that use their power over you? What is the most appropriate way to deal with very powerful people?
- What can you do to avoid being overpowered?
- How can you avoid giving away your personal power to powerful people?

5. Leadership effectiveness:

- Describe the ways in which you plan to change your leadership in order to improve your effectiveness as a leader.

Epilogue Exercise: Your Personal Leadership Development Plan

The Personal Leadership Development Plan is the culmination of the exercises. It is your plan that you can use to guide your development. Used optimally, it can be a dynamic plan that you update on a regular basis to reflect your leadership experiences and changes in your thinking about your development.

Take several hours to complete the plan, integrating the exercises you have done with appropriate revisions in your thinking.

1. Your True North:
   - Write an essay to yourself, answering the question, "What is your True North?" How do you know when you are following it?

2. Intellectual development:
   - In what ways will you endeavor to deepen your intellect?
   - In what ways will you broaden your intellect?
   - What are the areas in which you would like to read and study?
   - What are the places you would like to live in or visit as part of your development?

3. Personal discipline and stress management:
   - Describe your plan for healthy eating.
   - Describe your personal exercise plan.
   - What are your sleep requirements? To what extent do you deviate from them?
   - Describe the practices you use to manage your stress, referring to the following areas:

     Meditating or sitting quietly

     Running or walking

     Exercising, working out, or competitive games

     Yoga or similar practice

     Prayer or reflection

     Talking to spouse, friend, or mentor

     Listening to music

     Watching TV or going to movies

     Other

4. Values, leadership principles, and ethical boundaries:
   - In order of importance, what are the values that are most important to you? (Mark those values that you consider inviolate with an asterisk.)

- What are the principles on which you base your leadership?
- What are the ethical boundaries that will guide your professional life?

5. Your motivations and motivated capabilities:
   - What are your extrinsic motivations?
   - What are your intrinsic motivations?
   - Make a list in rank order of your overall motivations.
   - What are your greatest capabilities?
   - What are your developmental needs?
   - What are your motivated capabilities?
   - What leadership situations optimize the use of your motivated capabilities?

6. Personal reflections:
   - What do you do to be reflective or introspective?
   - What are your spiritual or religious practices?
   - If you don't believe in such practices, how do you address life's existential questions?
   - What do you intend to do to strengthen your practices?

7. Building relationships:
   - Who are the most important people in your life?
   - Who do you feel you can be completely open with?
   - When you are distressed, who do you turn to?
   - Who are your mentors?
   - Which of your personal friends do you look to for counsel and advice?
   - Who do you look to for professional advice and counsel?
   - In what ways do you network with professional colleagues?
   - Would you like to form a support group? How will you go about it?

8. Leadership style:
   - What is your preferred leadership style?
   - What leadership style do you revert to under pressure? What are you doing to avoid reverting to this style?
   - In what ways are you developing your ability to use flexible styles?
   - How are you developing your ability to adapt your style to the situation you are facing and the capabilities of your teammates?
   - In what ways are you developing your ability to use your power more effectively?

9. Leadership development:

   • What are the experiences you need to develop your leadership?

10. Integration:

    • How are you going to integrate your personal life, family life, friendships, and community life with your professional life to become a better leader?

    • What sacrifices and trade-offs are you prepared to make to achieve your professional and personal goals?

11. Leadership purpose and legacy:

    • What is the purpose of your leadership?

    • How does your purpose relate to your True North, your life story, and your passions?

    • What kind of legacy would you like to leave in terms of

      Your family

      Your career

      Your friends

      Your community

12. Write an essay about what you would like to be able to say about your life story and your leadership at the end of your life and where you hope to find fulfillment from being an authentic leader.

References

Introduction

"America's Best Leaders." *US News & World Report,* Oct. 2006.

Collins, J. "Level 5 Leadership: The Triumph of Humility and Fierce Resolve." *Harvard Business Review,* July–Aug. 2005, p. 10.

George, B. *Authentic Leadership.* San Francisco: Jossey-Bass, 2003, pp. 18–25.

George, B., and McLean, A. *Kevin Sharer at Amgen: Sustaining the High-Growth Company.* Boston: Harvard Business School Publishing, 2006.

George, B., Mayer, D., and McLean, A. *Wendy Kopp and Teach For America.* Boston: Harvard Business School Publishing, 2006.

James, W. *Letters of William James.* Vol. 1 (1878).

Medtronic Mission Statement. Available online: www.medtronic.com/corporate/mission.html.

O'Reilly, C. "Leadership and Management: A Brief History of the Research." Unpublished presentation by Professor Charles O'Reilly, Stanford Business School, 2005, p. 9.

Chapter One

Barth, John. *Where Three Roads Meet.* Boston: Houghton Mifflin, 2005, p. 80.

Bartlett, C., and McLean, A. *GE's Talent Machine: The Making of a CEO.* Boston: Harvard Business School Press, 2003.

Clark, T. "Thoroughly Starbucked." *Willamette Week,* May 26, 2004. "Few people love pouring coffee all day, but these perks have made Starbucks' annual turnover rate just 60 percent, compared with an industry average of 200 percent."

Erikson, E. *Childhood and Society.* (Reissue ed.) New York: Norton, 1993.

George, B., and McLean, A. *Howard Schultz: Building Starbucks Community.* Boston: Harvard Business School Publishing, 2006.

George, B., and McLean, A. *Martha Goldberg Aronson: Leadership Decisions at Mid-Career*. Boston: Harvard Business School Publishing, 2006.

John Barth quote—from a conversation Barth had with Warren Bennis. Research interview with Warren Bennis, July 2005.

Schultz, H., and Yang, D. J. *Pour Your Heart Into It*. New York: Hyperion, 1999.

Timmons, H. "As BP Profit Soars, Browne Sets Last Day." *International Herald Tribune*, July 25, 2006.

Chapter Two

Daniel Vasella quoted by Clifford Leaf in *Fortune*, Nov. 18, 2001.

Davis, A. "Closing Bell: How Tide Turned Against Purcell in Struggle at Morgan Stanley." *Wall Street Journal*, June 14, 2005.

Davis, A. "Mack, Back by Popular Demand." *Wall Street Journal*, July 1, 2005.

Davis, A., and Smith, R. "Delayed Reaction: At Morgan Stanley, Board Slowly Faced Its Purcell Problem." *Wall Street Journal*, Aug. 5, 2005.

George, B., and McLean, A. *Richard Grasso and the NYSE, Inc. (A)*. Boston: Harvard Business School Publishing, 2005.

George, B., and McLean, A. *Kevin Sharer at Amgen: Sustaining the High-Growth Company*. Boston: Harvard Business School Publishing, 2006.

McLean, B. "Brahmins at the Gate." *Fortune*, May 2, 2005.

Mulcahy, A. Address at Harvard Business School, Spangler Auditorium, Apr. 4, 2005.

Thomas, L., Jr. "Exile from Wall Street." *New York Times*, Aug. 21, 2005.

Chapter Three

"America's Best Leaders." *US News & World Report*, Oct. 2006.

Bennis, W., and Thomas, R. *Geeks and Geezers: How Era, Values, and Defining Moments Shape Leaders*. Boston: Harvard Business School Press, 2002.

Coelho, P. *The Alchemist: A Fable About Following Your Dream*. (Reprint ed.) San Francisco: HarperCollins, 1995.

George, B. *Profile of Steve Rothschild . . . In His Own Words*. Boston: Harvard Business School Publishing, 2005.

George, B., and McLean, A. *Marilyn Carlson Nelson and the Carlson Companies' Renaissance*. Boston: Harvard Business School Publishing, 2005.

Mandela, N. *Long Walk to Freedom: The Autobiography of Nelson Mandela*. Boston: Little, Brown, 1994.

Oprah Winfrey information taken from her interview for the American Academy of Achievement. Available online: www.achievement.org/autodoc/page/win0int-1.

Chapter Four

"America's Best Leaders." *US News & World Report*, Oct. 2006.

Delphic Oracle. Inscription on the Oracle of Apollo at Delphi, Greece, sixth century B.C. *The Columbia World of Quotations*, 1996. The words are traditionally ascribed to the "Seven Sages" or "Seven Wise Men" of ancient Greece and specifically to Solon of Athens (c. 640–c. 558 B.C.).

George, B., and McLean, A. *Tad Piper and Piper Jaffray*. Boston: Harvard Business School Publishing, 2005.

Goleman, D. *Emotional Intelligence: Why It Can Matter More Than IQ*. New York: Bantam Books, 1995.

Reingold, J. "The Fall and Rise of David Pottruck." *Fast Company*, Sept. 2005, p. 56.

"2006 CEO of the Year." *Chief Executive Magazine*, Apr./May 2006.

Whyte, D. *Where Many Rivers Meet*. Many Rivers Press, 1990.

Chapter Five

Jim Burke quotes from visit to Harvard Business School, 1994.

George, B., Singh, S., and McLean, A. *Narayana Murthy and Compassionate Capitalism*. Boston: Harvard Business School Publishing, 2005.

Huntsman, J. *Winners Never Cheat: Everyday Values We Learned as Children*. Philadelphia: Wharton School Press, 2005.

Palmisano, S. "The Globally Integrated Enterprise." *Foreign Affairs*, May/June 2006.

Chapter Six

The concept of integrating one's motivations with one's abilities originated in the System for Identifying Motivated Abilities. Available online: http://www.sima.co.uk.

John W. Gardner quote from interview Gardner had with Warren Bennis. Research interview with Warren Bennis, July 2005.

Chapter Seven

George, B., and McLean, A. *Tad Piper and Piper Jaffray*. Boston: Harvard
    Business School Publishing, 2005.
George, B., and McLean, A. *Anne Mulcahy: Leading Xerox Through the Perfect
    Storm (A)*. Boston: Harvard Business School Publishing, 2006.
George, B., and McLean, A. *Howard Schultz: Building Starbucks Community*.
    Boston: Harvard Business School Publishing, 2006.

Chapter Eight

Anders, G. "Are You on the Right Track? Part 2." *Fast Company*, Nov. 2000.
George, B., and McLean, A. *Philip McCrea: Once an Entrepreneur . . .*
    Boston: Harvard Business School Publishing, 2006.
Anne Mulcahy. Address at Harvard Business School, Spangler Auditorium,
    Apr. 4, 2005.

Chapter Nine

George, B. *Profile of Steve Rothschild . . . In His Own Words*. Boston: Harvard
    Business School Publishing, 2005.
George, B., Mayer, D., and McLean, A. *Andrea Jung: Empowering Avon
    Women*. Boston: Harvard Business School Publishing, 2006.
George, B., Singh, S., and McLean, A. *Narayana Murthy and Compassionate
    Capitalism*. Boston: Harvard Business School Publishing, 2005.
Oliver, M. *New and Selected Poems: Volume 1*. Boston: Beacon Press, 1992.

Chapter Ten

Class discussion, IMD International, Lausanne, Switzerland, Apr. 2003.
George, B., and McLean, A. *Marilyn Carlson Nelson and the Carlson
    Companies' Renaissance*. Boston: Harvard Business School
    Publishing, 2005.
George, B., and McLean, A. *Anne Mulcahy: Leading Xerox Through the Perfect
    Storm (A)*. Boston: Harvard Business School Publishing, 2006.
George, B., and McLean, A. *Anne Mulcahy: Leading Xerox Through the Perfect
    Storm (B)*. Boston: Harvard Business School Publishing, 2006.
George, B., and McLean, A. *Martha Goldberg Aronson: Leadership Decisions at
    Mid-Career*. Boston: Harvard Business School Publishing, 2006.
Morris, B. "The Accidental CEO." *Fortune*, June 23, 2003, p. 58.

Chapter Eleven

George, B., and McLean, A. *John Whitehead: A Life in Leadership*. Boston: Harvard Business School Publishing, 2005.

George, B., Singh, S., and McLean, A. *Narayana Murthy and Compassionate Capitalism*. Boston: Harvard Business School Publishing, 2005.

George, B., and McLean, A. *Kevin Sharer at Amgen: Sustaining the High-Growth Company*. Boston: Harvard Business School Publishing, 2006.

Leaders' style categories and definitions are adapted from Goleman, D., "Leadership That Gets Results." *Harvard Business Review*, Mar.–Apr. 2000.

Epilogue

Roosevelt, T. "The Man in the Arena." Speech at the Sorbonne, Paris, France, Apr. 23, 1910.

Appendixes

Elements of "Knowing Your Authentic Self" Exercise: Goleman, D. "What Makes a Leader?" *Harvard Business Review*, Jan. 2004.

"Honing Your Leadership Effectiveness" Exercise: The leaders' style categories and definitions are taken from: Goleman, D. "Leadership That Gets Results." *Harvard Business Review*, Mar.–Apr. 2000.

"Your Greatest Crucible" Exercise: Bennis, W., and Thomas, R. "Crucibles of Leadership." *Harvard Business Review*, Sept. 2002.

"Your Motivations and Motivated Capabilities" Exercise: The concept of integrating motivations with capabilities used in this exercise originated in the System for Identifying Motivated Abilities, but the exercise itself is entirely that of the authors.

Index